French Tapestry

A. MILLE-FLEURS TAPESTRY: A MOUNTED KNIGHT

FRENCH TAPESTRY

by

ROGER-ARMAND WEIGERT

translated by

DONALD AND MONIQUE KING

FABER AND FABER

24 Russell Square

London

First published in mcmlvi
by Société Encyclopédique Universelle Paris
First published in England in mcmlxii
by Faber and Faber Limited
24 Russell Square London W.C.1.
Printed in Great Britain by
Robert MacLehose & Co. Ltd Glasgow
All rights reserved

TO THE MEMORY
OF MY PARENTS

Contents

Illustrations

COLOUR PLATES

MONOCHROME PLATES

between pages 32 and 33

Illustrations

Illustrations

CHAPTER I

Generalities

DEFINITION. Since the middle ages, the word 'tapestry' has served to designate various types of work, which differ in technique, in appearance and in use. For the purpose of the present book its application is restricted to works in wool and silk, in which warp threads and weft threads have been interlaced by hand, on a loom, so as to produce a woven fabric, ornamented with human figures, landscapes or decorative motifs. All other interpretations are excluded from the definition, and especially the erroneous extension of the word 'tapestry' to include needlework or embroidery, of which the most celebrated instance is the embroidered hanging known as the Bayeux tapestry.

HIGH-WARP AND LOW-WARP. There are two kinds of tapestry, high-warp tapestry and low-warp tapestry; they are variants of the same technique. Identical in appearance, they are distinguished by the differing positions of the warp threads during the process of weaving. In high-warp tapestry the warp is stretched vertically on the loom; in low-warp tapestry it is horizontal. Thus there are considerable structural differences between high-warp looms and low-warp looms, differences which impose different operating techniques on the respective weavers.

TECHNIQUE. The high-warp loom comprises two wooden rollers (*ensouples*), arranged horizontally one above the other in the same vertical plane, and supported by two uprights (*cotrets*); the latter rest on the ground and are connected by a crossbar at the top. The warp threads are wound on the rollers, and fixed in position by a metal rod (*verdillon*) which fits into a groove running from one end of the roller to the other. The distance between the rollers may be adjusted by means of screw-clamps in the uprights, so as to obtain the tension in the warp which is indispensable for weaving. As weaving proceeds, the completed sections of the tapestry are wound on to the lower roller, thus exposing new sections of the warp.

The warp, which is of the same colour throughout, is divided into two separate sheets or series, firstly by a string (*ficelle de croisure*), and secondly by a glass tube (*bâton d'entre-deux*). Around each thread of the back series — from the point of view of the weaver sitting at the loom — is passed a cotton loop, the heddle (*lice*), which is attached to a rod, the heddle-rod (*perche à lices*). These heddles enable the weaver to pull the whole of the back series of threads to the front.

HIGH-WARP WEAVING. When the preparation of the warp (*ourdissage*) and of the loom is complete, the weaver, using tracing paper, transfers the outlines of the design, or cartoon (*carton*), on to the warp threads. These outlines serve merely as a rough guide for the weaver who, as he works, is obliged, in order to verify the details of design and colour, to turn round constantly to consult the cartoon itself, which is set up behind him.

For the actual process of weaving, the weaver (*tapissier, licier*) takes a bobbin (*broche*) in his right hand; this accessory, a kind of shuttle, is loaded with dyed wool, to form the coloured weft. Then, slipping his left hand between the two series of threads, the weaver passes the bobbin from left to right. Next, grasping the heddle-rod in his left hand, he pulls the back series of threads to the front, and passes the bobbin back again between the two series from right to left. These two passages of the bobbin form what is called a *duite*. The *duites* are beaten down first of all with the pointed end of the bobbin, and then, in the case of large monochrome surfaces, with an ivory comb. Innumerable repetitions of the *duite* constitute the tapestry. Since the weaver works from the back of the tapestry, he is equipped with a movable mirror to enable him to check the appearance of the front.

LOW-WARP WEAVING. The low-warp loom is more closely related to the normal shaft loom and is equipped with treadles controlling the movement of the warp threads, which are stretched horizontally. Besides this fundamental characteristic, another special feature of low-warp weaving is the fact that the cartoon is placed underneath the warp, so that on the front of the tapestry (the weaver, it must be remembered, is working from the back) the composition appears reversed. The cartoon must therefore be reversed in relation to the initial design in order that the latter may be correctly reproduced in the finished work.

Fixed low-warp looms, on which it was impossible for the weaver to check the front of his work, were replaced after 1757 by a swinging loom, perfected by Vaucanson.

TEXTURE. In the middle ages, tapestry warps were coarse, with no more than four or five threads per centimetre (about ten or twelve to the inch). The construction of the loom, on which our information is incomplete, seems to have allowed only a relatively weak tension of the warp. As a result, apparently, of this lack of rigidity, the threads lie in slightly different directions in the different parts of the finished tapestry; this defect is sometimes an advantage, accentuating the expressive character of the work. Can it be assumed that the weavers deliberately introduced these irregularities, from the second half of the fourteenth century onwards, with a view to enhancing the appearance of their products? This has been alleged, but it seems difficult to confirm or to disprove. All that can be said with certainty is that, following the example of the weavers of Paris and Arras, the Tournai weavers of the fifteenth century made skilful use of such expedients as varying the density of the weft threads, hatching with two colours, and arranging the junctions of colours in such a way as to produce slits in the fabric. Without dwelling unnecessarily on technical points, it may be said that, since the middle ages, the texture of the weave has grown progressively finer in proportion as the influence of painting has come to dominate the aesthetics of tapestry.

The Gobelins factory, which was distinguished for the neatness, regularity and, at times, almost mechanical perfection of its weaving, used six or seven warp threads per centimetre (about fifteen to eighteen per inch) in the seventeenth century and seven or eight (about eighteen to twenty per inch) in the eighteenth.

The nineteenth century was blind to the disadvantages of excessively fine textures, which favoured an inappropriate virtuosity, to the detriment of the real qualities of tapestry. Beauvais used ten, or even as many as sixteen, warp threads to the centimetre (about twenty-five, or forty, to the inch).

Since that time, saner views have prevailed. At present the Gobelins factory uses no more than five or six threads per centimetre (about twelve or fifteen per inch).

WOOL. While wool, hemp, linen and even, in more recent times, cotton, have all served for the warp, wool alone has remained the indispensable constituent of the tapestry weft — sometimes in association with silk, and gold or silver thread.

In the middle ages the best wools seem to have been prepared at Arras, whence references to fine Arras thread (*fin fillé d'Arras*) as opposed to Paris thread (*fil de Paris*).

SILK. Silk was used for parts of the weft from a very early date. Only light coloured silks were employed — never dark tones. They served for details which required more refined execution, for skies and horizons, for highlights on draperies, ornaments and flowers. Silk was used for the representation of hair, but never for flesh.

GOLD AND SILVER THREAD. From the fourteenth century onwards, the most sumptuous tapestries included, besides wool and silk, threads of gold (really silver-gilt) and silver, known as Cyprus threads (*fils de Chypre*); these were at first manufactured at Genoa, and only later in France. By being drawn through a wire-drawing apparatus and then flattened by hammering, the metal was rendered thin enough to be wound on a silk thread, covering it completely. The manufacture was the subject of severe regulations until the end of the seventeenth century, when it was almost entirely abandoned.

DYEING AND DYESTUFFS. The tapestry-weavers seem to have obtained at a very early date the privilege of dyeing the raw materials which they used. It appears to be impossible, however, to confirm the dates mentioned in this connection by some well-informed authorities.

The middle ages possessed only a limited number of pure colours. The wools, treated with tartar, were dyed in tones whose fastness has been proved by several centuries of use. The dyes were of vegetable origin. A cruciferous plant, woad (*guède, vouède* in northern France, *pastel* in other regions), provided blues; weld (*gaude*), a biennial plant, gave yellows; madder (*garance*) provided reds; a decoction of crushed madder root gave brownish reds.

Lastly scarlet, produced from insects (originally kermes, subsequently the cochineal insect), conferred, after its introduction into Europe about 1563, a lasting renown on a family of dyers — the Gobelins family, whose establishment was at the gates of Paris, on the banks of the Bièvre. This family gave its name to the site on which rose the famous factory founded by Colbert in 1662.

Generalities

From 1665 onwards, the Gobelins factory possessed its own dyeworks, directed by a Dutchman, Jacques Van Kerkhove, who had brought to France the secret of tin scarlet (*écarlate à l'étain*), also known as Dutch scarlet (*écarlate de Hollande*).

The knowledge of mordanting, the fixation of dyes by the use of alum, tin, iron and chrome, had long since multiplied the number of colours available. These substances made it possible to obtain various tones, from light to dark, of a single colour. At the same time, as a result of the discovery of America and closer relations with the Orient, new dyeing techniques were introduced. They were not considered an unmixed gain. Colbert's instructions of August 1669, with additions of March 1671, give strict directions on dyeing in general, and on dyeing for tapestries in particular.

Further regulations, new scientific research, and the authorization to utilize indigo, still further extended the repertoire of the dyers in the eighteenth century. These advances reinforced certain trends which were to prove particularly unfortunate for the future of tapestry. Changes of taste, which had begun to make themselves felt in Flanders as early as the middle of the sixteenth century, now demanded that a tapestry must be an exact reproduction of the cartoon provided by the painter, whereas, in earlier periods, the weaver had the right to make his own personal interpretation of the design. Thus it became necessary to match the colours of the wools meticulously to the colours of the painted model. To achieve this, comprehensive colour scales had to be created. Eventually they amounted to a total of thirty thousand shades distributed in nearly a thousand colour scales, each of thirty-six tones, ranging from light to dark.

The unfortunate effects of the enrichment of the colour scales were not limited to the reduction of the craft to a mere imitation of painting, and the removal of all initiative from the weavers. A further consequence was the diminished concern for the subsequent evolution of the colours of the tapestry and the inevitable fading of dyed wools when exposed to light.

The brilliant results obtained by the use of dyestuffs which were formerly forbidden, by the application of mordants, by chemical compounding and diluting, carried out without regard to the fastness of the colours, often proved ephemeral. The excessive use of soft and delicate tones, the addition of greys to other colours, and the intermediate shades produced by juxtaposing two *duites* of different colours produced equally unfortunate effects.

It was in vain that the chemist Quemizet endeavoured to introduce reforms designed to limit the damage produced by researches which were empirical rather than scientific.

Not until the middle of the nineteenth century did the chemist Chevreul seriously reduce the number of colours by the use of a chromatic circle with equidistant spacing for each shade. Chevreul's researches were based on the fact that the three primary colours, blue, red and yellow, are optically equidistant from each other. Despite the reduction, his system still included one thousand four hundred and twenty different tones.

His work met with a mixed reception and failed to produce all the desired results.

Nineteenth-century tapestries still continued to suffer from the consequences of a multiplicity of colours and the fugitive nature of some of the dyes.

The adoption of synthetic dyes by the Gobelins in 1911 served only to augment the difficulties, despite their undeniable advantages. Notwithstanding the success of the synthetic dyes, the use of the natural fast dyes, weld, madder, cochineal and indigo, was resumed at the Gobelins factory in 1939. This led to the rediscovery of the different degrees of fastness of the various tones and to a renewal of the liberty to interpret, rather than reproduce, the cartoons, which is indispensable to the best work in this medium.

TRAINING. Intended as it was to preserve and perfect the skills of the craft, the training of tapestry-weavers was always subject to strict regulations. The statute of the weavers of 'Saracen stuffs' (*tapis sarrasinois*), in the *Livre des métiers* of Etienne Boileau, which served as the charter of the high-warp weavers from 1303 down to the seventeenth century, laid down the conditions of apprenticeship, as well as other regulations touching the professional life of the workers. Like the 'Saracen' weavers, the high-warp weavers were at first allowed to have one apprentice for a period of eight years; later they were allowed two, apart from their children 'born lawfully in wedlock'. At Tournai, on the other hand, according to a regulation of 1380, the apprenticeship of high-warp weavers lasted only four years, a period which was later reduced to three years. At Paris, as at Tournai and other centres, enrolment as a master, once the apprenticeship had been completed, was dependent on the production of a master-piece. These general rules were confirmed, in the main, by letters patent of Louis XIII — dated October 1618, and revised on several occasions — which fixed the length of apprenticeship at six years.

Besides these apprenticeships, which might be described as personal or private, there also existed, from the sixteenth century onwards, a kind of collective apprenticeship.

The earliest experiment in collective apprenticeship was that of the *hôpital de la Trinité*, where Henri II sought to provide a professional training for orphans, the *Enfants bleus*, by teaching them high-warp weaving. Again, the letters patent granted by Henri IV in 1607 to François de la Planche and Marc de Comans, the two Flemish weavers whom he had summoned to set up tapestry workshops in Paris, laid special stress on the training of apprentices, 'all of them French.' But the first real school dates from the foundation of the Gobelins, in 1662. This was reorganized in 1737 and on several occasions in the nineteenth century. In the intervals, the prescribed curriculum, based on instruction in drawing, was not always respected; the apprenticeship was often spent in the factory itself, where the pupils were employed on tasks of varying degrees of difficulty. More recently, the Gobelins has given a sound artistic and technical training, divided into four stages: elementary level, advanced level, academy, and tapestry school.

Like the Gobelins, the royal factory of Beauvais, founded in 1664, had an obligation to train 'French apprentices', 'as many as may be.' In addition to the school 'for pupils and apprentices of the craft of tapestry' dating from the early days of the factory, a free drawing school 'for the youth of Beauvais' was added in 1750.

Drawing schools were likewise founded in the eighteenth century at Aubusson. In the next century, a small school of industrial design, organized by the town in 1869, became the nucleus of the school of decorative art, inaugurated in 1884. A new workshop-school was opened in 1946 for the purpose of training pupils in reading and executing cartoons with numerical notation for the colours, a technique which is deemed indispensable for the future development of the craft.

WORKING ARRANGEMENTS. The guild statutes were not concerned only with the professional training of the weavers; they also laid down strict rules for the work itself. As has already been mentioned, the high-warp weavers of Paris undertook, in 1303, to follow the regulations promulgated in 1290 for the 'Saracen' weavers. The adhesion of the newcomers led to the addition of a number of new clauses to the original statutes; one of these clauses prohibited all work made up by sewing, sanctioning only that which was woven in one piece.

Under the system devised by Colbert for the Gobelins, the heads of the workshops undertook to supply tapestries at contract prices; they were themselves responsible for paying the weavers, originally on piece-work rates, and subsequently on task-work. The most expert weavers, the *officiers de tête*, were entrusted with the weaving of the faces and flesh-parts, which demanded a higher degree of skill.

Task-work, abolished at the Gobelins at the Revolution, survived at Beauvais until 1829, and continued in use in the Aubusson workshops.

DESIGNS AND CARTOONS. By the nature of their work the weavers are executants; they interpret, or they copy, as the taste of their period demands, a model produced by a designer or painter.

A contract, signed in 1525 on behalf of the church of the Madeleine at Troyes, has often been quoted in this connection; it provides a detailed account of the various operations which preceded, at that period, the actual weaving of the tapestry.

It confirms, in particular, that the designs (*patrons*) were merely coloured sketches. They were intended only as a guide for the weavers, who could adapt them in accordance with their own ideas and with the limitations of their own materials and techniques.

The history of the principal French tapestry workshops which follows will show that, from the seventeenth century onwards, this freedom of the weavers became gradually more and more restricted. The designs supplied to them, though still retaining something of the character of a guide, grew more detailed and finished. Finally, the nature and aesthetics of tapestry were transformed, when the painter Jean-Baptiste Oudry succeeded, thanks to his position at the Gobelins and Beauvais, in imposing on the weavers the principle of exact reproduction of the cartoon (*carton*), which thenceforward replaced the design (*patron*). In this way tapestry became the slave of painting, providing woven copies of pictures in oils. The fact that from 1739 onwards, the more important models made for the Gobelins, Beauvais, and even Aubusson, were exhibited at the Salon, is proof of this. The weavers developed an extraordinary skill in the distribution and juxtaposition of the unstable and impermanent shades of fugitive dyes. They trained themselves in the use of broken tones and adopted finer and finer warps, in order to reproduce exactly the appearance of the models. The results thus obtained, however, diverged more and more from the ancient laws and traditions of tapestry design.

From the second half of the eighteenth century down to the first third of the twentieth the models designed for tapestry weaving were entirely subjected to the laws of the painted picture. By the use of a mechanism which was devised at the Gobelins after 1750 the weavers were enabled to utilize the original paintings.

The revival of the art of tapestry, which made its appearance in France about twenty-five years ago, has completely transformed this conception of the relationship between the weavers and their models, which dominated the craft for so long. With the intention of restoring to tapestry the lustre of its finest periods, the artists have endeavoured to return to 'medieval methods'. Animated by the zeal of the newly converted, they have simplified their designs until some of them are no more than line-drawings. They reduced, very judiciously, the number of tones, and advocated the re-adoption of coarser warps. Finally, the Aubusson workshops have introduced an innovation for which the inventors forecast decisive effects — the use of cartoons with a colour code. Less detailed than the cartoons of the eighteenth century, these offer greater scope to the initiative of the weavers. Their novelty, apart from the modernism of the designs, lies in the fact that they show only the outlines of the different patches of colour, while the colours are merely suggested by numbers running from one to thirty-two. Within a range of thirty-two tones, the choice and distribution of the actual colours used in the weaving are at the discretion of the individual worker.

BORDERS. Although they were not, as has been asserted, an invention of the Renaissance period, decorative borders became common only in the sixteenth century. The opulent ornamental borders of the seventeenth century were replaced, in the eighteenth, by woven representations of carved and gilded frames. This device, in an age which transformed tapestry into an imitation of painting, served to enhance the illusion that wall-hangings were really pictures.

MARKS. The tapestries of the *Lives of St. Piat and St. Eleuthère*, made at Arras in 1402 for the cathedral of Tournai, bore a lengthy inscription, which has long since vanished, giving the names of the donor and the weaver. Though not universal, this must have been common practice in the middle ages. It recurs in the set of the *Life of St. Peter* made for the cathedral of Beauvais, presumably at Tournai, in 1460.

In 1397, a regulation issued by the Tournai magistrate instituted an obligatory mark for tapestries woven with 'high warp and bobbin'. This mark, to be affixed by the inspectors of the craft, called *esgards* or *revards*, consisted of a lead seal bearing the arms of the town, and served as a guarantee of the quality of the raw materials and of the weaving.

Generalities

The statute promulgated by the emperor Charles V in 1544, which was designed to regulate the manufacture of tapestry in Flanders, laid down that each hanging must have, woven into it, the mark of the weaver or contractor, and the mark of the town where the work was carried out. Although it applied only to Flanders, this statute helped to promote the use of marks in the majority of the tapestry weaving centres of western Europe. They were adopted by most of the French workshops.

INSCRIPTIONS. The more important tapestries of the middle ages have inscriptions. Some are intended to indicate the names of the personages represented, and are placed beside them or on their clothing. Others extend to several lines at the top or bottom of the tapestry and serve to explain the episodes depicted. These inscriptions are sometimes translated into Latin, but more often they are in French. Occasionally they show the linguistic peculiarities of particular places or districts, thus indicating the provenance of the work. There are even instances in which the inscriptions constitute the principal motif of the tapestry, as in the case of the *Angels carrying the Instruments of the Passion* at Angers cathedral.

While some inscriptions were composed by clerics, others were the work of poets. The scholar Quicherat published, long ago, the 'twelve moral poems for use in tapestry' by Henri Baude (about 1430 — after 1490).

At the Renaissance, explanatory texts were first relegated to the borders and then fell into disuse. Later periods restricted themselves to small inscribed cartouches, forming part of the border ornament.

The desire to apply the 'lessons of the middle ages' has led some modern painters and designers to include brief inscriptions in their cartoons for tapestry. These are generally distinguished either by obscure and hermetic symbolism, or by deliberate naivety.

SUBJECTS. A sudden change in tapestry style, about the beginning of the fourteenth century, replaced the ornamental designs of animals and heraldry, which had been generally current until that time, by figure compositions.

Although by no means neglected, religious subjects drawn from the Old and New Testaments, the life of Christ, of the Virgin, of the saints, or of the patrons of the churches for which tapestries were made, tended to be outnumbered by secular subjects. Inspired, in general, by literary sources, these betray a marked curiosity concerning the ancient world. Humanism, as yet unconscious, made its appearance, and turned to such themes as the Trojan Wars, the story of Jason, and Alexander and his conquests. The classical heroes competed with the Nine Worthies, beside whom such modern heroes as Bertrand Du Guesclin also took their place. The strife, battles and festivals of contemporary history were not forgotten, but attracted less interest than the fantastic adventures of the romances of chivalry, the legends of Charlemagne and his peers, and those of the knights of the Round Table. Other themes which enjoyed great success were allegories, scenes of courtly life, stories of Cupid, moralities, pastorals, peasant subjects and rustic scenes.

Both before and after the Renaissance the subjects chosen for representation in tapestry were those which appealed to a cultured *élite*. Antiquity, or rather the legends of antiquity, were generally favoured, but never to the exclusion of other themes. Along with the *Triumphs of Petrarch*, some of the older subjects still survived. Whether religious, mythological, allegorical, or compounded of fact and fiction, they reflected the evolution and progress of human thought.

Later, influences emanating from Flemish workshops renewed the vogue for 'verdures', or rural landscapes. Without human figures, they exhibit scenes in which nature is carefully arranged and coordinated, the trees, bushes and plants being distributed with calculated negligence. Their popularity continued in the seventeenth and eighteenth centuries.

Another stream of influence originating in Flanders, but this time mingled with currents from Italy, led the sixteenth century to take the first step in subjecting tapestry to painting, by imposing on the former the subjects of the latter. The dominance of pictorial themes was to become more and more absolute. Tapestry subjects, whether religious, mythological or historical, became indistinguishable from, and followed the same evolution as, the subjects of painting.

The nineteenth century and part of the twentieth, showing a greater capacity for material production than for original creation, adopted an eclecticism of dubious value and continued to utilize the old themes, with modifications to suit current tastes.

The revival of tapestry since the 1939–45 war has produced a radical break with this tradition. Abstract and ornamental compositions are now commoner than narrative subjects; the latter, if used, receive a completely new interpretation.

TAPESTRIES IN PRIVATE AND PUBLIC LIFE. In the royal and princely residences of the middle ages tapestries afforded an effective insulation against cold. They adorned the state rooms of innumerable houses; they also served to form cosy compartments in large halls. Eventually, bed hangings, seat covers, and even rugs for the floor were made to match the wall hangings. From this use of matching tapestries, arose the custom of weaving sets comprising a number of hangings, which depict the successive episodes of a story. This practice persisted down to the nineteenth century.

'Chambers of tapestry' gave their owners an opportunity of displaying their wealth or high station. They did not remain permanently fixed in the same positions, but were accumulated in store rooms so that changes could be made without difficulty. These changes might be dictated by vanity, by pleasure, or simply by habit, a different selection of tapestries being hung for each season. Kings and princes carried tapestries with them on their journeys; warriors carried them on their campaigns. These removals necessitated the employment of carts, trunks, transport animals and craftsmen.

From houses, tapestries passed into churches. Besides glorifying God and the saints by the subjects depicted, they served a strictly practical purpose by enclosing and insulating sections of the nave and aisles that might be required for special purposes; narrow bands of tapestry (*dosserets*) adorned the backs of the choir-stalls and protected their occupants from draughts.

In addition to houses and churches, tapestries also invaded the streets. They took their place in the urban scene as temporary backcloths for public ceremonies. Without regard for the appropriateness of the subject represented, religious and secular tapestries were hung indiscriminately along the routes of processions, on the occasions of royal entries, receptions for notable visitors, and popular festivals. There are few descriptions of public ceremonies, from the middle ages to the Revolution, which fail to make a reference to some choice tapestry.

The introduction at the Renaissance of more complex monumental decoration, including painted ceilings, did not seriously prejudice the manufacture of tapestries.

During the seventeenth century, wall hangings remained an indispensable adornment of the comfortable interior; while the rich ordered tapestries from workshops of repute, their poorer contemporaries utilized brocatelle, or the so-called tapestry 'from the gate of Paris'.

The engravings of Abraham Bosse, dating between 1630 and 1650, show that people did not hesitate to nail pictures or mirrors on their tapestry hangings. The desire to cover the entire wall-surface, at Fouquet's château of Vaux-le-Vicomte, or at Versailles, led to the introduction of pieces woven to hang between the windows (*entre-fenêtres*) or over doors (*portières*). Tapestries were even woven to fit a particular architectural feature, following the precedent of a piece (from a set of *Arabesque Months*) which was made at the Gobelins to fit the back of a niche in the study of Louis XIV at the Trianon (now in the Louvre).

The finely carved panelling, with details in delicate colours or gilding, which covered the walls of the fashionable eighteenth-century room, still retained a place for tapestries. Reduced to a suitable size, they became an integral part of the interior decoration, and were framed, like pictures, with narrow mouldings. At the same time the furniture was adorned with tapestry covers which matched the wall panels.

Tapestries remained indispensable ornaments of the drawing rooms of the nineteenth and the beginning of the twentieth century. They then suffered a momentary eclipse, but have since regained the lost ground. Thanks to the transformation of their design and technique in the last twenty years, they now have countless opportunities of moderating the rectilinear character of the modern dwelling.

DESTRUCTION AND PRESERVATION OF TAPESTRIES. The aesthetic transformation wrought by the Renaissance endangered the survival of many fourteenth and fifteenth-century tapestries. The seventeenth and eighteenth centuries likewise disdained them, despising their coarse execution and their 'Gothic' style, and treating them with small mercy. Illuminating anecdotes might be quoted in this connection from the *Historiettes de Tallemant Des Réaux*, under Louis XIII and Louis XIV, or from the *Souvenirs de la baronne d'Oberkirch*, on the eve of the Revolution. The fall of the monarchy led to the loss of innumerable tapestries. They were destroyed, either because they showed 'the odious marks of feudalism', or for more straightforward reasons, from which cupidity was not absent.

The first half of the nineteenth century showed little interest in tapestries; the Romantic movement paid them only scant attention. It is true that the initiative of an enlightened prelate, in 1843, was successful in saving part of the *Apocalypse* of Angers, and that Mérimée helped to preserve the set of the *Lady with the Unicorn*, but many other pieces, which are now the pride of public or private collections, continued to be put to the most surprising domestic uses!

But these aberrations are ancient history. Thanks to the officials of the historical monuments commission (*Monuments historiques*), to the curators of the great collections, to enlightened municipalities and ecclesiastical authorities, and to the vigilance of art-lovers, tapestries are now among the best-preserved treasures of the artistic patrimony of France.

STUDY AND KNOWLEDGE OF TAPESTRIES. In 1838, A. Jubinal published *Les Anciennes Tapisseries*, accompanied by an album of line-engravings: this was the earliest work dealing with the craft of the tapestry-weaver. It was only towards the end of the nineteenth century, however, that the attention of scholars came to be directed more seriously to this subject. They quickly discovered that, apart from the intrinsic interest of these works, which are often of outstanding quality, tapestries are also a unique source of information on the history of painting, of illumination, of costume, and of social customs. Soon, local historians began to investigate. Their painstaking research brought to light documents which made it possible to reconstruct the careers of obscure or unknown workshops, and to identify their productions. From that moment the subject was launched. Monographs appeared, general works provided accurate summaries, bibliographies were published. French tapestry had its historians and specialists, among whom we cannot omit to mention at least the names of J.-J. Guiffrey (1840–1918), J.-J. Marquet de Vasselot (1871–1946), Maurice Fenaille, who compiled the *État général des tapisseries des Gobelins*, and Cyprien Pérathon and Louis Lacrocq, who studied the productions of Aubusson.

Exhibitions, such as the retrospective exhibition organized in connection with the international exhibition of 1937, and the incomparable exhibition at the Musée d'Art Moderne in Paris in 1946, which was followed by others in the great cities of Europe and America, attracted the attention of a wider public. Captivated by this sumptuous display, and by the manifest technical and aesthetic revival of the craft, the world at large became aware that tapestry is among the most refined creations of French art.

CHAPTER II

The origins and early history of tapestry in the West

THE PARIS WORKSHOPS IN THE FOURTEENTH CENTURY

Most of the civilizations which preceded our own Western civilization were acquainted with some form of ingenious but rudimentary loom, on which it was possible to interlace warp threads and weft threads so as to produce textiles which, technically speaking, are of the same type as tapestry. These products, which may be stout or fragile according to the nature of the raw materials employed, show ornaments and figures which are formed by the weft threads, and which are equally visible on the back and on the front of the work.

Among early examples are fragments of Chinese silk textiles of the type known as *k'o-ssu*; these attained a remarkable perfection under the T'ang dynasty (A.D. 518–906).

Like the ancient Peruvian civilization, which remained isolated by its geographical situation, and like the Chinese civilization, whose influence was felt by way of the trans-Asian trade routes, the Mediterranean cultures also produced textiles woven by the tapestry method at an early date. Though they will not be discussed in great detail, they must certainly be mentioned, since they are the remote but direct ancestors of the high-warp tapestries woven in Western workshops during the middle ages.

TEXTILES OF THE MEDITERRANEAN BASIN. The Egyptians, like other peoples of antiquity, seem to have possessed tapestries. This appears to be proved by a representation of a loom, closely resembling a high-warp loom, among the paintings of the hypogeum of Beni-Hassan, dating from about three thousand years before our era. But the Egyptians of the time of the Pharaohs utilized linen for a long period before they knew or used wool and silk. Apart from polychrome pieces found in the tombs of Thutmosis IV and Tutankhamun (15th–14th century B.C.), now in the Cairo museum, their tapestries are almost entirely unknown.

Babylon and Niniveh excelled in the weaving of tapestry hangings, which were admired in both Greece and Rome. As to Greek weaving, passages from the *Iliad* and the *Odyssey* refer to the golden shuttle of Calypso and the loom of Penelope. Representations of such objects in vase paintings have been the subject of prolonged discussions among scholars. It is said that the Parthenon was adorned with tapestries after designs by Phidias.

The conquests of Alexander, which brought Greece into direct contact with the Orient, spread the fame — and provoked imitations — of the sumptuous hangings woven in the workshops of Tyre and Sidon.

COPTIC TAPESTRIES. In contrast to the conjectures and hypotheses which make up the better part of our information regarding the pre-Christian period, the capital importance of Coptic art for the early history of tapestry in the West has been demonstrated by exhibitions of actual specimens, organized by the Musée des Gobelins in 1934 and 1935.

The Copts, at the time when the ancient Egyptian civilization was in decline, were grouped in the Nile delta and lower Egypt, intermingled with other peoples who had arrived by way of the sea or along the coasts. They quickly proved themselves to be skilful craftsmen and shrewd traders, able to adapt themselves to the customs and tastes of the peoples with whom they dealt.

The Romanization of Egyptian society led to the abandonment of the complex processes of mummification. The dead were now buried in their own garments which, from the second century onwards, were richly ornamented in styles probably derived from Syria. The trimmings of these garments were frequently made in a technique which was virtually identical with that of later tapestries, coloured woollen weft threads being woven into the linen cloth in the areas where decoration was required. But the work of the Coptic craftsmen, like that of the Chinese, was not restricted to ornamental bands and medallions for robes; it also included larger panels and hangings.

LATER HISTORY OF TAPESTRY IN EGYPT. The earliest specimens of these Egyptian tapestries, excavated chiefly at Antinoe, near El-Amarna, have patterns in two colours only; the subjects are often derived from the Bacchic mysteries. Later, about the middle of the fourth century, ornament inspired by Sassanian Persia appeared alongside the Hellenistic motifs, contributing a marked heraldic stylization and lively polychrome effects. From these Hellenistic and Sassanian influences, a specifically Coptic style gradually emerged and was subsequently utilized for Christian subjects.

The Arab invasion of Egypt in 640 did not check the progress of this Coptic tapestry tradition, already several centuries old. The tradition simply adapted itself, once again, to the tastes of the conquerors. The period of transition extended down to the accession of the Tulunid dynasty, in 866. The powerfully stylized woollen tapestries of the Tulunid era (868–905), were replaced, under the Fatimids (909–1171), by polychrome weaving in silk. This work, a synthesis of various older stylistic currents, was distinguished, in the twelfth century, by continuous all-over patterns, which were reproduced, for the use of the caliphs, in all the territories of the Muslim empire. The crusades put an end to this efflorescence, which was nevertheless a subject of admiration for the Frankish nobles. The latter marvelled at the multiplicity of textiles produced by the infidels, and sought to acquire the delicate silks, the brocaded or embroidered tissues of Islam, in order to enrich the churches of their native land or to adorn the relics of their saints.

There can be no doubt that the booty and the purchases brought back by the crusaders must also have included woollen tapestries.

Were these a complete novelty for the West, or were they perhaps known already by way of Spain, of which a part was subjected to the Arab yoke from the eighth to the tenth century? The second hypothesis seems all the more likely since there is evidence that tapestry workshops already existed in France prior to the crusades. There are traces of them from about the end of the eighth century, fifty or sixty years after the Muslim invasion of France, which was halted and thrown back at the battle of Poitiers in 732.

Evidence of French Tapestry Workshops, Eighth to Twelfth Century. The want of precision in the texts, the ambiguity of the words tapestry (*tapisserie*) and carpet (*tapis*), used to describe the products of these workshops, lend themselves to various interpretations; *tapis* may denote true tapestry, but it may equally well mean a pile carpet, or a plain cloth with a pattern added by needlework.

Of what nature were the tapestries woven at the instigation of Radon, abbot of Saint-Vaast, near Arras, when he was rebuilding his church at the end of the eighth century? Was his example followed by St. Angelme at Auxerre in 840? Were they really carpets that Abbot Robert bought, or had made, for the abbey of Saint-Florent-lès-Saumur? What are we to think of the hangings representing the twenty-four elders of the Apocalypse and the panels with likenesses of ferocious beasts, presented to the same abbey by Abbot Mathieu de Loudun in 1132? As for the Poitiers workshop, was it really the great reputation of its work that inspired a commission from an Italian bishop in 1023? Such questions might be multiplied without improving the prospect of obtaining any decisive answer. The problems which they raise can only be noted for consideration, along with the questions of origin, identification and dating posed by certain pieces of weaving which have survived in Germany.

POSSIBLE WORKS OF GERMAN MONASTIC WORKSHOPS, TWELFTH TO THIRTEENTH CENTURY. A textile in several colours, from the treasury of the church of St. Gereon in Cologne, now divided between the Musée des Tissus at Lyon, the Germanisches Museum in Nuremberg and the Victoria and Albert Museum in London, has been variously attributed.

Decorated with a series of medallions in Byzantine-Sassanian style, enclosing bulls attacked by griffins, it has all the technical characteristics of tapestry. While some authorities have considered it to be pure Byzantine work, others maintain that it was woven about 1200, after a Byzantine model, by a monastic workshop in the Rhineland.

A similar origin has been postulated for the three sets of hangings at Halberstadt cathedral. Originally thought to be of the eleventh century, they have since been assigned to the end of the twelfth or the beginning of the thirteenth century.

The hangings at Quedlinburg cathedral, representing the curious story of the *Marriage of Mercury and Philosophy* from the *Satyricon* of Marcianus Capella, a late Latin writer popular in the middle ages, are known to have been made about 1200 by the Abbess Agnes II and her nuns. The work consists of tufts of wool, which are knotted on to the warp threads, and subsequently cut with scissors to make an even pile. This is the technique of Oriental rugs, and may well be that of the 'shaggy carpets' (*tapis velus*), which are so often referred to in medieval texts.

THE OSLO TAPESTRY. If they were known in the monastic workshops of the Rhineland in the twelfth and thirteenth centuries, the Oriental weaving techniques must presumably have been utilized in other areas and countries of Western, and even Northern, Europe.

This assumption is borne out by a tapestry of the Romanesque period in the museum of decorative arts in Oslo, which is particularly noteworthy for its representation of a mail-clad horseman, in the style of the figures of the so-called Bayeux tapestry. Discovered at Baldishol, in Hedmark, the fragment formed part of a series symbolizing the *Twelve Months,* of which only the scenes representing April and May have survived. This is assumed to have been intended for use as secular furnishing, but it is as likely to have been made in a monastic, as in a lay, workshop.

TAPISSIERS NOSTREZ: TAPISSIERS SARRASINOIS. Summarizing the foregoing paragraphs, we may say that the knowledge of tapestry-weaving was acquired from Orientals by a sequence of events which cannot be exactly reconstructed, and that the craft was first practised in the West in monastic workshops. Like the other minor and luxury arts, it subsequently abandoned these sanctuaries. As a demand arose for tapestries to enhance the comfort of daily life, so workshops of lay artisans sprang up to supply it. But the Book of Trades, initiated by the provost of Paris, Étienne Boileau, about 1263, which contains the earliest information on this subject, mentions among the manual trades only *tapissiers nostrez* and *tapissiers sarrasinois.*

The discussions and explanations of these two terms have come to an end only for want of fresh evidence; the latest interpretations are by no means the least complicated.

It has been supposed, with some probability, that the *tapissiers nostrez* wove ordinary stuffs or, rather, stuffs without pile. The adjective *nostrez* may have been applied to weaving techniques which had become naturalized, as against techniques of more recent importation. The latter were presumably the province of the *tapissiers sarrasinois,* who must have been specialists in the production of knotted pile fabrics, in the Saracenic or Oriental manner. The Quedlinburg hangings, mentioned above, may give a more or less accurate idea of this class of work, which was revived, in the seventeenth century, in Savonnerie carpets.

ORIGIN OF THE HIGH-WARP WORKSHOPS OF PARIS. Although obviously different from true Oriental work, the products of the *tapissiers sarrasinois* must have been fairly closely related to it technically. An addendum to the statutes of the *sarrasinois* weavers decreed that the same rules should apply to 'another class of weavers called high-warp weavers'.

This decision brought to an end a dispute which had arisen between the two groups. Ten high-warp weavers undertook 'on behalf of themselves and the generality of their craft, to observe the regulations enacted'. We may conclude, following J.-J. Guiffrey, that in March 1303, the date of this extremely important document, the high-warp technique had been practised in Paris for at least fifty years, the minimum period in which its practitioners are likely to have grown sufficiently numerous to combine in the attempt to found an independent craft-guild.

By the beginning of the fourteenth century, therefore, the Paris workshops were firmly established as the heirs of a craft tradition handed down from many earlier civilizations. In them the Western tradition of tapestry came to birth, and set out on the road which it has followed down to our own time.

PARIS

During the first two thirds of the fourteenth century the history of the high-warp workshops of Paris remains obscure, for the rare documents give little precise information, and actual tapestries are entirely lacking.

The earliest references date from 1316 and 1317. In 1326, in the inventory of the property of Queen Clémence of Hungary, widow of Louis le Hutin, we find several entries which may relate to tapestries. It is uncertain whether these were high-warp tapestries. Thereafter, references to tapestries (*tapisseries*) and carpets (*tapis*) become commoner; in general, the two terms appear to be interchangeable. It may be noted that, from 1350 onwards, King John the Good acquired no less than two hundred and thirty seven *tapis*. Decorated with *fleurs de lis* and shields of arms, these were intended for his own apartments and those of his sons, and were supplied by craftsmen or merchants who were in all probability Parisians — Clément le Maçon, Jehan Du Tremblay, and Philippe Doger or Dogier.

CHANGES IN THE STYLE OF TAPESTRIES ABOUT 1360. Down to about 1360, high-warp tapestries, supposing that the examples mentioned above were really such, had only relatively simple designs — geometrical patterns of straight lines and circles, and heraldic devices. These now began to be replaced by birds and small animals (*bestelettes*). Within a few years, as was shown by J.-J. Guiffrey in his *Histoire générale des arts appliqués à*

I. THE APOCALYPSE OF ANGERS

(A) THE SON OF MAN SPEAKS TO ST. JOHN

(B) THE ANGEL SHOWS ST. JOHN THE WOMAN COMBING HER HAIR

II. THE APOCALYPSE OF ANGERS

AN ELDER

III. THE PRESENTATION IN THE TEMPLE

Musée du Cinquantenaire, Brussels

IV. THE STORY OF ST. PIAT AND ST. ELEUTHÈRE

Tournai Cathedral

V. THE HUNT OF THE BOAR AND THE BEAR

Victoria and Albert Museum, London

VI. THE STORY OF CLOVIS: FOUNDATION OF THE CHURCH OF THE HOLY APOSTLES;

THE DEFEAT OF GONDEBAUD; THE MIRACULOUS STAG

Reims

VII. SCENES FROM THE WAR OF TROY
Drawing in the Cabinet des dessins, Museé du Louvre

VIII. STORY OF ST. PETER

Museum of Fine Arts, Boston (Mass.)

l'industrie (1913) the woven designs underwent a veritable revolution. Instead of the rudimentary patterns fashionable about the middle of the century, the high-warp weavers were producing religious and secular scenes, all sorts of figure compositions, landscape subjects, and even scenes of contemporary life.

By 1370, the revolution was complete, and thenceforward the inventories merely record further progress in the same direction.

NEW IMPETUS TO TAPESTRY UNDER CHARLES V. The transformation of tapestry-style during the second half of the fourteenth century was due to both general and particular causes, all of them linked with the accession of Charles V, with his personal tastes, and with the growing importance of Paris.

Since the thirteenth century, Paris had been acknowledged as the intellectual capital of the West. Its influence was felt throughout Europe, and persisted in the fourteenth century, despite the defeats suffered by Philip VI and John the Good. A genuine court began to form about the sovereign. A new wealth and luxury made themselves felt in most fields related to the fine arts. Such an environment could not fail to encourage the development of tapestry, which now, without losing its utilitarian function and character, began to achieve a new refinement of execution. Its rise was all the more rapid since the weavers received numerous commissions from Charles V and from his brothers, the Dukes of Anjou, Berry and Burgundy. The demands of these enlightened patrons, these initiators of great works of art, provided an effective stimulus to the weavers of the time, among whom the most distinguished was Nicolas Bataille.

NICOLAS BATAILLE. A considerable amount of general information may be extracted from the documents, assembled by J.-J. Guiffrey, relating to the career of Nicolas Bataille, who was one of the principal high-warp weavers of the late fourteenth century.

As supplier to the royal family by appointment, Nicolas Bataille delivered to the Crown, between 1387 and 1400, the approximate date of his death, about two hundred and fifty *tapisseries* and *tapis*.

Among these, works of great value appear alongside quite insignificant pieces. This strange association of disparate objects suggests that Nicolas Bataille was not only a talented craftsman, but also, and no less successfully, a contractor and middleman. He is sometimes referred to as a 'dealer in *tapis sarrazinois*', while the earliest mention of his name, in 1373, relates to a sale of Arras tapestries.

On the other hand, it was as a citizen of Paris, *civis parisiensis*, that he sold, in 1376, two complete chambers of tapestries to the Duke of Savoy, Amadeus VI, known as the Comte Verd.

By this time, the good fortune of Nicolas Bataille had led him to take service with the luxury-loving Duke Louis of Anjou.

As *valet de chambre* and confidential man of business for the duke, he had already undertaken commissions for him prior to 1373. In the following year, in spite of the commissions of the Comte Verd, he received payments from Anjou's exchequer in respect of a high-warp *tappiz* with figures, containing the story of Hector; other works followed, among which was a little *tapy* representing the Seven Temperaments.

Having thus had occasion to appreciate the merits of Nicolas Bataille, it was natural that the Duke of Anjou should turn to him when he decided to commission another set of tapestries. For what building was this intended? We do not know. But, contrary to the generally accepted hypothesis, René Planchenault has established that it cannot have been the chapel of the castle of Angers, which has since been demolished and replaced with another, smaller, edifice.

Commissioned about 1379 and completed at an unknown date, this work of Nicolas Bataille consists of a set of hangings of quite exceptional importance. In spite of numerous vicissitudes, this set has survived to our own day, still together, even if incomplete.

This astounding and moving masterpiece, the oldest surviving set of medieval tapestries, is the *Apocalypse* of Angers.

THE APOCALYPSE OF ANGERS

Since about 1850, a voluminous literature has accumulated around the *Apocalypse* tapestries of Angers. It is hardly possible to repeat and examine here all the observations contained in these writings. The publications extend from the studies of Louis de Farcy, in the last century, down to the recent, and extremely interesting enquiries undertaken by René Planchenault since 1941.

To begin with, it must be mentioned that on the death of the Duke of Anjou, in 1384, the *Apocalypse* tapestries descended to his son, Louis II. In 1400, they were sent to Arles for the wedding of this prince and Yolande of Aragon. Later, they became the property of the son of this couple, King René of Anjou, who bequeathed them to Angers cathedral. The bequest took effect in 1480, but Anne de France, Duchess of Bourbon, the daughter of Louis XI, retained one piece, which was belatedly handed over to the chapter about 1490. Thenceforward, the *Apocalypse* hangings served to adorn the architectural beauties of the church on the occasion of solemn religious festivals. Thrown out in 1782, and sold by the Domaines in 1843, they were bought back for three hundred francs by Monseigneur Angibault, Bishop of Angers, who returned them to the cathedral. Shortly afterwards, the tapestries underwent repairs and restorations of dubious value, supplementing the similar, but less drastic work carried out in the sixteenth and seventeenth centuries. These restorations, the changes made in the arrangement of the subjects and in the details of the iconography, and the loss of about twenty scenes have substantially altered the original appearance of the set. Fortunately, in spite of these vicissitudes, it retains, on the whole, its original technical, compositional and stylistic features, which may be regarded as characteristic of the aims and achievements of this period in the history of French tapestry.

THE DESIGNER OF THE APOCALYPSE TAPESTRIES. The *Apocalypse* tapestries are equally important for the understanding of Parisian painting at the close of the fourteenth century. Nicolas Bataille and his subordinates, despite their manual dexterity, were, from the very nature of their training, interpreters and not originators. The production of the models and designs which were prepared, according to the technical traditions of the time, for the guidance of the weavers, had perforce to be entrusted to a professional designer. This designer is known. He was one of the Flemish artists who, under several French kings, took advantage of the excellent political and commercial relations existing between France and the County of Flanders to establish themselves in Paris. His name was Jean de Bondolf (not Bandol), and he was known as Jean or Hennequin of Bruges. From 1371 onwards, he held the offices of painter and *valet de chambre* to the king. The accounts of the Duke of Anjou leave no room for doubt that this man was indeed the designer of the tapestries. They record payments to Hennequin of Bruges from 1375 to 1379 'for drawings and designs made by him for the said tapestry of the Apocalypse'. In January 1379, the duke granted him a further sum, payable by quarterly instalments until 1381, 'by reason of the good services which he has done him in making certain designs.'

ANTIQUITY OF THE APOCALYPSE THEME. In choosing for his tapestries the subject of the *Apocalypse*, the terrible preface to the Last Judgment, as related by St. John, the Duke of Anjou was following a well-trodden path.

About the end of the eighth century, the abbot Beatus, of Liebana in Asturias, composed a commentary on the Apocalypse. His work became an official text of the Spanish church, and many copies were made between the tenth and twelfth centuries. Illuminated copies brought back to France by pilgrims visiting St. James of Compostella exercised an undeniable influence on sculpture, by introducing a wealth of new subjects. After a brief eclipse, the Apocalypse theme was brought back into favour about 1250 by a new cycle of miniatures, this time originating in England. Its relationship with the Spanish cycle remains rather obscure.

MS. FR. 403 OF THE BIBLIOTHÈQUE NATIONALE. Stylistic analysis of the miniatures of the numerous Apocalypse manuscripts of the second, or English, cycle, has made it possible to divide them into several distinct groups. One of these, originating in England or northern France in the thirteenth century, served as the prototype for other illuminations and, at a later date, for woodcut illustrations. To this group belongs an *Apocalypse*, formerly the property of Charles V, which is now preserved in the manuscript department of the Bibliothèque Nationale under the registration number Ms. fr. 403.

It is stylistically related to an Apocalypse manuscript at Oxford.

As a result of the studies of A. Giry (1876), great importance was formerly attached to Ms. fr. 403. His theories, which appeared to be supported by an article contributed by Maxime Petit to the periodical *Le Moyen Age* in 1896, long held the field. Yet a study by Léopold Delisle, in 1901, was to prove that the final solution of the question had not been reached.

THE CAMBRAI-METZ GROUP OF MANUSCRIPTS. Without denying the theory of A. Giry that Ms. fr. 403 was lent by Charles V to the Duke of Anjou, or the possibility that Jean de Bruges may have consulted it while working on the designs of the Angers tapestries, Léopold Delisle established beyond doubt that the artist must also have utilized other manuscripts. The strength of this argument lies in the fact that scenes which do not appear in Ms. fr. 403 and which had been assumed until then to be original compositions of Hennequin de Bruges, were found to exist in another, different group of Apocalypse manuscripts. The most characteristic specimens of this group belong to public and private libraries in Paris, Namur, London and — most notably — to the libraries of Cambrai (No. 422) and Metz.

It is clear from this that no single manuscript can be said to be the true and unique source of the designs prepared by Hennequin de Bruges. It must be presumed that the Duke of Anjou was able to bring together temporarily a number of different Apocalypse manuscripts from various princely libraries, thus giving the painter the opportunity of selecting the motifs most suitable for rendering in the tapestry technique.

STYLE AND TECHNIQUE OF THE APOCALYPSE TAPESTRIES. It is clear that the designs of the *Apocalypse* tapestries were dependent on late fourteenth-century miniature-painting. But this did not prevent Nicolas Bataille and his fellow-workers from introducing the technical and stylistic effects characteristic of their own craft.

Although the designs are very primitive in character, they are nevertheless of high artistic quality. The simplified forms which evoke the landscape setting of the scenes — the trees, the fortified towns, the clouds — show a spontaneous sense of decoration which is rarely found in later tapestries.

Following the traditions of miniature painting, the earliest scenes of the hanging are set against plain backgrounds. This must have struck the weavers as rather severe and monotonous, for in later pieces they sought to make more extensive use of arbitrarily stylized flowering trees and shrubs. Later still, renouncing all attempts at a logical imitation of nature, they devised backgrounds covered, as those of miniatures sometimes were, with scrolls, vine branches, flowers and other ornament. On little flags, and on the wings of butterflies, appear at regular intervals the arms of the Duke of Anjou. Those of the Order of the Cross, which he founded, and of Jeanne de Laval, wife of his successor René I, are later additions.

The plain and regular weaving gives the tapestries an expressive ruggedness, which was enhanced by the occasional audacity or awkwardness in the execution, now partially obscured by later restorations.

In accordance with normal medieval methods, the warp is coarse, with about twelve or thirteen threads to the inch (five per centimetre).

The colours are limited to a scale of about fifteen tones, which are juxtaposed with little attempt at modelling. This limited colour-scale gives the composition a remarkable unity. The pure colours, blue, red and green, have lost little of their liveliness. The broken tones, browns, greys and flesh tints, have grown paler, but their simultaneous loss of strength has not upset the general harmony.

COMPOSITION OF THE APOCALYPSE TAPESTRIES. Originally, the *Apocalypse* set consisted of seven hangings, each about sixteen and a half feet high, and of lengths up to about eighty feet. The total length seems to have been between about four hundred and fifty and five hundred and twenty-five feet.

Each hanging showed first of all an old man seated beneath a Gothic canopy, and absorbed in meditation on the Scriptures. Then came fourteen symbolic scenes, divided into two horizontal bands, each of seven scenes, with alternately red and blue backgrounds. According to tentative reconstructions, which have not been accepted without reserve, the second and third hangings differed from the rest and showed only fifteen subjects in all — eight in the second, and six in the third, plus the figure in meditation.

Between the two bands of scenes was a brown strip with verses corresponding to the scenes above, in white or red Gothic characters about two and a half inches high. There was a similar strip beneath the scenes of the lower band. These inscriptions have disappeared. Ornamental strips at the top and bottom of the tapestries have survived in part; none of them is complete, but some preserve two-thirds or three-quarters of the original depth. So as to convey to the spectator the idea that the scenes represented were taking place between heaven and earth, the upper strip showed the sky, with angels playing instruments or holding armorial bearings, while the bottom strip showed a green and blossoming earth, where birds, rabbits and other small animals disported themselves.

The initials which occur in several of the scenes have given rise to speculation; they may have been added after the original weaving, in honour of subsequent owners.

The mutilation which the set has suffered has caused the loss of twelve complete scenes. Eight others have survived in fragmentary condition. By adding these to the seventy existing scenes, we arrive at a total of ninety scenes — a figure which has recently been disputed. We cannot enumerate them individually. In general, they are faithful translations of the miniatures which were intended to illustrate the texts of the principal Apocalypse manuscripts, already mentioned.

THE 'ELDERS'; ATTEMPTS AT IDENTIFICATION. As for the elders, who appeared enthroned at the beginning of each of the seven original pieces of the set, occupying the entire height of the hanging, their identity remains uncertain. The field is all the more open to hypothesis since these figures do not appear in the Apocalypse manuscripts, and are an invention of Hennequin de Bruges. Can they represent the Duke of Anjou himself? This has been suggested, on account of the banners with his arms, and the butterflies whose wings are charged with the heraldic bearings of Anjou and Brittany. Or are they not rather abstractions, under the dominion of the mystic figure seven, beloved of the Hebrew prophets, which recurs throughout the Book of Revelation? Or could they be the representatives of the seven churches of Asia, the seven doctors, as Henri Focillon once suggested orally, or simply St. John himself?

These are all unanswerable questions. To the evocative power of the *Apocalypse* of Angers, one of the most impressive works of art left to us by the middle ages, they add the mysterious fascination of the inexplicable.

OTHER WORKS OF NICOLAS BATAILLE. The *Apocalypse*, which was woven with surprising rapidity by Parisian weavers established temporarily at Angers, was by no means the last major work produced by Nicolas Bataille and his craftsmen.

As a result of a gap in the archives, we do not know what became of them between 1379 and 1387. By the latter date, the Duke of Anjou was dead and we find Bataille again, as has been mentioned above, supplying the royal household with minor works, which contrast strangely with the Angers *Apocalypse*.

These modest productions did not prevent him from executing for the Duke of Touraine, in 1389, a high-warp tapestry with the *Story of Theseus and the Golden Eagle*, a subject derived from a romance. Among much other work, there were considerable deliveries of tapestries to the Duke of Burgundy in 1395. They included *Knights and ladies*, the *Castle of Sincerity*, the *Story of Godefroy de Bouillon*, and two scenes of *Shepherds and Shepherdesses*, as well as a hanging with the *Story of Bertrand du Guesclin*. About the same period, in 1390, Nicolas Bataille supplied the Duke of Orleans with three tapestries or sets of tapestries which were no less remarkable. These were the *Story of Pentéasillée* (sic), *Queen of the Amazons*, that of *Beuve de Hanstonne* (sic), derived from the epic of Beuve de Antonn or Hampton, and the *Adventures of the children of Renaud de Montauban* (the four popular sons of Aymon) *and of Riseus de Ripemont*. But none of these tapestries, nor the chapel-hanging representing the *Tree of Life*, with prophets and fathers of the church on the branches, and the trunk surmounted with a crucifix, could vie with the set of the *Jousts of Saint-Denis*, begun by Nicolas Bataille in 1397.

The *Jousts of Saint-Denis* were made in collaboration with Jacques Dourdin and completed in 1400. Executed 'entirely in figure-work of gold and fine Arras thread', they commemorated the admission of the Duke of Orleans, brother of Charles VI, and of his cousin, Duke Louis II of Anjou, into the order of knighthood, an event which was celebrated with memorable festivities in May, 1389.

JACQUES DOURDIN. Following the death of Nicolas Bataille, which took place before 1400, his widow continued for a time to direct his workshop, the pre-eminence of which was now threatened by rivals. Among these was the workshop of Jacques Dourdin. Dourdin, who was associated with Bataille in weaving the *Jousts of Saint-Denis*, was evidently his principal competitor, although the names of many other Parisian weavers are known to us. He was buried in 1407 at the charnel-house of the Innocents. Between 1386 and 1397, he executed seventeen sets of tapestries for the Duke of Burgundy; Queen Ysabeau of Bavaria and the Duke of Orleans were also among his clients.

A detailed enumeration of the works of Jacques Dourdin and those of his rival Pierre Baumetz, or de Baumetz, added to the list of those of Nicolas Bataille, would demonstrate the prodigious activity of the Paris high-warp workshops at the end of the fourteenth century. It would also underline the intimate relationship between tapestry and the beliefs, the knowledge and the customs of the age. In tracing the later history of the craft, we shall find evidence of a similar relationship at all periods.

Apart from the *Apocalypse* set, only two other important works can be attributed to the Paris workshops. These are, firstly, the remains of a set of *Nine Worthies*, and secondly, a *Presentation in the Temple*.

THE NINE HEROES. In 1932, the Metropolitan Museum of New York bought a tapestry which had formerly been in the collections of Chabrières-Arlès and Baron A. Schickler in France, and of Clarence Mackay in America. It showed *King Arthur* enthroned in an elaborate architectural setting, between niches occupied by other figures. This first acquisition was joined, in 1947, by other similar panels and fragments, which had long been utilized as curtains in the château of Martinvast, near Cherbourg, the property of Baron A. Schickler; these were presented to the Museum by John R. Rockefeller, junior, and George A. Douglas.

Patient reconstruction and painstaking restoration have succeeded in reconstituting several hangings, which are now exhibited at the Cloisters, a branch of the Metropolitan Museum. In addition to the *King Arthur* already mentioned, these show *Alexander, Caesar, David* and *Joshua*, who were all members of the group of *Nine Heroes* so often depicted in the middle ages. Seated in the same way in architectural settings, they are likewise accompanied by other figures in niches at the top and sides of the tapestries.

The researches of Mr. James J. Rorimer, to whose efforts the resurrection of this extremely important work is due, tend to prove that the set of the *Nine Heroes*, which originally consisted of three large hangings, closely resembles the Angers *Apocalypse* in technique, colour and style. Inspired by manuscripts from the circle of André Beauneveu, they were probably woven about 1385, either by a Flemish master, perhaps from Bruges, or by the workshop of Nicolas Bataille, or, again, by a workshop under his influence.

The set of *Heroes* was made for the Duke of Berry, brother of John the Good, whose arms appeared on the David and Joshua panels. Mr. Rorimer, who believes that it is possible to trace in the Cloisters tapestries relationships not only with manuscripts from the collection of the Duke of Berry, but also with the frieze of the ducal palace at Bourges and with stained glass at Bourges cathedral, is inclined to believe that the *Nine Heroes* were formerly associated with a companion set of *Nine Heroines*, likewise surmounted by the arms of Berry; such a set is known, from inventory references, to have belonged to King Charles VI, the Duke's nephew.

THE PRESENTATION IN THE TEMPLE. Contemporary with, or a little earlier than the set of *Heroes*, the *Presentation in the Temple*, at the Musée du Cinquantenaire in Brussels, is likewise distinguished by the simplified, sculptural aspect of the draperies and by the calm and serene expression of the figures; the latter have, once again, been compared with sculpture of the Valois period, with miniatures and with stained glass. Apart from similarities, in composition and execution, with the Angers *Apocalypse*, a relationship has been pointed out between the female figures in the tapestry and the miniature of the Virgin, by André Beauneveu, in the *Hours of the Duke of Berry*. The attribution to the Paris workshops is now contested, in favour of Arras, but the tapestry shows the same well-mannered reticence, the avoidance of exaggerated effects, which we have already observed in the Angers *Apocalypse*. These features seem to have been characteristic of the Paris workshops; but both they, and the workshops themselves, were soon to disappear. With the defeat at Agincourt in 1415, the Hundred Years War took a decisive turn for the worse. The Paris workshops were submerged by the miseries of the time, and the star of Arras was in the ascendant.

CHAPTER III

Franco-Flemish tapestry
down to 1450

ARRAS

The foundation of the high-warp workshops of Arras probably dates, as in Paris, from the late thirteenth century. There is no useful purpose to be served by endeavouring to discover which of the two great centres, linked as they were by so many commercial and other ties, was the earlier. But whereas the Parisian weavers were dispersed or ruined by the English occupation (1418–36), the prosperity of the Arras workshops suffered no ill effects. Their fame became international, and a last echo of their prestige survives to this day, for the name Arras, like the name Gobelins, still exists in several European languages as a synonym for tapestry.

In 1369, the marriage of Marguerite of Flanders, daughter of Count Louis de Mâle, presaged the attachment of Arras to the Duchy of Burgundy, which actually took place in 1384. The alliance between Duke Philip the Good and the King of England (1419) allowed the Arras workshops to continue to draw their supplies of wool from across the Channel and to export their products in the reverse direction. It was not so much to their commercial links with foreign countries, however, as to the patronage of the Dukes of Burgundy, those shrewd protectors of art and letters, Philip the Bold (1341–1404), son of King John the Good and brother of Charles V, John the Fearless (1371–1419) and Philip the Good (1396–1467), that the Arras workshops owed their most brilliant successes. These carried far and wide the name of this flourishing city, the capital of a frontier province open to every current of French art, yet sensitive also to influences from Flanders and the region of the Meuse. This remarkable development attained its full flowering about the middle of the fifteenth century, and continued, not without difficulty, until, following the death of Charles the Bold on the battlefield of Nancy, Arras was captured and annexed by the troops of Louis XI, in 1477.

At this date, and indeed much earlier, other Flemish towns possessed tapestry workshops which were well known or on the way to becoming so. These included not only Lille, Valenciennes and Cambrai, to which we shall return briefly, but also Enghien, Audenarde, Brussels and, above all, Tournai, which formed part of the royal domains of France down to the treaty of Madrid, in 1526.

FRANCO-FLEMISH TAPESTRIES. The products of the Tournai workshops, which also numbered the court of Burgundy among their most faithful customers, formed part, like those of Arras, of the great intellectual and artistic movement inspired by the pageantry of the 'great dukes of the West'. For this reason, as well as by virtue of their geographical and historical situation, the Tournai workshops, like those of Arras, must be considered in any study of French tapestry and its evolution. One cannot, on the basis of misleading considerations of nationality, exclude their works and proclaim them Flemish. Still less so, since neither Arras in Artois, nor Tournai in Hainaut, forms part of Flanders.

In accordance with the excellent formula of Gaston Migeon, it is enough to note that Arras tapestries, and Tournai tapestries prior to 1526, are 'specifically Flemish, Burgundian by their geographical character, and Franco-Flemish by their adherence to a style which was common to both France and Flanders'.

This definition is all the more apt since, apart from the very few documented sets, it has so far proved practically impossible to make any clear division between the products of the Arras workshops and those of Tournai.

Both centres utilized religious and secular subjects drawn from the same sources; both created and developed styles which, if not identical, are certainly very closely related, and have given rise to much discussion and argument.

It is true that certain differences have been suggested. M. Guillaume Janneau believes that it is possible to distinguish certain technical habits of the Tournai weavers — treatment of form, tricks of weaving, and choice and distribution of colours, especially blue. Writers on the Tournai workshops note that tapestries woven there often have the names of the figures inscribed in Gothic characters on their garments, and that the figures themselves hold scrolls with inscriptions, also in Gothic letters, the initial letter being blue.

Lastly, in a thesis submitted to the École du Louvre in 1932, Mlle. Margerin indicated considerable differences between the flowers, the stiff tufts of grass, the dry tree trunks and flattened leaves of Arras, and the less schematic plant forms of Tournai.

Without underrating the value and importance of these observations, it does not seem that they are always sufficiently convincing to permit the establishment of a genuine line of demarcation between the products of these two great northern centres of tapestry weaving. Nor is this surprising when we consider that weavers of the same family, such as the Du Moulin and Sarrazin families, worked both at Arras and at Tournai, and that there were numerous artistic links between the two towns.

WORKSHOP OF BAUDOIN DE BAILLEUL. CONNECTIONS BETWEEN ARRAS AND TOURNAI. The researches of Abbé (later Chanoine) Lestocquoy, curator of the Diocesan Museum of Arras, have emphasized the extent and importance of the contacts between the workshops of Arras and Tournai, which had already been noted by Mme. Crick-Kuntziger, curator at the Musée du Cinquantenaire in Brussels.

Apart from the *Story of St. Piat and St. Eleuthère*, woven at Arras in 1402 for the cathedral of Tournai, such exchanges are exemplified by Bauduin de Bailleul, a well-known painter established at Arras, who in 1449 designed the eight cartoons for the famous *Gideon* set, woven at Tournai by Robert Dary and Jean de L'Ortye. In fact, the workshop of Bauduin de Bailleul supplied designs for both centres.

Without multiplying examples indefinitely, it should perhaps be mentioned that in 1446 a weaver of Arras, Wuillaume au Vaissel, delivered to Duke Philip the Good a tapestry which was intended to complete a 'chamber of verdure' supplied by Jehanne Pottequin, widow of Jean Baubrée, of Tournai. Three years later, in 1449, the same Wuillaume au Vaissel wove a hanging of the *Resurrection* for the abbot of Saint-Waast, after a design 'painted in tempera on coloured canvas' by the painter Jacques Daret. This Jacques Daret, who had then been established for twenty odd years at Arras, where he and his followers produced works in the Tournai style, had been a pupil, along with Roger van der Weyden, of the Tournai painter Robert Campin, who has been identified, as has Daret himself, with the mysterious Master of Flémalle.

SURVIVAL OF THE ARRAS WORKSHOPS AFTER 1477. In addition to the uncertainty caused by complexity of the artistic and commercial relations between the workshops of Arras and Tournai, recent discoveries have introduced new complications. While it remains true that the decline of the Arras workshops began about 1450, it can no longer be maintained that their activity was ruined and destroyed by the siege of 1477. This event, which was followed by the sack and occupation of the town by the troops of Louis XI, has long been held to mark the close of the Gothic period in French tapestry.

It now appears, however, that decisive documentary evidence proves that the industry continued at Arras, though no doubt on a reduced scale, after 1477. It seems, indeed, to have persisted down to the end of the fifteenth century, or the first quarter of the sixteenth. In this case, it must be admitted that some surviving tapestries of these later periods may well have been woven at Arras. This opens the door to many possibilities.

All these considerations suggest that attributions of Franco-Flemish tapestries to Arras in the nineteenth century, and to Tournai in the twentieth, must be accepted with considerable caution. In any case, it must be emphasized that their acceptance is subject to such modifications as may be proved necessary by future archival discoveries, by new stylistic comparisons, and by additional information derived from unpublished or little-known tapestries.

ARRAS: WORKSHOPS AND ATTRIBUTIONS

The origins of the tapestry workshops of Arras remain, like those of the other great centres, shrouded in obscurity.

It was long considered, largely as a result of the work of J.-J. Guiffrey, that their foundation or development was due to the patronage of the Countess Mahaut of Artois, great-niece of St. Louis and wife of Otto IV, Count Palatine of the Rhine, who governed Artois from 1303 until her death in 1329.

This account, which has become traditional, is not corroborated by the relatively limited purchases of tapestries made by Mahaut of Artois, which were, furthermore, divided between Arras and Paris. Moreover, the researches and observations of Abbé J. Lestocquoy suggest another, and more likely hypothesis.

According to this, the foundation of high-warp workshops at Arras was the result of decisions taken by the aristocracy and principal citizens of the town, with a view to counteracting the competition, and consequent decline, which was threatening their manufacture and trade in woollen cloth.

As shrewd businessmen, accustomed to speculations and to monopolies in the various branches of economic activity — wine, beer, cloth, weapons — they fixed on high-warp weaving, which was just beginning to be practised and which seemed capable of great development. The craft was all the more interesting from their point of view, since it was the most likely to profit from the perfection attained by the woollen industry of Artois, the skill of its dyers, and its artistic and intellectual resources.

LACK OF INFORMATION ON ARRAS TAPESTRIES. Despite the interest of the published documents and the number of tapestries which have been attributed to Arras workshops, there exists, as we shall see, only one set of tapestries which is definitely known to have been woven there: the *Story of St. Piat and St. Eleuthère*, in the treasury of Tournai cathedral.

Apart from this, we have only suppositions, based on the facts available, and the sometimes contradictory observations of scholars who, for a century, have been working on problems created, as often as not, by themselves, rather than by the works studied.

THE BEGINNINGS OF HIGH-WARP WEAVING AT ARRAS IN THE FOURTEENTH CENTURY. A few brief references to commissions, some 'cloths' with arms or ornament recorded in inventories, and the names of some high-warp weavers (Isabeau Caurée, of Halennes, producer, merchant, or dealer, in 1313; Jean de Thelu, in 1328; Thomas le Cardeur, in 1342) prove the existence of a nascent tapestry-weaving industry at Arras from 1313 onwards. But there is nothing to suggest the rapid extension and development which was to take place thirty or forty years later.

At that time numerous workshops made their appearance, producing works in 'fine Arras thread' and 'Cyprus thread' (gold and silver spun on silk). Their activity increased in the second half of the century, when they began to be patronized by the wealthiest customers.

The Duke of Burgundy, Philip the Bold, a client of the Parisian merchant and weaver Nicolas Bataille, who also sold Arras tapestries from time to time, was quick to support the craftsmen of his own dominions. His commissions provided the final impetus necessary for the success of the Arras workshops.

PHILIP THE BOLD AND THE ARRAS WORKSHOPS. An inventory of seventy-five tapestries collected by Philip the Bold (1404), and various entries in accounts, are our principal sources for the subjects treated by the Arras workshops during the first thirty or forty years of their expansion.

In general, they show the same variety, the same wide-ranging inspiration, as the contemporary productions of the Paris workshops. The episodes chosen are similar; their diversity is the same. There are some particularly eloquent examples among the purchases of Philip the Bold, some of them from Jean Cosset, one of the most active of the Arras high-warp weavers.

But it was Michel Bernard of Arras who wove, or arranged for the weaving of the famous *Battle of Roosebecke*, commemorating the victory of Charles V and Louis de Mâle, brother-in-law of Philip the Bold, over the rebellious Flemings.

THE BATTLE OF ROOSEBECKE. Put on the looms in 1387, five years after the event which it celebrated, the tapestry of the *Battle of Roosebecke*, woven of wool, with details in silk and Cyprus thread, was fifty-six ells long by about seven and a quarter ells high, i.e. about four thousand square feet. Its weight and unwieldy size led to its being divided, in 1406, into three pieces, which were again subdivided into two. In this condition it figured for the last time in the inventory of the Emperor Charles V in 1536, where it is described as 'very old and worn'.

Despite an apparent preference for secular subjects, the Arras workshops of the period of Philip the Bold also wove tapestries with religious themes. In their designs for these the artists showed imagination and ingenuity, as can be seen from the *Story of St. Piat and St. Eleuthère*, where both the scenes and the details are remarkable for their unconventional character.

THE STORY OF ST. PIAT AND ST. ELEUTHÈRE. An inscription, which disappeared in the sixteenth century, but which was fortunately recorded, proclaimed that 'These cloths were made and completed / in Arras by Pierrot Feré, the year one thousand four hundred and two / in December the month of grace / Please ye to God and all saints / pray [tous saincts priez] for the soul of Toussaint Prier.' The beneficiary of this naive pun on his name, Toussaint Prier (d. 1437), clerk of the chapel of Count Louis de Mâle, had been almoner to Philip the Bold before becoming a canon of Tournai cathedral. It was for this cathedral that he commissioned the *Story of St. Piat* (who was the apostle of the Tournai region in the third century) *and St. Eleuthère* (first Bishop of Tournai, in the sixth century). The pictorial narrative, accompanied by explanatory texts, seems originally to have comprised eighteen scenes, in two tapestries, which were no doubt intended to adorn the backs of the choir-stalls on feast days. Only fourteen scenes remain, six of St. Piat and eight of St. Eleuthère. Woven in fine wools, including only about a dozen colours, which are dominated by pure tones, they are surrounded by a border of later date. The whole is about seventy-five feet long by seven and a half feet high.

The designer is unknown. As for Pierrot Feré, a prominent citizen of Arras, his name does not occur in the accounts of the Dukes of Burgundy, which mention the middlemen, the dealers, more often than the weavers.

As the starting point — as far as our knowledge goes — of Arras production, the *Stories of St. Piat and St. Eleuthère* are characterized by a new realistic note and by facial types which incline towards vulgarity. The relationship with the art of Van Eyck, and the homely realism of the landscapes and accessories bear witness to an artistic environment more Flemish than French. In the crowding of the figures, there are reminiscences of the fourteenth century style of the school of illuminators who inspired the designer and cramped his attempts at freedom and fantasy. But in this overabundance, which remains balanced and disciplined despite the absence of perspective, we see foreshadowed the type of drawing and composition which is characteristic of the fifteenth-century tapestries attributed to Arras.

ARRAS TAPESTRY. FIRST THIRD OF THE FIFTEENTH CENTURY. Among these works it is possible to isolate an early group, distinguished by its archaic or archaising style.

It includes, firstly, *Five pieces with courtly subjects*, with details in gold thread, which formed part of the Peyre bequest and are now exhibited at the Musée des Arts Décoratifs in Paris. Inspired by an unidentified romance, these tapestries show scenes of courtly life. As in the *Offering of the Heart* (Davillier gift to the Musée de Cluny, 1955), a tapestry influenced by the style of the brothers Limbourg, the illuminators of the Duke of Berry, and as in other scenes of similar inspiration in the hands of private collectors or dealers, the plant forms, like the treatment of the sky, show a characteristic simplification. But this is by no means uniform and is, in fact, subject to considerable variation. Elements of this generally rather naive stylization recur in the long, narrow *Resurrection* (about eight feet long by two and a quarter feet high; Davillier gift to the Musée de Cluny, 1955), which is obviously earlier than the *Offering of the Heart*, and of finer weave, with silver-gilt threads. They seem to be still more apparent in the plant forms of a scene derived from the *Romance of Jourdain de Blaye*, in the municipal museum of Padua.

The *Hunts*, from Chatsworth, and the *Passion of Christ*, at the Seo of Saragossa, have also been included in, or related to, this archaic group.

IX. TAPESTRY OF THE SACRAMENTS: EXTREME UNCTION (detail)
Metropolitan Museum of Art, New York

X. STORY OF ALEXANDER (detail)
Palazzo Doria, Rome

XI. THE KNIGHT OF THE SWAN
Church of St. Catherine, Cracow

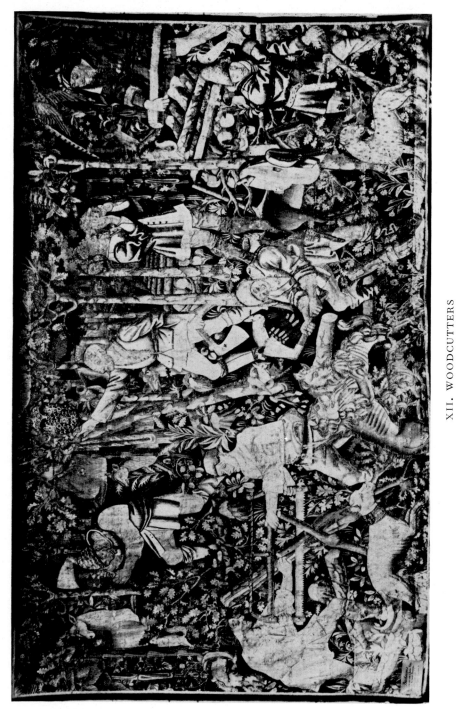

XII. WOODCUTTERS

Tapestry with the arms of Nicolas Rolin, chancellor of Burgundy

Musée des Arts Décoratifs, Paris

XIII. FAMOUS WOMEN: PENELOPE

Museum of Fine Arts, Boston

XIV. TAPESTRIES OF CHANCELLOR ROLIN: ST. ANTHONY
Hôtel-Dieu, Beaune

XV. LIFE OF THE VIRGIN: THE VISITATION
Church of Notre-Dame, Beaune

XVI. STORY OF SUSANNA (detail)
Musée Marmottan, Paris

THE CHATSWORTH HUNTING TAPESTRIES. After forming part of the original furnishings of Hardwick Hall, the set of *Hunts* was removed to Chatsworth House, in Derbyshire, about the end of the sixteenth century, and reassembled in its original form in 1902. It is now in the Victoria and Albert Museum.

Dated by specialists to the second quarter or middle of the fifteenth century, it comprises four hangings, devoted to the *Hunts of the deer, of the otter, of the wildfowl, and of the bear.* They are thought to have been inspired by the illuminations of the Hunting Book of Gaston de Foix, known as Gaston Phébus, written about 1370; the same is probably true of some fragments of similar tapestries, a *Falconry* in the Minneapolis Museum, U.S.A., and the *Boar-hunt* in the Burrell Collection, Glasgow.

Many theories have been put forward with regard to the origin of these hangings.

As between Tournai and Arras, where Jean Walois, one of the best-known high-warp weavers, is known to have supplied tapestries to several princes, the balance of opinion has been in favour of Arras.

This attribution to Arras is strengthened, moreover, by a number of details of technique and composition, of which the most telling are perhaps the 'kidney-shaped flints', noted by Mme. Crick-Kuntziger as occurring on the ground in the scene of the *Bear-hunt.* These stones, rare and unusual in the Tournai region, are common in Artois.

The great size of the Chatsworth *Hunts* (each over thirteen feet high, and up to forty feet long) is as striking as the breadth of their design and the subtlety of their colouring. The weaving, which is of remarkable virtuosity despite its relatively coarse texture, produces an effect of extreme elegance, thanks to the judicious handling of the colour-junctions.

In front of gnarled trees and bushes with bunches of rigid leaves, forming a very high horizon, the groups and single figures (some participating in, some standing aside from the activities of the chase), the animals, the buildings, and the vistas opening into animated landscapes are disposed in studied confusion, in such a way as to preserve both the unity of the whole and the harmony of the various individual scenes of which each tapestry is composed.

These features are not the effects of chance or improvisation. They are the expression of a considered programme, a universally held conception of tapestry, which was reaffirmed in many other works, including the *Passion of Christ* at the Seo of Saragossa.

THE PASSION CYCLE: SARAGOSSA, BRUSSELS, THE VATICAN, ANGERS. The two tapestries of the *Passion*, at the Seo of Saragossa, a gift from King Ferdinand the Catholic to his son Bishop Alonso, are among the earliest tapestries devoted to the dramatic events of the life of Christ. Related to the *Stories of St. Piat and St. Eleuthère* by similarities of design which range from the architectural to the vegetable forms, and comparable with the *Courtly Scenes* from the Peyre bequest in the Musée des Arts Décoratifs, they are closest of all to the Chatsworth *Hunts*, which they resemble in spirit, in dimensions and in the arrangement of the compositions.

Another similar composition, forty years or so later in date, but certainly based, despite considerable variations, on the same cartoon, was formerly in the Somzée collection, and is now in the Musée du Cinquantenaire in Brussels.

Less fluent and less spontaneous in design than the Saragossa *Passion*, the Brussels *Passion*, woven in wool and silk, without gold, is nevertheless more stylish and impressive. The scale and massing of the figures reinforce the monumental aspect of the whole.

A companion piece to the Cinquantenaire tapestry has been discovered in the Vatican. A gift from the Spanish royal family to Pope Leo XIII, it shows the Entry to Jerusalem, the Last Supper, and the Betrayal.

The provenance of the Brussels-Vatican *Passion* remains uncertain. It has been attributed to Tournai. At the same time, certain details of the design, and the presence on the ground below the Crucifixion of the 'kidney-shaped flints' already noted in the Chatsworth *Bear-hunt*, have made it impossible to avoid the conclusion that the cartoons at least were of Arras origin. Probably the weaving also was carried out at Arras.

A third Passion, the *Passion* of Angers cathedral, is later than the Brussels-Vatican *Passion*. It was formerly in the church of Saint-Saturnin at Tours, to which it was bequeathed by Pierre Morin, treasurer-general of the Finances, in 1555. The scenes of the first Angers piece recur in a tapestry at the Museum of Fine Arts in Boston, U.S.A.; some further episodes have been added. Chanoine Urseau has made comparisons between the Angers *Passion* and the embroidered panels in the church of Saint-Bernard at Romans (1555).

Apart from other isolated pieces with Old and New Testament subjects of uncertain provenance, an *Annunciation*, acquired by the Metropolitan Museum about 1945, which is presumed to be a remnant of the *Life of the Virgin* made for Philip the Good and presented to Pope Martin V, can be

B. THE CHATSWORTH HUNTS: FALCONRY (detail)

associated with the *Passion* of Saragossa, Brussels and the Vatican. These tapestries confirm the formulation of characteristic aesthetic principles in the Arras workshops. The full development of these principles is seen in the *Story of the mighty King Clovis*, at Reims cathedral.

THE STORY OF CLOVIS. Despite an attribution to Tournai, the *Story of the mighty King Clovis* seems to find its natural home among the productions of Arras, by reason of its design, its style and its dimensions. Ought it not be included in the class of battle pieces, of which the *Battle of Roosebecke*, begun in 1387, and its probable companion piece, the *Battle of Liège*, sold to Jean the Fearless by Ryfflard Flaymal in 1413, were doubtless the most distinguished examples?

Armoured warriors, disposed in tiers, fill the entire field of the hangings, apart from the flowery mead below and the explanatory inscriptions in quatrains above. They are locked in furious combat. The laws of perspective are ignored; no thought of composition seems to direct the arrangement of this disarray, which is nevertheless, once again, meticulously organized. The prevailing impression is of opulence and great decorative power, in spite of a colour scheme which lacks brilliance, and could even be described as sombre. The costumes, which are always of the most sumptuous kind, are, by the usual anachronism, transposed into fifteenth-century style.

It has been claimed that the features of Charles VII may be recognized in those of Clovis. In that case the set would probably have been woven in the years around 1440. Its fate can be traced for more than five centuries. The six hangings of the *Story of Clovis* served, with other choice tapestries, to decorate one of the banqueting halls at the wedding of Charles the Bold and Margaret of York in 1468. They subsequently passed to the Austrian royal house, on the marriage of Mary of Burgundy, daughter of Charles the Bold, with Maximilian of Austria. Found in the baggage of the Emperor Charles V after the precipitate raising of the siege of Metz (1552), they fell to Duke François de Guise, later passing into the possession of his brother Charles de Guise, Cardinal of Lorraine. The latter gave them to the cathedral of Reims in 1573.

Three pieces were still in existence in 1840. Only two now remain. The first represents *the Coronation of Clovis, the Battle, and the Siege of Soissons*; the second includes the *Foundation of the church of Saint-Pierre-et-Saint-Paul at Paris, the Defeat of Gondebaud, King of the Burgundians*, and *Clovis crossing the Loire guided by a white stag before doing battle with Alaric, King of the Visigoths*.

THE 'CAPTURE OF JERUSALEM BY TITUS'. A similar impetuosity of movement, an identical avoidance of empty spaces, the same want of perspective, with the background as detailed as the foreground, appear again in the four fragments of the *Capture of Jerusalem by Titus* in the church of Notre-Dame-de-Nantilly at Saumur. The largest shows warriors with grotesque faces, in the strange architecture which passed at that time for Oriental. A coronation scene, the *Coronation of Vespasian*, has been compared with the *Coronation of Clovis* at Reims. Among the various inscriptions, the capital letters J.R. or R.J. have not yet been satisfactorily explained, despite some plausible attempts. Some remains of the same set seem to be divided between the Musée des Arts Décoratifs in Lyon (Musée des Tissus), the Museum für angewandte Kunst in Vienna, and private collections. A repetition of the left-hand section of one of the Saumur fragments, with the ground covered with flowering plants in the manner of late fifteenth and early sixteenth-century tapestries, is in the Museo Nazionale in Florence (Bargello). Several specimens of the *Capture of Jerusalem* have been reproduced in sale-catalogues, or are preserved in the great museums, for example, the Metropolitan Museum of New York. It has been supposed that these various versions may have some connection with the examples, of uncertain provenance, recorded in the inventories of Jacqueline of Bavaria, widow of Charles VI's second son, in 1419, of Pope Paul II in 1457, and of Anne de Bretagne in 1514.

Like other compositions which will be discussed in detail at a later stage (the *Story of Tarquin* at Zamora cathedral, and those of *Trajan and Herkenbald* and *Julius Caesar* in the museum of Berne), the *Capture of Jerusalem by Titus* belongs to one of the cycles of antique subjects which were woven quite frequently in the workshops of Arras and Tournai. Inspired by old chronicles, by romances, by manuscripts in the collection of the dukes of Burgundy, these enjoyed a lasting success with princes and wealthy citizens.

THE CYCLE OF THE TROJAN WAR. The prolonged success of the *Capture of Jerusalem* was equalled by that of the cycle of the Trojan War.

The latter subject inspired innumerable sets of hangings. A rapid survey of them will provide typical illustrations of the questions, difficulties and hypotheses which arise from the study of medieval tapestries.

Accounts of the Trojan war, popular since the tenth and eleventh centuries, enjoyed renewed favour with the thirteenth century *Romance of Troy* (*Roman de Troie*), by Benoît de Sainte-More, and the fifteenth century *Collection of the stories of Troy from its foundation to its fall* (*Recueil des histoires de Troie depuis sa fondation jusqu'à sa ruine*), written by Raoul

Le Fèvre for Philip the Good. The culmination of a long series of texts composed over a period of several centuries, the work of Raoul Le Fèvre took its place on the shelves of the ducal library alongside sixteen other manuscripts on the same theme. Like its predecessors, it went far beyond the strict limits of the misfortunes of Ilion, to include the story of Jason's quest for the Golden Fleece (a topical subject in view of the foundation of Philip the Good's order of chivalry in 1429) and the Labours of Hercules, who twice destroyed Troy, and was the legendary ancestor of the house of Burgundy.

The tapestries were concerned only with the misfortunes of Troy. Executed at intervals over a period of about fifty years, they have survived in fairly considerable numbers. A set of four pieces is in the cathedral of Zamora, in Spain; it has been attributed to Tournai, but confirmation is wanting. The Victoria and Albert Museum in London owns the tapestry including the *Meeting of Penthesilea and Priam, Penthesilea doing battle at the side of the Trojans*, and the *Arming of Pyrrhus*, which is traditionally said to have hung at the château of Bayard in Grésivaudan; after being presented by A. Jubinal to the French Imperial Library, it was reclaimed and sold by his heirs. At the court-house of Issoire there were formerly a number of fragments of the last third of the fifteenth century with the names of the Greek and Trojan heroes woven above the figures. Their fate is unknown. Panels of the early sixteenth century still remain in the commercial court at Montereau; they were formerly at the château, not of Varennes, but of Saint-Ange, built by Anne de Pisseleu. The *Funeral of Hector*, from the château of Sully, was formerly in the Kann collection. It is easy to extend the list of these Troy tapestries, all with the same densely packed crowds of figures. In Florence there are the three pieces from the Schouwaloff collection, later the Beckendorf collection. The *Andromache and Hector*, with *Hector and Priam* below, from the Dolfus and Clarence Mackay collections, is in the Metropolitan Museum in New York. Ignoring chronological order, which can hardly be established in these few lines, we may add, in Spain, *Penthesilea slain by Pyrrhus*, in the collection of the Duke of Alba, and, in America, *Ulysses and Diomedes at the court of Priam*, the fragment at the Rhode Island School of Design. A fragment in the Raoul Heilbronner sale in 1923 showed *Achilles and the siege of Troy*, with inscriptions in French and Latin. Lastly, we must not omit the set which was hung in the Painted Chamber at Westminster in the time of Charles II, and which was sold after 1800. Its appearance is preserved in the drawings in Indian ink which were acquired by the Victoria and Albert Museum at the Gardner sale in 1924.

THE DRAWINGS OF THE TROY CYCLE IN THE LOUVRE. Another set of pen-drawings, which entered the collections of the Louvre about 1898, also permits some interesting comparisons. Executed on paper which is held to have been manufactured in Laon or Soissons after 1463, they show the episodes of the Troy cycle which appear in the Victoria and Albert Museum tapestry and in the Zamora cathedral pieces.

The question whether the Louvre drawings are original designs for the cartoons or, as is more probable, copies after existing hangings, is of no great importance. Their very existence reveals that, at a given moment, these tapestries or replicas of them were assembled in one place, which is in itself a weighty argument in favour of a common origin.

For most of the hangings, the identification of the place of manufacture, which would be an extremely useful piece of knowledge, is rendered difficult by the fact that scenes of the Trojan war were produced in almost all the medieval tapestry-weaving centres. They were woven in Paris, where in 1396 Jacques Dourdin sold to Philip the Bold a tapestry of *Hector of Troy*, which was to be presented to the Grand Master of the Teutonic Order. They must have been woven at Arras, and they were certainly woven at Tournai, where, in 1472, a tapestry of the *Destruction of Troy* was bought from Pasquier Grenier for presentation to Charles the Bold.

These indications, which are too vague and imprecise to permit any firm conclusions, must be considered in conjunction with the fact that, at the period when most of these Troy subjects were executed, which can be fixed from the details of costume and accessories as the middle or second half of the fifteenth century, or even the beginning of the sixteenth, the Arras workshops had for some time been in a stagnant condition.

THE DECLINE OF THE ARRAS WORKSHOPS. The commission for the *Gideon* set, given by Philip the Good in 1449 to the Tournai workshops, has been considered, rightly or wrongly, as the first sign of the decadence of the workshops of Arras. The violent controversies which divided local scholars over this question in the nineteenth century have succeeded in complicating the problem. The only hope of resolving it lies in an impartial critical study of the few surviving documentary references, which have been too often wrenched from their original sense to serve partisan arguments.

We do not know whether the loss of clientele which the Arras workshops suffered, probably as a result of the unexplained decision of Philip the Good, was a slow or a rapid process, but it is certain that they continued to weave tapestries after 1449. Production continued down to the siege of 1477 and, as has been mentioned above, there was probably some activity even later. It is quite possible, therefore, that we possess at least a few tapestries woven at Arras during this period, which seems to have been one not so much of decadence as of slow decline. The increasing importance of Tournai has suggested the attribution to that centre of large numbers of Franco-Flemish tapestries made after 1450. But apart from certain hangings which can be assigned to, or otherwise associated with Tournai, on the basis of textual evidence, many such attributions must be treated with great reserve. The most important of these doubtfully attributed tapestries will be studied in the following chapter, which deals with Franco-Flemish production from 1450 onwards.

CHAPTER IV

Franco-Flemish tapestry
from 1450 onwards

TOURNAI

Tournai, a French enclave surrounded, until the middle of the sixteenth century, by the territory of the Dukes of Burgundy, holds an important place in the history and the development of the art of tapestry. This statement implies no limitation or diminution of the prestige of Arras, which is universally known for its achievements in the same field. As has been noted in the preceding chapter, the work of the two towns exhibits close parallels and, at times, a similarity of style sufficiently exact to give rise to uncertainties and doubts on questions of attribution. It would be rash to assert, however, that the Tournai workshops began life as branch-establishments of those of Arras, or that they reproduced the cartoons or undertook the surplus commissions of the latter.

Nothing could be more detrimental to sound research in this field than the attempt to establish non-existent connections between the production of these two independent centres.

It would be no less fallacious to assume that, in 1402, the Tournai workshops were insufficiently developed to be entrusted with the commission for the *Story of St. Piat and St. Eleuthère,* which was woven in Arras for the cathedral of Tournai. The same line of reasoning would lead to the conclusion that the execution of the *Gideon* set at Tournai in 1449, after designs painted in Arras, was a proof that the Arras workshops were hopelessly decadent by the middle of the fifteenth century.

Speculations of this kind are unlikely to lead to any positive result. In the absence of firm documentary evidence, all that can be done is to note these facts of 1402 and 1449, without indulging in sterile commentaries.

In the same way it should be noted, without launching into further hypotheses that the high-warp weaving referred to at Tournai in the course of the fourteenth century was important enough, by 1398, to form the subject of regulations issued by the magistrate of the town.

THE 1398 REGULATIONS. The regulations of 1398 for the manufacture 'of tapestry, high-warp and pile cloth (tapisserie, hauteliche et drap velu) made at Tournai' are the oldest document of this type from the group of workshops which are often called, with deliberate vagueness, 'North French workshops.'

Other regulations followed, and they suggest the growing importance of the production of narrative tapestries at Tournai. Nevertheless, despite the references collected by E. Soil in his book *Tapisseries de Tournai* (1892), little is known on this subject prior to the weaving of the *Gideon* set, begun in 1449.

THE 'GIDEON' SET. This set was extolled by all the chroniclers as 'the richest hanging ever to enter court of king'. It was made to adorn the chapter-hall of the Order of the Golden Fleece, founded in 1429 by the Duke of Burgundy, Philip the Good. For various reasons, the Biblical hero Gideon was chosen in place of Jason. As has already been mentioned, the cartoons for the eight hangings of the set, with a total length of 112 ells (about 325 feet) were executed by the painter Bauduin de Bailleul at Arras, and translated into tapestry at Tournai by Robert Dary and Jean de l'Ortye, 'merchant manufacturers of tapestry.'

Completed in 1453, the *Gideon* set formed a splendid setting for the festivals of the house of Burgundy, and of its heirs, the Kings of Spain. In 1555, at the time of the abdication of Charles V, it was hanging in the palace of Brussels, and it was still in Brussels at the end of the eighteenth century. It is believed to have been carried off by the retreating Austrians in 1794, after which nothing is known of its fate. Its loss is all the more regrettable since it might well have furnished criteria for the attribution of several other very important sets which have been assigned sometimes to Arras, sometimes to Tournai. Among these are the *Story of St. Peter* and the *Sacraments*.

THE 'STORY OF ST. PETER' SET. The set of the *Story of St. Peter*, which was made for Pierre de Hellande, Bishop of Beauvais, comprised ten tapestries, of which six remain at Beauvais, one is in the Musée de Cluny and one in the Boston Museum. Some fragments in the antique trade, now in America, belonged to the tenth piece.

The *Story of St. Peter*, as is indicated by the word *'paix'* scattered everywhere in great profusion, was intended to commemorate the end of the Hundred Years War. In the catalogues of all exhibitions of French tapestries since 1946 it has been assigned to Arras, but this should not be allowed to obscure the fact that it has also been repeatedly attributed to Tournai.

This second attribution is not without substance. It is supported by a possible relationship with a set of painted hangings, which are unfortunately lost; they represented the *Life and Passion of St. Peter* and were painted in 1443 by Henri de Beaumentiel, after designs by Robert Campin, for the chapel of Saint-Pierre at Tournai.

As against this, the first hypothesis is supported by the stylistic analogies which have been detected, despite the lapse of sixty years, between the *Story of St. Piat*, which is known to have been woven at Arras, and the *Story of St. Peter*. Further comparisons have been made with the arcaded miniatures executed in the abbey of Saint-Waast at Arras.

These arguments seem for the moment to have carried the day. But the two opinions are not so contrary as they appear, for both tend to confirm the identity of style which characterized the work of Arras and of Tournai about the middle of the fifteenth century. It would seem to be simple prudence not to depart too far from this idea, which is reinforced by study of another series related to the *Story of St. Peter* — the *Sacraments* set, which seems certainly to have been woven at Tournai.

THE SEVEN SACRAMENTS. The unusual subject of the *Sacraments* seems to have been distributed in two rows, one above the other; the various scenes, divided by colonnettes, were accompanied by inscriptions. The surviving scenes of the lower row are *Baptism*, *Marriage* and *Extreme Unction* (New York, Metropolitan Museum), and *Ordination* (with *Confirmation* [?]; London, Victoria and Albert Museum). From the upper part, which showed the prefiguration of the sacraments in the Old Testament, there remain *Baptism* (Naaman in the Jordan), *Confirmation* (Jacob and his children), *Marriage* (Adam and Eve), and *Extreme Unction* (anointing of David). Lastly, Mme. Crick-Kuntziger has identified in the Burrell collection (Glasgow Art Gallery) the prefiguration of *Communion* (Abraham and Melchisedek), which has suffered some alterations and additions.

In addition to its aesthetic and iconographical interest, the set of *Sacraments* thus partially reconstituted possesses documentary interest of the first importance. In 1936, following the discovery of an unpublished document, M. Paul Rolland advanced the hypothesis that the *Sacraments* represent the remains of a gift made in 1475 to the church of Saint-Quentin in Tournai by Pasquier Grenier, one of the principal tapestry-contractors of the town. Although certain reservations have been expressed, especially with regard to the rather rash identification of a group of figures in the Burrell tapestry as Pasquier Grenier and his family, this hypothesis has been accepted by the best-qualified specialists.

PASQUIER GRENIER. Pasquier Grenier was enrolled as a citizen in 1447. In three documents of 1449, he is referred to as a '*marcheteur*', or weaver of low-warp tapestry ('*tapisserie à la marche*'). Like the prominent Arras weavers, he was also engaged in the wine trade. His business was continued by his sons Antoine and Jean, as well as by other members of his family.

Thanks to the perfection and charm of his work, Pasquier Grenier was frequently employed by the Dukes of Burgundy.

In 1459, he sold a *Story of Alexander* to Philip the Good, and in 1461 a *Passion of Our Lord* and a chamber of tapestry with *Peasants* and *Wood-cutters*. In 1462, the Duke bought of him the *Story of Esther and Ahasuerus* and the *Knight of the Swan*. In 1466, there are references to 'chambers of *Orange-trees*' and of *Woodcutters*, intended for the Duchess of Bourbon and the Duchess of Gelderland. Finally, in 1472, when Charles the Bold, son and successor of Philip the Good, received a tapestry of the *War of Troy* from the *magistrat du franc* of Bruges, this too was supplied by Pasquier Grenier.

This documentary evidence is valuable, for most of these subjects are found not only in the archives, but also in existing tapestries of about the third quarter of the fifteenth century. These documents and tapestries thus provide some welcome landmarks in the difficult and complex study of Tournai production from about 1450 to 1475.

THE STORY OF ALEXANDER. The *Story of Alexander*, which was sold by Pasquier Grenier to Philip the Good in 1459, was numbered among the most sumptuous tapestries of the Burgundian collection and included details in silk and Cyprus gold thread. In addition to seven wall-hangings, it comprised the indispensable accessories of the 'chamber of tapestry' — canopy, dossal, cover and valances. Two of the hangings have been preserved; they illustrate several episodes, including *Alexander's Flight in the Air* and *Alexander's Descent into the Sea*. They now belong to Prince Doria, in Rome. The presence of gold or silver threads, which had been doubted by several authors, has been verified, after close study, by Mme. Crick-Kuntziger, and seems to clinch the identity. The subjects are derived from the *Livre des Conquestes et Faits d'Alexandre le Grand*, compiled by Jean Wauquelin for the Count of Estampes, first cousin of Philip the Good. This was one of the fabulous romances which were so much appreciated on account of their flattering references to the origins, the grandeur and the destiny of the Burgundian court. The same compilation by Jean Wauquelin — rather than the twelfth-century version of the *Romance of Alexander* by Lambert de Tors — probably served as the source for three fragments of another *Story of Alexander* from the former Aymard collection. These, showing the *Combat of Alexander and Nicolas*, *Philip of Macedon and his Barons*, and *Men-at-arms*, now belong to the municipal collections of Paris (Petit Palais).

THE 'STORY OF ESTHER AND AHASUERUS'. The six pieces of the set of *Esther and Ahasuerus*, bought by Philip the Good from Pasquier Grenier in 1462, were intended for Cardinal Geoffroy, Bishop of Arras. Other examples of the *Story of Esther* adorned a room of the ducal palace at Bruges on the occasion of one of the marriages of Charles the Bold, in 1468; pieces with the same subject figure in the inventory of Margaret of Austria (1523). The *Story of Esther* was obviously a fashionable subject and several specimens have survived. Two pieces, in the Musée Lorrain at Nancy, are said, rightly or wrongly, to be booty from the collections of Charles the Bold. They show *Vashti refusing to attend the banquet of Ahasuerus* and *Ahasuerus deciding to repudiate Vashti*; the subjects are explained by French inscriptions above.

A replica of the scene of *Vashti refusing to attend the banquet* is in the Louvre (Albert Bossy gift). It is less complete than the Nancy version; both specimens are mutilated. The *Story of Esther* recurs in examples in the Minneapolis Museum, in a private collection and in the cathedral of Saragossa.

'THE KNIGHT OF THE SWAN'. The date of execution of the *Story of the Knight of the Swan* is apparently determinable within narrow limits. It is likely to have been subsequent to the theatrical presentation of a rhymed poem, which forms part of the Godefroy of Bouillon cycle, concerning the *Knight of the Swan*, a supposed ancestor of the house of Burgundy. This presentation took place on the occasion of the Vow of the Pheasant, at Lille, in 1454, in which the participants took an oath to wage war against the enemies of the Cross. The set must certainly have been completed, however, by 1462, when Philip the Good paid Pasquier Grenier for its execution.

One fragment of the *Knight of the Swan* belongs to the Museum für angewandte Kunst in Vienna; a second, more important, fragment is in the church of St. Catherine in Cracow.

The style of the architecture, landscape and perspective, the elegance and nobility of some of the faces, and the clarity of the scenes, notwith-standing their complexity, are indications of French influence.

Traces, in the inscriptions, of the dialect of the Tournai area show that the designer of the cartoons of the *Knight of the Swan* and of related sets was a native of, or at least resident in, that neighbourhood. Vestiges of archaism, which are apparent in several of the sets, seem to support the view that they were designed in the same studio or by pupils of the same master. Mme. Crick-Kuntziger has suggested the circle of the old Robert Campin, who died in 1444. Subsequently, Abbé Lestocquoy has drawn attention to Bauduin de Bailleul, to whom reference has been made in the preceding chapter.

SCENES OF THE TROJAN WAR. The identity of inspiration, and the artistic relationships and interchanges between the two great centres of Arras and Tournai pose — and this must be emphasized even at the risk of appearing repetitive — some extremely complicated problems. The solutions adopted by the various authorities have rarely been subjected to comparison and evaluation, and are often contradictory. In considering them for the first time in the course of a general survey it is only prudent to exclude excessively rigid interpretations. This caution is undoubtedly appropriate in the case of the scenes from the *Story of Troy*. The principal examples have already been referred to in the chapter devoted to Arras. Were they in fact woven simultaneously, or at different periods, in both centres? Were they woven only at Arras? Or only at Tournai? Is it apposite to recall, in this connection, that Tournai contractors, such as Haquinet le Scellier or Jacques Descamaing (1491), sometimes sub-contracted work to, or employed, weavers of Audenarde or Louvain? The sale of the tapestry of the *Destruction of Troy* by Pasquier Grenier in 1472 is one of the few contemporary references which we have, but it is hardly possible to affirm that the Metropolitan Museum fragment is a product of his work-shop. We shall shortly have occasion to mention a *Story of Hercules*, woven at Tournai, and derived from a literary source in which this story appears as a preamble to the Story of Troy.

THE 'WOODCUTTERS'. On more than one occasion, in 1461 and 1466, the Tournai archives record the sale by Pasquier Grenier of tapestries with figures 'such as peasant folk and woodcutters who are seen working and labouring in the woods in divers ways', a theme which differs from his usual repertory.

These references have been linked with a tapestry of *Woodcutters*, bearing a coat-of-arms which has been identified as that of the Chancellor of Burgundy, Nicolas Rolin (died 1461); this is in the Musée des Arts Décoratifs, Paris.

Belonging to the same group, but of various dates, are the *Shepherds* at the Musée du Cinquantenaire in Brussels (formerly Somzée collection), the *Vine-dressers* or *Gipsies* exhibited at the Gobelins in 1928, and the *Lord administering justice* from the former Figdor collection (Copenhagen, Kunstindustrimuseum). Another tapestry with *Woodcutters* at the Musée des Arts Décoratifs in Paris (which also possesses a third piece, intermediate between this and the former) has been attributed to Jean Grenier, son and successor of Pasquier Grenier. The attribution seems to have been a little over-hasty. It provides an occasion, however, to mention the extent to which a popular prototype might be repeated and modified and to record the sale, made by Jean Grenier to Philip the Fair in 1505, of 'a chamber . . . made with figures of woodcutters'.

VARIOUS WORKSHOPS. Pasquier Grenier (died 1493), notwithstanding his importance, his princely customers, his sales to Le Puy, to Lyon, to Reims, and his branches or warehouses at Bruges and Antwerp, was by no means the only tapestry-contractor at Tournai in the second half of the fifteenth century. Other workshops existed, among which were those of Haquinet le Scellier (died before 1483) and Willaume or Guillaume Desreumaulx (died 1483).

The compositions woven in these workshops were very similar to those of Grenier and all seem to share in a common Tournai style which was current from 1450 until after 1475. This style is found in the tapestries of the *Old and New Testament*, the *Story of Ahab* and the *Story of Jephtha*, in subjects drawn from ancient and modern history, such as *Queen Semiramis* (Metropolitan Museum), *Julius Caesar*, the *Battle of Roncevaux*, *Herkenbald*, and the *Portuguese Victories*, as well as in mythological themes.

THE OLD AND NEW TESTAMENT: THE HANGINGS OF THE ABBEY OF SAINT-BERTIN. The set of hangings ordered by Guillaume Fillastre, Abbot of Saint-Bertin at St. Omer, and at the same time Bishop of Tournai (1461–73), must have been among the earlier productions of these Tournai workshops. They represented the 'story of the Old and New Testament, including the Passion of Our Lord'. The hangings, which must have been numerous, were despatched to Saint-Bertin in consequence of a dispute between the bishop and the canons of Tournai cathedral. The design of the set is preserved only in a series of forty-four rather rudely drawn miniatures in the Library of St. Omer. The tapestries themselves have disappeared, with the exception of two pieces, comprising three scenes from Genesis, in the St. Omer Museum.

AHAB AND JEPHTHA. The *Story of Ahab,* a subject which was treated from time to time by the tapestry-weavers of the fifteenth century, is almost unrepresented among surviving tapestries, apart from the *Judgment of the House of Ahab* (Boston Museum). This piece is characterized by the intense expressions of the faces, a method of suggesting dramatic emotion with limited technical resources which recurs in the *Story of Jephtha.*

A strange chance has brought together two identical and contemporary specimens of the *Story of Jephtha* in the superb collection of the Seo or cathedral of Saragossa. The explanatory inscriptions show the same peculiarities of dialect as have been noted in those of the *Knight of the Swan.* The employment of the same dialect and various other indications — though they do not prove, as some authors have suggested, that the *Story of Jephtha* was woven in the workshop of Pasquier Grenier — do at least testify to a common origin in Tournai.

THE BERNE TAPESTRIES: 'ADORATION OF THE MAGI', 'TRAJAN AND HERKENBALD', 'CAESAR'. The Berne tapestries are said to have been booty from the baggage of Charles the Bold after the disaster of Grandson or the battle of Morat (1476). This is plausible enough for a piece with a blue ground and the arms and motto of Philip the Good or Charles the Bold, but it seems doubtful for the *Adoration of the Kings,* the earliest of the group. The place of origin of the *Trajan and Herkenbald,* and *Julius Caesar* tapestries is open to dispute, but it seems likely that they were woven at Tournai.

The hanging comprising several scenes illustrating the *Justice of Trajan and the Story of Herkenbald* was probably given to the cathedral of Lausanne by Bishop Georges de Saluces, whose episcopate terminated in 1461. It is said to have been transferred to Berne at the time of the Reformation. The *Story of Herkenbald* includes two scenes, reproducing, more or less accurately, the paintings executed by Rogier van der Weyden in 1441 for the Brussels Town Hall; the latter were destroyed by the bombardment of 1695.

Like the scenes of the *Justice of Trajan*, the designs of the *Story of Julius Caesar* are characterized by a certain confusion. Their colouring is rather gloomy and lacking in brilliance. The inscriptions in verse, and hence the scenes themselves, are derived from a thirteenth-century manuscript of the *Faits des Romains*, which belonged to Philip the Good. After being in the possession of Louis of Luxemburg, Comte de Saint-Paul, the *Story of Julius Caesar* later passed to Charles the Bold. The latter gave it to Guillaume de La Baume (died 1490), who added his arms. *The Story of Julius Caesar* is said to have been seized by the Swiss at the sack of the château of La Baume.

THE 'BATTLE OF RONCEVAUX'. The large size of the Berne tapestries was surpassed by the dimensions of a hanging representing the *Battle of Roncevaux*, which was cut into smaller pieces at an early date. The important fragment in the Musée de Cinquantenaire in Brussels (formerly Somzée collection) may be reunited in imagination with the no less important fragment in the Bargello, Florence, which was identified by Mme. Crick-Kuntziger in 1931. Portions of the design are missing between the two fragments and at the bottom of the Brussels piece.

Woven for some unidentified dignitary of the court of Burgundy, the *Battle of Roncevaux*, like so many other tapestries, was inspired by a literary source, which has been identified, and by other derivative texts. The scenes depicted in the tapestry follow the original text closely and are designed with assurance, despite an appearance of confusion. Details of composition and style link the *Battle of Roncevaux* directly with the group of tapestries woven at Tournai in the third quarter of the fifteenth century.

The dialect forms employed in the verse inscriptions of the *Battle of Roncevaux* provide further evidence in support of this association.

THE 'PORTUGUESE VICTORIES'. The furious mêlée of the *Battle of Roncevaux* meets its match in the *Portuguese Victories*, which have been preserved for several centuries in the collegiate church of Pastrana, a little town in the province of Guadalajara, Spain. Replicas of three of the tapestries have been woven in modern times. These three hangings, each about thirty-six feet long, represent the *Landing under the walls of Arzila*, and the *Siege* and *Capture* of this African town. A fourth tapestry shows the *Occupation of Tangier*. The events commemorated in the Pastrana tapestries occurred in the month of April, 1471.

XVII. THE VINTAGE
Musée de Cluny, Paris

XVIII. THE THREE CORONATIONS (detail)
Sens Cathedral

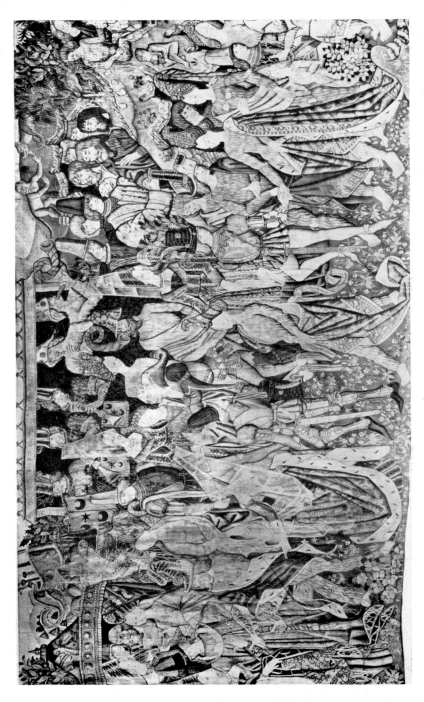

XIX. THE DANCE OF THE WILD MEN AND WOMEN

Church of Notre-Dame-de-Nantilly, Saumur

XX. CAVALCADE or FALCONRY
Church of Notre-Dame-de-Nantilly, Saumur

XXI. THE PRESENTATION OF THE ROSES
Metropolitan Museum, New York

XXII. THE WINGED STAGS

Musée des antiquités de Normadie, Rouen

XXIII. THE SHEPHERDS
Musée des Gobelins, Paris

XXIV. THE NOBLE PASTORAL: WORKING IN WOOL AND SHEEP-SHEARING

Musée du Louvre, Paris

The catalogue of the exhibition of Portuguese art in Paris, in 1931, mentions that the cartoons were the work of the great Portuguese artist Nuño Gonçalves, court-painter to King Alfonso V (died about 1481). This positive attribution is repeated and elaborated in the catalogue of the Portuguese-Flemish-Spanish exhibition at Bordeaux, in 1954, but in neither case is any documentary evidence adduced.

The despatch of designs or cartoons by Nuño Gonçalves to Tournai, if it were to be backed by satisfactory evidence, would be a striking proof of the international renown which the tapestry-workshops of the town enjoyed, and which brought them commissions from potentates of countries remote from their own immediate neighbourhood.

HERCULES. Among such commissions was probably that for the *Story of Hercules.*

Thanks to M. Jacques Bacri's identification of the coat-of-arms, we know that the *Story of Hercules* belonged to Cardinal Charles de Bourbon, Bishop of Lyon, a nephew of Philip the Good. The weaving must have taken place between 1476, the year in which Charles de Bourbon became cardinal, and 1488, the year of his death. The *Story of Hercules* has been divided into three pieces, of which one is in the Musée des Gobelins, one in the Musée du Cinquantenaire, Brussels (former Somzée collection), and one in a private collection (1934). The composition was inspired by the *Recueil des histoires de Troie*, which was composed in 1464, at the instigation of Philip the Good, by his chaplain Raoul Lefèvre.

There are other attributions to Tournai which must be treated more cautiously. They cannot, however, be omitted from a general survey in which inevitably, owing to the absence of contemporary descriptions and the rarity of documentary references, a great many hypotheses have to appear alongside the established facts. For this reason we must mention here, even at the risk of digressing, at least two controversial works, the *Dance of the Wild Men and Women* at Notre-Dame-de-Nantilly, Saumur, and the set of the *Story of Susanna* in the Musée Marmottan, Paris.

THE 'DANCE OF THE WILD MEN AND WOMEN'. The tapestry of Notre-Dame-de-Nantilly has for many years attracted attention on account of its curious subject. At one time it was suggested that this gathering of men and women, dancing and conversing together, some clad in the brilliant fashions of the second half of the fifteenth century, while others are covered with the fleeces of animals, must refer to the notorious 'Dance of the Burning Men' at the Hôtel Saint-Pol in 1393, in which Charles VI so nearly perished. This identification, which was already abandoned by Jules Guiffrey, may be rejected without regret in favour of a more rational explanation. The piece must represent a scene from some courtly romance, which has unfortunately not yet been identified.

It is difficult to determine the origin of this tapestry, despite the over-ingenious reading of some letters, which appear in the border of the dress of one of the figures, as the signature of the Tournai citizen Lambert le Fève. Is it the work of a settled or an itinerant workshop? Was this workshop in fact established in northern France or elsewhere? It might be possible to take a first step towards the solution of the problem if we could explain what subject was represented in the five tapestries with 'figures of wild men' which, after being found in a cupboard, were recorded in an inventory of the abbey of Saint-Waast at Arras in 1597.

THE 'STORY OF SUSANNA'. Hardly more conclusive is the evidence concerning the origin of the *Story of Susanna*, which consists of eight scenes in five hangings. Its incorporation by Soil in his work on Tournai (1892) scarcely merits the name of hypothesis; none the less, it cannot be rejected out of hand.

The armorial bearings which appear in the tapestries are stated by Soil to be later than the tapestries themselves; this remains to be proved.

The arms in question are those of Bénigne de Cirey and his wife, Guillaumette Jacqueron, both from Burgundian families; their marriage must have taken place at the end of the fifteenth or the beginning of the sixteenth century. But this identification provides no evidence either for or against an origin in Burgundy rather than in northern France. The uninterrupted contacts between Flanders and the hereditary possessions of the Dukes of Burgundy, the possible despatch of the Nuño Gonçalves cartoons to Tournai, the existence of itinerant workshops, which will be discussed in the following chapter — these facts seem to open the door to every possibility. Even supposing the set to have been woven at the time of the marriage of Bénigne de Cirey and Guillaumette Jacqueron, it is quite possible that it may have been derived from older cartoons. An additional complication, which might some day turn out to be the vital factor, is the circumstance that the explanatory inscriptions of the *Susanna* set resemble those of painted hangings preserved at Reims. This similarity, which does not extend to the scenes themselves, does little more than show that the two series were based on a common literary source. The latter has not yet been identified.

THE TOURNAI WORKSHOPS AT THE END OF THE FIFTEENTH AND BEGINNING OF THE SIXTEENTH CENTURY. Whether or not it was woven at Tournai, the *Susanna* set is not inconsistent with the normal and logical development of the Tournai workshops. The '*marcheteurs*' (low-warp specialists) and other weavers who had directed production in the third quarter of the fifteenth century were replaced by a new generation. Among the busiest workshops were those of at least two of the four sons of Pasquier Grenier; all four had inherited designs from their father. Antoine Grenier numbered among his clients the Cardinal d'Amboise, to whom he sold tapestries for the episcopal palace at Rouen (1497) and for the château of Gaillon (1508). His brother, Jean Grenier (died 1519), was no less active. He furnished the Archduke Philip the Fair with numbers of tapestries, and it was he who supplied a set of the *City of Women* in six pieces, which was presented by the magistrate of Tournai to Margaret of Austria when she was appointed governor of the Low Countries in 1513. Tapestries with *Woodcutters*, including the fragments in the Musée des Arts Décoratifs in Paris, have been attributed to Jean Grenier.

Besides the Grenier family, another distinguished name, from 1491 onwards, and especially after 1510, is that of Arnould Poissonnier (died 1522), from whom the Emperor Maximilian I made important purchases. Then there are the Sarrasin family, the weavers Burbure, de Cassel, and others, who also, in varying degrees, contributed to the prosperity of the Tournai workshops.

Besides the new contractors and craftsmen, the passage of time naturally brought changes in the choice of subjects and in the style of the designs.

Religious and historical themes continued to be favoured. Among others, a piece recording a contemporary event, the *Siege of Dijon in 1513* in the Dijon museum, has been attributed to Tournai; it is marked with the letter 'G', but it is not likely that this refers to the Grenier family. Apart from these historical subjects, which had now become traditional, it seems possible to distinguish a fashion for certain allegorical compositions, based on the scientific interests of the time. Thus a tapestry of *Arithmetic* in the Musée de Cluny, which once formed part of a set of *Seven Liberal Arts*, has been attributed to the Tournai workshops.

To the same cycle may belong *Music* (Boston, Museum of Fine Arts), *Rhetoric* (Paris, Musée des Arts Décoratifs), *Astronomy* (Homberg collection), and *Archimedes and Ptolemy at the feet of Arithmetic and Astronomy* (Rochester Memorial Art Gallery).

FAMOUS WOMEN. The designers of tapestry-cartoons at the end of the fifteenth and the beginning of the sixteenth century did not restrict themselves to personifications of abstract sciences. They also represented, in the guise of heroines of antiquity and of the Old Testament, the virtues by which these ladies were distinguished. This set is known as the *Famous Women*. Consisting of ten pieces, it began with Virtue, beneath a canopy whose two supports were carried by unicorns; the remaining pieces presented in turn a rather curious collection comprising Lucretia, Penelope, Virginia, Dido, Susanna, the Cimbrian women, Hippo of Athens and Judith.

A set of *Famous Women* was in the possession of Ferry de Clugny, a canon of Autun, to whom it is said to have been given by his patron Mary of Burgundy, wife of Maximilian I. It may well be, however, that the tapestries were ordered by Ferry de Clugny himself. He was Bishop of Tournai from 1473 onwards and received a cardinal's hat in 1480, after an earlier nomination to the cardinalate had been nullified by the death of Pope Paul II (died 1471). Ferry de Clugny died in Rome in 1483. The tapestries, of which the *Dido* piece included his arms accompanied by a cardinal's hat, must presumably have been on the looms, though not necessarily completed, between 1480 and 1483. Clugny, however, on account of the war with Louis XI, whose troops occupied Tournai from 1477 onwards, had transferred his see to Bruges. We are thus left in doubt as to the place where the weaving was carried out. Mme. Crick-Kuntziger, who has directed her attention chiefly to the questions of the design, and the designer, supposes that it is likely to have been Bruges rather than Antwerp.

Most of the tapestries of the set of *Famous Women* were destroyed in a fire at the end of the eighteenth century at the château of Thenissey, in Burgundy. Only fragments remain, among them those of *Penelope* and the *Cimbrian Women*, which since 1926 have been in the Museum of Fine Arts in Boston.

It is not only the inherent charm of the sumptuously clad Penelope which has attracted the attention of scholars, but also the strange likeness between her and the *Lady with the Unicorn* in the Musée de Cluny. Another link between the two is the hanging, with flowerets on a green ground, which appears behind Penelope.

Once again, these connections pose many problems, which are all the more delicate in view of the importance of avoiding lines of research which might tend to favour inadequately based conclusions.

THE SCENE OF THE 'STORY OF PERSEUS'. One aspect of these problems has recently been attacked by Mme. Crick-Kuntziger, who had the good fortune to discover and publish, in 1954, an unknown tapestry representing the *Story of Perseus*. The female figures in this hanging show resemblances with *Penelope* and the *Lady with the Unicorn*. The deductions derived from these resemblances will be found in the paragraphs devoted to the latter series (Chapter V, below).

THE 'MORALITY OF SUPPER AND BANQUET'. Among the subjects woven in the Tournai workshops at the end of the fifteenth and the beginning of the sixteenth century, the moralities were the most successful. We may justifiably draw this conclusion from the number of replicas of the *Morality of Supper and Banquet* which are known from documentary evidence and from specimens preserved in public and private collections.

Soil mentions four tapestries with figures 'after the manner of Banquet', delivered by Colart Bloyart to Philip I the Fair, Archduke of Austria, in 1501, and six large pieces of the *Story of Banquet* woven by Jean Grenier in 1505. The cartoons of these may have belonged to Pasquier Grenier, for there exists a mock-letter, supposedly addressed to Philip the Good, which described similar subjects. It was nevertheless a different text, the *Condamnation de Banquet*, published in Paris in 1507 by Nicolas de la Chesnaye, which served as the source for the five tapestries in the Musée Lorrain at Nancy.

The latter were long considered to have formed part of the booty taken from Charles the Bold. But a recent study by M. Pierre Marot has shown that the set formerly numbered nine tapestries, of which four large pieces and two small ones seem to have been acquired by Duke Antoine about 1511.

There are also, in addition to the *Lady Experience* in the collection of the Duke of Fernan Nuñez, two other slightly earlier pieces with restored borders. One of these, including a subject which is lacking at the Musée Lorrain, *Banquet leading the guests to his house*, was exhibited at Venice in 1952.

The borders of the Nancy set, consisting of a double row of bunches of flowers, fastened with ribbons, and sometimes with a valance adorned with bells beneath the upper row, can be found, in more or less the same form, in other tapestries. Mme. Crick-Kuntziger has pointed out that certain details of style, such as the rendering of the folds of the draperies and the taste for head-ornaments of ostrich plumes, recur throughout the group.

This group, one of the last to come off the Tournai looms before the decline of the industry there, includes the *Story of Judith*.

THE 'STORY OF JUDITH'. This set is represented by a piece from the former Somzée collection, now in the Musée du Cinquantenaire in Brussels. A partial replica, lacking a border, has circulated in the antique trade, while a second tapestry, presumably a companion-piece to the first, is in a private collection.

In accordance with usual practice, the two tapestries include several successive episodes of the story. They date from the beginning of the sixteenth century. At this period, between 1516 and 1522, the workshop of Arnould Poissonnier is known to have sold several sets with this subject. Mme. Crick-Kuntziger has pointed out, without drawing any conclusion from the fact, that cartoons were supplied to Poissonnier's workshop by Antoine or Anthonin Ferré, who qualified as a master in Tournai in 1503.

SETS WITH EXOTIC SUBJECTS. The other tapestries belonging to the same group offer more unexpected subjects. They include the hangings or fragments from the château of Dreux-Brézé, the *Triumphal March*, the *Lion-Hunt* and the *Ships*, of which there is possibly another specimen in the Azurara palace at Lisbon (Riccardo da Espirito Santo collection); to these may be added the partial replica in the Nationalmuseum of Stockholm (left side restored; by Gilles le Castre in Poissonnier's workshop [?]), with its procession of giraffes, and the piece in the museum of Barcelona. These hangings, with their marching animals and human figures, reflect the taste for exotic motifs which had been launched by the Portuguese voyages of discovery. It must have been compositions of this type which appear in the Tournai archives as tapestries 'after the manner of Portugal and India' (1504), as 'people and savage beasts after the manner of Calicut' (1520), as the 'voyage of Caluce' (1513) and as the 'caravan'.

VERDURE TAPESTRIES. Alongside the sets with exotic subjects, the archives mention several tapestries with plant-ornament or landscape subjects, of the type known as 'verdures'. Such tapestries had always formed part of Tournai production. They occur in the inventory of the property of Arnould Poissonnier, and Pasquier Grenier had sold them fifty years earlier. Among other verdure tapestries attributed to Tournai is one in the Musée des Arts Décoratifs, Paris, with children playing amid birds and flowers (beginning of the sixteenth century).

★　　★　　★　　★　　★

The prosperity of the Tournai workshops, which reached its height at the beginning of the sixteenth century, was destined to suffer a series of crushing blows — notably the sieges of 1512 and 1521 — as a result of political events. The authority of the King of France was succeeded by that of the King of England; finally, having been reoccupied for a short time by the French, the town was ceded to the Emperor Charles V. An epidemic of plague added its ravages to the disastrous effects of the political situation. The tapestry workshops suffered the full rigours of these calamities. Their activity declined rapidly and by the second half of the sixteenth century was almost insignificant. By that period, however, Tournai had long since ceased to be French territory.

CHAPTER V

French tapestries of the fifteenth and early sixteenth centuries

While Arras and Tournai were still enjoying the fruits of their success, and had not yet been overtaken by the inevitable decline, tapestry workshops were set up in various other towns of northern France. There is evidence for their presence at Lille, Amiens, Cambrai and Valenciennes. But they remained little more than isolated experiments, which failed to found a real tradition. The theory of a local provenance for the *Tournament* tapestry in the museum at Valenciennes has been contested. This hanging, woven about the beginning of the sixteenth century, with a border of pomegranate-pattern and coats-of-arms, seems to show signs of Germanic origins, though this might well be due merely to the employment of a German-trained designer.

In Paris, as a result of a long series of political and economic disasters, a great outbreak of plague in 1418, and the beginning of the English occupation, most of the arts of luxury entered upon a period of inactivity. The tax-list imposed by the English in 1421 refers to only two tapestries. Only a very small number are mentioned under the reigns of Charles VII (died 1461), Louis XI (died 1483) and Charles VIII (died 1498).

Nevertheless, it must be supposed that tapestry-production was resumed in Paris fairly rapidly. How else can we explain the purchase in 1460, by the canons of Angers cathedral, of six pieces of the *Story of St. Maurice*, from Brie d'Espagne, merchant or weaver of Paris? The *St. Maurice* set has disappeared, but there is still at Angers cathedral an important fragment of the *Story of St. Maurille*, which was bought by the chapter from Pierre Dupuys, residing in Paris, in 1461. Despite excessive restoration, there is still considerable charm in the scene where the saint, in the capacity of gardener, is digging a flower-bed full of little flowers. The latter show a free interpretation of natural forms, whereas the trees of the background are still stylized.

French Tapestries of the Fifteenth and Early Sixteenth Centuries

In 1484, the magistrate of Tournai commissioned a craftsman of Paris to supply a chamber of tapestry to a nobleman of the French court.

About the same period, tapestry-weavers were active in the territories of the Dukes of Burgundy, which were reunited with France in 1477. Soon after, tapestry-looms were also set up in the district of La Marche, where their activity has continued down to our own day. But it was the centre of the kingdom — the region of Bourges, residence of Charles VII, of Tours, residence of Louis XI, of Angers, residence of Charles VIII, and of Blois, residence of Louis XII — that was best placed to produce tapestries in a characteristic French style, free, in the main, from foreign influences.

The arts of luxury could hardly exist and prosper except in the neighbourhood of the court; hence it was in the region of the Loire that the Paris weavers took refuge, and resumed the exercise of their profession.

The transitional works which presumably preceded the full development of their style are lost or unrecognized; their mature works have survived only in relatively small numbers.

These French tapestries of the end of the fifteenth and the beginning of the sixteenth century are grouped, without any attempt at more precise attribution, under the general heading of 'workshops of the Loire region'. Itinerant workshops must also have played a part in this development. They evidently included weavers from Arras and Tournai, refugees from the wars that afflicted their native cities, as well as local and Parisian craftsmen. One imagines that they wandered from town to town, from castle to abbey, ready to settle down for a few months or a few years, according to the commissions that they might receive from great nobles or richly endowed prelates. Such hypotheses, though they cannot claim to be an exact account of the actual conditions of work, for which documentary evidence is not yet forthcoming, nevertheless cannot be very far from the truth. They provide at least a plausible explanation for the appearance, over a period of about forty years, of considerable numbers of religious tapestries executed for churches or monasteries situated in various parts of the old kingdom of France. Despite their late date and relatively advanced style, these tapestries are still legitimate offspring of the traditions of the middle ages. Executed in a technique which, by reason of its slow and laborious nature, is always prone to archaism in style, but which can be equally favourable to modernism when the occasion offers, they permit us to follow the progressive erosion of the old culture, the old artistic conceptions, before the new currents of the Renaissance.

THE TAPESTRIES OF THE HÔTEL-DIEU AT BEAUNE. For want of more precise information it is usual to attribute to an itinerant workshop, or one temporarily settled in the area, the tapestries of the Hôtel-Dieu at Beaune. This hospital was founded by one of Pasquier Grenier's customers at Tournai, Nicolas Rolin, chancellor of Burgundy from 1421 to 1461, and by his wife, Guigone de Salins. The tapestries, executed about 1450 and intended as covers for the sick-beds 'on solemn feast-days', are of an elegant simplicity, with their ornament 'of turtle-doves, with the shields-of-arms of the founders'. Lopped branches, stars and the motto 'Seulle' complete the design of the thirty pieces which have survived from the original set of thirty-one. The same red ground recurs in two other hangings, made for the chapel of the foundation, in which the centre of the field is occupied by a figure of St. Anthony dressed as a hermit; these figures show an undeniable affinity with the sculpture of the Burgundian school.

Three further fragments, discovered in chests in recent years, must have belonged to other series, which are now lost.

THE 'LIFE OF THE VIRGIN'. Several decades later in date than the Hôtel-Dieu tapestries, the *Story of the Life of the Virgin* was intended as a gift from Cardinal Jean Rolin, son of Nicolas Rolin, to the church of Notre-Dame at Beaune.

By a contract dated 13th September 1474, Pierre Spicre (died 1478), one of a family of Burgundian painters, who had previously worked in the cathedral of Lausanne, undertook to paint 'the designs of the stories of Our Lady'. These were completed and paid for in 1475, in which year Spicre received a further commission from the chapter of Notre-Dame for the 'design of the story of the contemplation of St. Bernard'.

It is generally agreed that the weaving of the *Life of the Virgin* must have been delayed or interrupted for reasons of finance, and that it was eventually completed 'in the year of Grace m.V^c' (1500; an indisputable date, woven into the tapestry), thanks to the generosity of Hugues Le Coq, canon and archdeacon of Beaune.

Intended as they were to be hung around the choir, above the main arches, the tapestries of the *Story of the Life of the Virgin* are only just over six feet high. There are five pieces, which together form a band (known as 'ceinture' or 'litre') comprising seventeen principal subjects. The latter are isolated in arcaded compartments, a compositional device which had already been employed in the *Life of St. Peter*, given to Beauvais cathedral by Guillaume de Hellande. The ground is enlivened with flowering plants and pecking birds. At two different points, figures of donors, including

Hugues le Coq, are introduced among the scriptural characters; they are evidently later additions to the original designs. The absence of hieratic formulae and the fresh observation of nature lend this set a special charm. As with most contemporary sets, speculations regarding its place of origin have failed to arrive at any useful conclusion. An origin in Burgundy, an area open to artistic influences from the north, has much to recommend it.

THE 'THREE CORONATIONS'. We are no better informed concerning the provenance of the tapestry of the *Three Coronations* preserved in the treasury of Sens cathedral, to which it was given by Cardinal Louis de Bourbon-Vendôme, Archbishop of Sens from 1536 to 1557. The latter is said to have inherited it from his uncle, Cardinal Charles de Bourbon, Archbishop of Lyon from 1446 to 1488, who also possessed the *Story of Hercules* which has already been mentioned in the chapter devoted to Tournai.

The *Three Coronations* — those of the Virgin, of Bathsheba and of Esther, a subject suggested by the *Biblia pauperum* — were cut into pieces in 1759, in order to replace an altar-piece of precious metal which had been melted down by order of Louis XV, but they were re-integrated in their original form by the French Historical Monuments commission in 1926. The design, which is of a symbolical character, is conceived in the manner of Van der Weyden or Dirk Bouts, and has been reproduced in the tapestry technique with great delicacy. The gold and silver threads, which mingle with the coloured silks and wools, enhance the rare and precious quality of the work, which also differs from the normal productions of the tapestry-weavers by its much closer adherence to the painted cartoon.

THE 'CAVALCADE' OR 'FALCONRY'. In spite of the exceptional character of the *Three Coronations* tapestry, it seems best to classify it, for the present, with other hangings of uncertain origin.

Specific attributions of these works to France or to Flanders are commonly based only on the assumptions or prejudices of the author concerned.

This is the case with a band of tapestry, a fragment of a large hanging, in Notre-Dame-de-Nantilly at Saumur, which has been attributed to Tournai; it represents ladies and gentlemen riding out to hunt. Various other fragments have been compared to it. To these may be added, in spite of its coarser style, a fragment in the town hall of Regensburg.

THE 'PRESENTATION OF THE ROSES'. In conjunction with the *Cavalcade* or *Falconry* of Notre-Dame-de-Nantilly it is appropriate to mention the fragments which make up the three pieces known as the *'Presentation of the Roses'*. These belong to the Metropolitan Museum, having formerly figured notably in the Sigismond Bardac collection. They show a number of figures, clad in the fashions of the reign of Charles VII, disposed, without any coherent spatial relationship, against a background consisting of vertical bands of various colours, powdered with rose-sprays. These bands have an heraldic significance; they recur, for example, in five drawings of the Gaignières collection (Bibliothèque Nationale, Cabinet des Estampes) representing tapestries formerly at the château of Le Verger, the seat of Pierre de Rohan, Maréchal de Gié (1451–1513).

The red, green and white bands of the *Presentation of the Roses* are the colours of Charles VII. They appear again in the hangings of the parliament-hall at Vendôme in 1458, as represented in a miniature by Jean Fouquet in the *Boccaccio* of the Staatsbibliothek, Munich.

THE 'WINGED STAGS'. The frontispiece of the same book shows winged stags holding a shield charged with *fleurs-de-lis*, the personal arms of Charles VII. Similar stags, wearing the royal crown of France as a collar, with the royal shield of France attached as a pendant, appear in a tapestry at the Musée des Antiquités, Rouen.

Contrary to earlier suppositions, this is apparently to be connected, not with Louis XI, but with Charles VII. Hence the date of the tapestry must be put back considerably; a study by M. Paul Martin places it between 1430 and 1450.

Of the new stylistic elements which appear in the *Winged Stags*, perhaps the most important is the treatment of the small flowering plants.

The practice of powdering the backgrounds of tapestries with flowers was an old one. It appears already in the *Apocalypse* of Angers, and was common throughout the fifteenth century in both France and Flanders. Thus the presence of flowers, growing in the grass, or scattered on the ground, is less significant than the manner in which they are treated or the type to which they belong. As the older conventions of design were relaxed, so the flowers were transformed, and approached more and more closely to nature. Finally, innumerable naturalistic flowering plants, of great variety and delicacy, were scattered broadcast over the backgrounds and became the characteristic feature of an important class of tapestry.

MILLE-FLEURS TAPESTRIES. Tapestries of about 1500, with blue or pink backgrounds powdered all over with little flowers, are sufficiently numerous to be considered as an independent group, known as *mille-*

fleurs (thousand flowers) tapestries. Their delightful naturalism, their civilized refinement, and the harmony of their colours place them among the most accomplished creations of French taste. Inspired by a deep feeling for nature, the *mille-fleurs* tapestries multiply the flowers of garden and of field. Amid their slender leaves and tender petals, beneath the bushes laden with fruit, we sometimes see animals, sheep, dogs, birds, the small creatures of meadow and forest. These serve as an accompaniment to themes of a secular character — scenes of rural life, or the amusements and pastimes of the great. It might be an interesting study — which no one, it seems, has undertaken — to trace the possible relationships between *mille-fleurs* tapestries and the (admittedly rather later) poets of the Pléiade.

Mille-fleurs tapestries, despite the diversity of the scenes represented, show some interesting duplications or variants of individual motifs. A child in the *Courtly Life* at the Musée de Cluny reappears in one of the two *Allegories* of the former Martin Le Roy collection, but in clothes of a different colour. A halbardier and a nobleman in the *Courtly Life* (which has a blue ground) recur in a tapestry (with a pink ground) in the Art Institute of Chicago; they appear once more, with insignificant changes, in the supposed *Miracle of St. Julian* in the Louvre. Lastly, a fountain, in a *Concert* at the Musée des Gobelins, closely resembles another in the *Hunt of the Unicorn* set, formerly at the château of Verteuil.

These analogies are not fortuitous. Though they offer no proof of common origin, they do throw some light on the ill-defined relationship between the designers and the weaving-workshops, or perhaps between the different workshops themselves. The number of pieces known, the relatively brief period during which they were woven, and the wide variations in quality tend to suggest the existence of a number of workshops responding to the demands of a transitory fashion, rather a single workshop devising variations on a theme which had met with popular success.

In face of the impossibility of localizing the manufacture of the *mille-fleurs* tapestries, they are generally said to have been woven by itinerant workshops 'in the Loire region'. This is an hypothesis rather than an attribution. Hence some authors have been tempted to claim certain examples as products of Tournai. Since Tournai belonged to France down to the first quarter of the sixteenth century and, though an enclave in foreign territory, maintained lively contacts with the rest of the kingdom, these conjectures are in principle unobjectionable. A tapestry with little flowers hangs behind Penelope in the set of *Famous Women* that belonged to Ferry de Clugny, Bishop of Tournai, as has been mentioned in the preceding chapter. But to replace a traditional hypothesis by a new hypothesis, however attractive or ingenious it may be, does require some form of proof. Such proof has not yet been forthcoming.

THE PRINCIPAL MILLE-FLEURS TAPESTRIES. The tapestries of the *mille-fleurs* group have, as yet, no established chronology, and are too numerous for them all to be mentioned individually. To avoid confusion, therefore, it will be best to limit the discussion to a few of the most important and representative pieces.

Some of the compositions are conceived in a rustic vein, such as the *Shepherds* of the Musée des Gobelins, with their naïve inscriptions, or those from the former Blumenthal collection, now in the Metropolitan Museum. Others move in more elegant society, such as the *Courtly Life* of the Musée de Cluny, whose six hangings, on a blue ground, may be distinguished as *Departure for the Hunt*, *Reading*, *Needlework*, *The Bath*, *The Walk* and *Scene of Dalliance*.

To the same class as the *Courtly Life* belong the *Falconry* or *Cavalcade* from the former Charles Mège collection (later G. and F. Blumenthal collection, now Metropolitan Museum), and the three *Concerts*, at the Louvre, the Gobelins and the Musée des Tapisseries at Angers (the last-named also known as the *Lady at the Organ*). The last two of these are said to have come from the château of Le Verger, the seat of Pierre de Rohan, Maréchal de Gié, not far from Tours.

THE 'NOBLE PASTORAL'. The peasants and nobles, who appear separately in the foregoing pieces, are intermingled in three other hangings, which are among the most perfect of *mille-fleurs* tapestries. After a long sojourn at the château of Serrant, in Maine, these entered the Louvre with the Larcade gift in 1949–50. M. Pierre Verlet has christened them the *Noble Pastoral*. Clad in costumes of an elegant simplicity, the lords and ladies mingle with the countryfolk to share in the *Dance*, *Fruit-gathering*, *Hopscotch*, *Sheep-shearing* and *Working in Wool*.

The coats-of-arms which appear in the tapestries have been identified as those of Thomas Bohier (died 1523), chamberlain of the King of France, and his wife Catherine Briçonnet (died 1526), the builders of Chenonceau. It does not, of course, follow that the *Noble Pastoral* was made for Chenonceau, but the identification of the original owners does at least suggest the possibility that the tapestries may have been woven in that area.

The rustic and aristocratic scenes of the *Courtly Life*, the *Concerts* and the *Noble Pastoral* give place to epic themes in the *Penthesilea, Queen of the Amazons* in the Musée des Tapisseries at Angers (probably the remains of a set of *Nine Heroines*, and slightly earlier than the other pieces discussed) and to mythological subjects in the *Hercules* of the Musée des Arts Décoratifs, Paris. Subjects drawn from allegory or romance appear in the two tapestries with red grounds in the former Martin Le Roy collection. But despite the charm of all these hangings, the finest of all *millefleurs* tapestries are undoubtedly the sets of the *Lady with the Unicorn* and the *Hunt of the Unicorn*.

THE 'LADY WITH THE UNICORN'. Among tapestries of the late fifteenth and early sixteenth centuries, the *Lady with the Unicorn* enjoys the same pre-eminence as the *Apocalypse* of Angers among tapestries of the fourteenth.

The set comprises six hangings, in each of which appear one or two female figures with, on one side, a lion, said to symbolize the ancient nobility of blood and, on the other, a unicorn, symbolizing the incorruptibility of the new nobility of the magistrature. The beasts hold banners and pennants, all bearing the same arms, 'gules, a bend azure, charged with three crescents argent.' These arms have been identified as those of Le Viste, a family of the higher bourgeoisie, originating in Lyon. Allied by marriage to several distinguished houses of Dauphiné and Provence, the Le Viste family also included a president of the parliament of Paris.

After the rejection of several earlier interpretations, it is now generally presumed that the theme of the set was the *Five Senses*. The subject of the sixth hanging (the *Lady and her attendant before a pavilion*) and the motto '*Mon seul désir*' ('My sole desire') accompanied by two single letters ('A' and possibly 'P'), remain unexplained. It is presumed to be a dedication to the lady, who here reappears for the last time between the two heraldic animals.

An unusual device, which recurs in the *Allegories* of the former Martin Le Roy collection, is the placing of the figures on a kind of blue islet, contrasting with the pink ground, and, like the latter, powdered with flowering plants and enlivened with small animals.

THE ORIGIN OF THE 'LADY WITH THE UNICORN'. Many hypotheses have been advanced concerning the origin of the *Lady with the Unicorn* tapestries, which, from 1660 until 1882, when they entered the Musée de Cluny, hung in the château of Boussac, in the Creuse district. They are said to have been made locally, in La Marche, in Lyon, in Touraine, or even in Tournai. In spite of the ingenious suggestions which have been made, the mystery remains. Yet it seems likely that at least a corner of the veil has now been lifted.

The resemblance between *Hearing*, or the *Lady at the Organ*, and the *Penelope* (Boston Museum) from the set of *Famous Women* which belonged to Ferry de Clugny, and the similarities between *Taste*, or the *Lady with the Parrakeet*, and figures in the *Story of Perseus*, published by Mme. Crick-Kuntziger in 1954, have put a new complexion on the problem. The three sets clearly have elements in common; even supposing that they were woven in the same region, we are still no nearer to knowing where that region was, but we can at least venture certain observations concerning the designer.

The tapestry of the *Story of Perseus* bears the arms of Charles Guillard or Guillart (1456–1537) and his wife Jeanne de Vignacourt; Guillard was counsellor of the parliament of Paris and held various other high offices. The hanging was presumably woven at the end of the fifteenth century, between 1480 and 1500.

The Guillard family, according to the researches of Mme. Crick-Kuntziger, were closely connected with the Le Viste family, whose arms appear in the *Lady with the Unicorn* tapestries. This suggests the tempting hypothesis that both families employed the same designer, whose talents could have been brought to their notice by the tapestries of Ferry de Clugny (died 1483). But the whereabouts of this last set at the end of the fifteenth and the beginning of the sixteenth century is unfortunately unknown, for it arrived at the château of Thenissey, in Burgundy, only in 1750. Moreover, even if we admit that the three series of cartoons are the work of the same designer, it is questionable whether we need look for him outside France or Burgundy. It is true that Ferry de Clugny, Bishop of Tournai, resided in Bruges from 1477 onwards and that there was in Bruges a designer of cartoons, Jennyn or Jan Fabiaen, none of whose works is known. But in the complete absence of other information, we cannot know whether Fabiaen may not have had rivals in his own chosen field, which was apparently that of heraldic subjects.

The arguments which have been advanced in support of one conclusion are equally favourable to another. Would it not have been possible for Ferry de Clugny, whose set was the earliest in date, to have obtained designs from a painter living in Burgundy or France just as easily as for the Guillard and Le Viste families to have obtained theirs from a painter in Bruges? Or could not these designs, originating in the north, perhaps have been carried into France by immigrant weavers from that region? Finally, do not the comparable results produced in the seventeenth and eighteenth centuries by the copying or imitation in other countries of Gobelins or Beauvais tapestries suggest that the common inspiration

XXV. COURTLY LIFE: THE DEPARTURE FOR THE HUNT
Musée de Cluny, Paris

XXVI. THE DEPARTURE FOR THE HUNT

Art Institute, Chicago

XXVII. COURTLY LIFE: THE BATH
Musée de Cluny, Paris

XXVIII. THE LADY WITH THE UNICORN
Musée de Cluny, Paris

XXIX. THE HUNT OF THE UNICORN: THE FOUNTAIN
Metropolitan Museum, New York

XXX. LIFE OF ST. MAURILLE
Musée des tapisseries, Angers

XXXI. LIFE OF ST. STEPHEN

Musée de Cluny, Paris

XXXII. LIFE OF ST. GERVAIS AND ST. PROTAIS

Le Mans Cathedral

traced in these three sets are no guarantee that they were actually woven in the same place?

THE 'HUNT OF THE UNICORN'. In the set of tapestries in the Musée de Cluny which have just been discussed, the unicorn, which was considered by the middle ages as a symbol of purity, plays only a subordinate role. In the *Hunt of the Unicorn*, on the other hand, it becomes the principal actor and, indeed, the subject of the tapestries. This enchanting set, formerly in the possession of the family of La Rochefoucauld, at the château of Verteuil in Charente, has now passed from the Rockefeller collection to the Metropolitan Museum in New York. The six hangings, bearing initials which are supposed to be those of François de la Rochefoucauld, grandfather of Francis I, show various dramatic episodes in the hunt for the symbolic animal.

Four of the pieces — the *Fountain, Crossing the River*, the *Chase*, and *Death of the Unicorn* — seem earlier in date than the other two — the *Unicorn at Bay*, and the *Unicorn held captive*.

THE 'ANGELS CARRYING THE INSTRUMENTS OF THE PASSION'. Although generally employed for secular subjects, *mille-fleurs* grounds were also used occasionally for religious tapestries, as for example in the *Angels carrying the instruments of the Passion*, in the Musée des Tapisseries at Angers.

In the three surviving pieces, kneeling angels, reminiscent of those seen in a number of wall-paintings, hold various instruments associated with the Passion of Christ. Beside each angel is a scroll bearing an eight-line inscription describing the torments to which Our Lord submitted and the moral lessons which they offer to humanity; these verses, composed, according to a chronicler, by King René, were reproduced in the chapel of the Grey Friars at Angers, now destroyed. At top and bottom of the tapestries appear crosses, of the type which the members of the order of Sainte-Croix-de-Bretonnerie wore on their breasts; these alternate with the coat-of-arms of Pierre de Rohan, Maréchal de Gié, either alone, or associated with those of his second wife, Marguerite d'Armagnac, surrounded with the knotted cord indicative of a widow. Presumably, therefore, the set of *Angels carrying the instruments of the Passion* was woven after the death of Pierre de Rohan, in 1513, for the priory of the order which he had built, in 1492, near his château of Le Verger, in Anjou.

At the time when the tapestries were made, the artistic device of the *mille-fleurs* ground had already been exploited for a considerable period. This may explain the exuberance of the backgrounds of these hangings, in which the plants have been scattered with an unusually lavish hand.

Another contemporary tapestry, with standing angels, who likewise hold Passion instruments, is in Notre-Dame-de-Nantilly at Saumur; with its simulated damask background, this is a rare example of the imitation in textile materials of the effects of stained-glass.

RELIGIOUS SETS OF THE END OF THE FIFTEENTH AND THE FIRST THIRD OF THE SIXTEENTH CENTURY. The tapestries with *Angels carrying the instruments of the Passion* provide a convenient transition to the study of the great religious sets of the end of the fifteenth and the beginning of the sixteenth century. Apart from a few examples, such as the *Life of St. Maurille*, which was ordered in Paris in 1460, the absence of documentary references makes their origins particularly difficult to determine. Often, the only reliable evidence regarding them is that offered by the building for which they were made and the coats-of-arms of the bishops or abbots who gave them. There is a general tendency to attribute their execution to itinerant workshops, but in most cases it is quite uncertain whether these were composed of French or foreign weavers. The same uncertainty extends to the nationality of the designers, and is only increased by consideration of the style. Obvious traces of northern influence appear frequently alongside other elements — facial types, costume, and even the general character of the compositions — which are entirely French.

Although it will be unnecessary to dwell on single pieces, or relatively unimportant examples, we must now examine the main sets, concentrating not so much on hypothetical regional characteristics as on the evidence of date.

THE 'LEGEND OF ST. QUENTIN'. Among the religious tapestries inspired by the *Golden Legend*, one of the earliest is probably the *Legend of St. Quentin*. This hanging, measuring about 11 feet by 26 feet, formerly in the Revoil collection, now belongs to the Louvre (at present exhibited in the Musée de Cluny). The various scenes are explained in eight octosyllabic quatrains. The French origin of the piece, which is of the period of Louis XI or Charles VIII, has not been disputed.

THE 'STORY OF ST. STEPHEN'. The *Story of St. Stephen*, now in the Musée de Cluny (acquisitions of 1880 and 1897), was given to the cathedral of Auxerre by Bishop Jean Baillet, son of a counsellor of parliament, in 1502. Like the *Story of the Virgin* at Beaune, completed two years earlier, it was made to be hung in the choir; hence it is no more than about 5 feet 6 inches in height; the eight hangings, comprising eighteen scenes, extend to a length of about 107 feet. The scenes depict the life and posthumous miracles of the martyr, following the apocryphal narrative of the *Golden Legend*. Certain details, such as the manner of planting vines (in three scenes) and the shape of the baskets used by the executioners, are based on Burgundian models. The same peculiarities recur in another tapestry, which can be most conveniently discussed here, in spite of its decidedly secular subject.

THE 'VINTAGE'. This tapestry, comprising two scenes, and known as *Pressing the Grapes* or *The Vintage*, was bequeathed to the Musée de Cluny in 1931 by Mme. Edouard Dolfus.

In spite of its resemblance to the rustic subjects woven at Tournai at the end of the fifteenth century, details of the costumes suggest that it was made after 1505.

The unforced effects, and the moderation which avoids both the exaggerated naturalism of Flanders and the over-sophistication derived from Italy, point to the same origin as is clearly proclaimed by the subjects themselves. The partial use of *mille-fleurs* backgrounds suggests hypotheses too complex to be evaluated here.

THE TAPESTRIES OF LA CHAISE-DIEU. An equally lengthy discussion would be required to deal fully with the problems raised by the fourteen hangings of La Chaise-Dieu, the ancient Benedictine abbey on the central plateau of France. Repeated cartouches contain the arms of Jacques de Senneterre, Abbot of La Chaise-Dieu from 1491 to 1518. The set, with its long inscriptions, accompanied by heads of prophets, has been attributed to French looms, possibly working in the abbey itself; more recently, however, a Flemish attribution has been favoured. Perhaps part of the set was woven in one place and part in another, though it is admittedly not easy to imagine the reason for such a procedure. Whether it is French or Flemish, however, its charm and decorative value remain the same. The designs present each scene from the *Life of Christ* in conjunction with two scenes from the Old Testament. According to Emile Mâle, the painter of the cartoons has simply copied the woodcut illustrations of two books which were common at the time, though now rare: the *Biblia Pauperum* and the *Speculum Humanae Salvationis*. The tapestries of Reims are another example of the powerful influence which the illustrated book was able to exercise, thanks to its wide circulation, on textiles and other arts, only a comparatively short time after the invention of printing.

THE 'LIFE OF ST. GERVAIS AND ST. PROTAIS'. Like the *Story of St. Stephen*, the *Life of St. Gervais and St. Protais* is enlivened by a wealth of humble, suggestive details, observed from everyday life. Here again, French verse inscriptions provide a running commentary on the action. The set derives an additional interest from the appearance in it of Italianate decorative elements. They are used, it is true, timidly and clumsily, but there can be no doubts as to the origin of these squared pillars, scallop-shells and medallions. The five hangings, comprising seventeen scenes, were completed in 1509. They were given to the cathedral of Le Mans, as a decoration for the choir, by Martin Guérande, who was secretary, first to Cardinal Philippe de Luxembourg, and later to his nephew, François de Luxembourg, Bishop of Le Mans. This set, which, despite its late date, still retains close links with the traditions of the middle ages, was considered by J.-J. Guiffrey as an example of thoroughly French work, in both conception and execution.

THE TAPESTRIES OF LE RONCERAY. Similar comments might be applied to the tapestries of the abbey of Le Ronceray, at Angers. These were woven under the Abbess Isabelle de La Jaille (1505–18), whose arms appear on one of the hangings. Until 1888, the set remained almost intact in the château of Le Plessis-Macé. Sold in that year, it is now divided between the Louvre, the Gobelins, the Boston Museum, the château of Langeais, the Leeds Castle collection and private collections in Paris and Amiens. These tapestries, like a lost set which is recorded as in the possession of Tours cathedral in 1539, illustrate the *Story of the Holy Sacrament*, in scenes derived in part from the Bible and in part from medieval literary compilations; among the latter was *Les Fleurs de l'histoire*, composed by Jean Marsal for one of the Dukes of Burgundy, possibly Philip the Good (died 1467). Eight of the preserved pieces are concerned with prefigurations of the mystery of the eucharist and of the divine sacrifice; thirteen others illustrate miracles (not shown in the Tours set) tending to prove the divine presence in the Holy Sacrament.

Of the various attributions proposed for the tapestries of Le Ronceray, those to Arras and to Paris have little to recommend them. The literary sources of the compositions, which point to Burgundy, suggest the hypothesis of manufacture in Flanders, in view of the political and artistic links between the two areas. An origin in Touraine is also possible, and it must not be forgotten that local workshops were established in the region of the Loire, and especially at Tours, where tapestry-looms were set up at least as early as the first third of the sixteenth century.

RELIGIOUS TAPESTRIES OF THE LOIRE REGION. The designers of the religious tapestries which are considered to have been woven in the Loire region long remained faithful to the models provided by their immediate ancestors, the miniaturists of the middle ages. The sophisticated and skilfully framed compositions which the Flemish tapestry-designers, under influence from Italy, were now beginning to produce, did not persuade them to make any hasty changes in their established practice.

In general, their works remained attractive, lively and expressive renderings of the stories depicted. Readily comprehensible in themselves, they still continued, with excessive precaution, to include explanatory inscriptions in French.

Besides the two fragments of the *Story of St. John the Baptist* (end of the fifteenth century) in the collegiate church of Saint-Julien or Saint-Jean-Baptiste at Angers, the *Story of St. Gervais and St. Protais* at Le Mans, mentioned above, the two pieces (originally twelve; beginning of the sixteenth century) of the *Life of St. Julian* in the same cathedral, and the *Passion* in the Musée des Tapisseries at Angers, mentioned above (Chapter III; end of the fifteenth century), we must mention here two scenes from the *Legend of St. Martin*, also in the Musée des Tapisseries at Angers. These are the remains of a set of six pieces presented to the collegiate church of Saint-Martin at Tours. One of the same scenes (heathens attempting to crush St. Martin beneath a tree) is reproduced in another *Story of St. Martin* at the church of Montpezat, near Cahors. The five hangings of the latter set, comprising fifteen scenes, are said to be copies of those given to the church of Montauban by Bishop Jean d'Aurioli, which were destroyed in 1557.

The Italian influences, seen in the ornamental details of the *Story of St. Gervais and St. Protais*, appear in a stronger and more developed form in the pilasters with arabesque decoration in the *Life of St. Florent*. This set was given by Abbot Jacques Le Roy, in 1524, to the abbey of Saint-Florent, near Saumur. Five hangings are in the church of Saint-Pierre at Saumur, and a sixth is in the Musée des Tapisseries at Angers; several others are lost.

Only three years separate this set, conceived in accordance with the traditional formulae of medieval tapestries, and the very different *Story of*

St. Saturnin, given by Jacques de Semblançay to the church of Saint-Saturnin at Tours in 1527, and now in the Musée des Tapisseries at Angers and the château of Langeais. But the significance of the brief interval between the two sets, to which scholars have drawn attention, is more apparent than real. It must not be forgotten that the *Life of St. Saturnin* was woven after designs by a Florentine painter established in Tours, Andrea Polastron (probably Andrea Squazella or Chiazella, a pupil of Andrea del Sarto), so that its Italianate features (use of perspective, classical architecture, pilasters ornamented with trophies) must be considered as direct imports from Italy rather than as the result of French assimilation of Italian formulae.

Thus, though it is an important testimony to the influence of foreign artists in Touraine, it cannot be taken to mark the end of an epoch or a decisive revolution in the style of French artists and craftsmen. In fact, it is chiefly significant as showing the existence of tapestry-workshops in Tours. The importance of these increased in the years that followed and reached its height in the workshop of the Duval family which, between 1546 and 1548, wove the ten tapestries of the *Life of St. Peter* (in the church of Saint-Pierre, at Saumur) after designs by Robert de Lisle, an Angevin artist, and Jehan Delaistre. In the second half of the century the Duval family was succeeded by others, among whom the presence of François Dubois, a 'native of the country of Flanders', is not without significance.

Since the *Story of St. Saturnin* is inadmissible as evidence, the advance of the tapestry-workshops towards a more Italianate style must be traced in two sets woven in another area. These are the *Life of the Virgin* and the *Story of St. Remi*, both at Reims, which constitute the last legacy, the swan song, of the Gothic tapestry tradition.

THE 'LIFE OF THE VIRGIN' AND THE 'STORY OF ST. REMI'. It remains to be determined whether the *Life of the Virgin* and the *Story of St. Remi*, which were executed between 1509 and 1532 and presented to the cathedral of Reims and to the church of Saint-Remi by Archbishop Robert de Lenoncourt, may justifiably be considered as French tapestries. Tournai has been mentioned in connection with them, but no decisive arguments have been adduced in support of this view. Nothing specifically Flemish can be discerned in the style of the figures or the composition of the scenes, which are much more suggestive of a French origin than of any foreign intervention.

The seventeen scenes of the *Life of the Virgin* are based, like those of the tapestries of La Chaise-Dieu, on woodcuts. In this case the sources are the illustrations of Books of Hours (including the page-borders), as well as those of the *Speculum Humanae Salvationis* and the *Biblia Pauperum*. A *Tree of Jesse* of the second decade of the sixteenth century, in an American private collection, reproduces the frontispiece of the *Hours of Reims* published in 1515; the same Renaissance-style borders, with vine-scrolls, candelabra and other motifs, recur in the tapestries of the cathedral.

The latter were intended to decorate the nave and are therefore of very large size. The scenes, which are accompanied by commentaries in French, are enacted beneath a portico in a developed Renaissance style. The centre of each composition is occupied by an episode from the *Story of the Virgin*, while on either side appears a prophet, who foretells her coming, and an Old Testament subject, which prefigures her. The essential character of the series is revealed in this persistence of medieval thought, on the very eve of the final triumph of Renaissance humanism.

The ten hangings, each divided into four compartments, of the *Story of St. Remi*, depict scenes from the life of the patron saint of the church to which Robert de Lenoncourt gave the set in 1531. His arms appear in association with those of the cathedral chapter. The figures represented are identified by French inscriptions.

The compositions testify to a more varied and copious invention than those of the *Life of the Virgin*.

THE 'TRIUMPHS OF PETRARCH'. The Reims tapestries mark the natural conclusion of a chapter devoted to French tapestries of the second half of the fifteenth and the beginning of the sixteenth century. There remain, however, two further sets of that period which cannot be passed over in silence. Less readily categorized than the secular and religious tapestries discussed hitherto, their themes are allegorical, in the *Triumphs of Petrarch*, and historical, in the *Kings of Gaul*. They were woven in two distinct workshops.

Six hangings of the *Triumphs*, inspired by the sonnets of Petrarch, which were so much appreciated in the later middle ages, belong to the former Austrian Imperial collections. Two similar pieces, the *Triumph of Time* and the *Triumph of Fame*, are in the Metropolitan Museum. Their archaic design and the rather dry handling of the compositions seems to place them at the end of the fifteenth or the beginning of the sixteenth century. The explanatory quatrains are in French. Formerly attributed to Arras or Tournai, the *Triumphs* have more recently been assigned to Touraine. This idea receives some support from the flowers that strew the ground, though it can hardly be said that these are very closely related to those of the *mille-fleurs* tapestries.

THE 'KINGS OF GAUL'. The set of the *Kings of Gaul*, comprising five hangings, in the cathedral of Beauvais, enjoys a rather more precise attribution. It is supposed to have been woven in Beauvais itself by an itinerant workshop, possibly of Flemish origin. This set is far removed from the simplicity of the *Equestrian Portrait of Charles VIII*, which appeared at the exhibition of French primitives in 1904 (former Schickler collection). The Kings of Gaul in question are those who reigned from the time of the deluge down to the period following the siege of Troy, but they are clad in costumes of the period of Francis I. They are inspired by a fanciful translation of Annius of Viterbo (1498), supplemented by the *Illustrations de Gaule et singularités de Troyes*, by Jean le Maire, printed at Lyon between 1509 and 1512. This set, which was given to the cathedral in 1530 by canon Nicolas d'Argillières, possesses, over and above its general interest, a particular archaeological interest on account of the views of buildings in Reims, of Notre-Dame in Paris, and of Beauvais cathedral itself, which appear in the backgrounds.

CHAPTER VI

The tapestries of the Renaissance

The framework of great events, of accessions or deaths of kings, which serves to subdivide the historical continuum into manageable lengths, is generally ill-adapted to a meaningful and intelligible presentation of the facts of art-history. The latter, especially when they concern techniques so intimately linked with everyday life as that of tapestry, are too much affected by constant and imperceptible variations, by inevitable time-lags in the adaptation of new aesthetic ideals to major and minor arts, for precise dates to have much meaning.

The principal secular and religious tapestries woven in the French provinces during the first third of the sixteenth century represent for the most part, as has been shown in the preceding chapter, a continuation and logical conclusion of the medieval formulae. The successive introductions of Renaissance elements, the encroachment of Italianism on French traditions, were confined to details of ornament and did not upset the structure and rhythm of the compositions. In adopting these innovations — important, but secondary — neither the designers nor the weavers modified their allegiance to the ancient principles of the craft. The moment arrived, nevertheless, when the Renaissance period succeeded in creating, imposing and exploiting a textile style adapted to its own special gifts and proclivities. The emergence of this style represented a profound revolution. In adopting it, tapestry renounced its prerogatives as an independent art and entered on a course which was eventually to reduce it to the status of an art of reproduction.

The decisive demonstration of this revolution took place, not in France, but in Flanders. It was the weaving, in the workshops of Brussels, between 1515 and 1519, of the *Acts of the Apostles*, after Raphael. The pictorial character, the perspective effects and the wide borders of this set came to be accepted as a sacrosanct archetype which for several centuries, despite all variations of detail, dominated every tapestry that was woven. Like other manifestations of the Renaissance spirit, the adoption of this

89

archetype was at least supported, if not imposed, by royal power. The proof is seen in the commissions given by Francis I to Flemish workshops, despite the existence of workshops in Paris. The tapestries executed by the Fontainebleau workshop or its associates assured the further propagation of the accepted model, but its development in France was soon to be brutally interrupted by the civil wars of the second half of the century.

TAPESTRY-WEAVERS IN PARIS IN THE SIXTEENTH CENTURY. Although ruined by the English occupation in the first half of the fifteenth century, the Paris workshops seem to have resumed their activity, even if only on a limited scale, after 1450. As has already been mentioned they received an order in 1460 from the chapter of Angers cathedral for the *Life of St. Maurille*, and another in 1484 from the magistrate of Tournai. These were certainly not isolated instances.

Though neither particularly numerous, nor particularly flourishing, tapestry-workshops continued to operate in Paris during the first half of the sixteenth century.

On the occasion of the marriage of Renée of France and the Duke of Ferrara in 1528, two Parisian manufacturers or merchants, Jean Pinel and Claude Bredas, supplied a set of over twenty pieces for the sum of 3,600 *livres*. About the same time, Francis I ordered a set woven with silk and gold thread from the Parisians Nicolas and Pasquel de Montagne. In 1552, one of their competitors, Pierre de Larry, undertook to execute for the Archbishop of Sens, Louis de Bourbon, six pieces of a *Life of Jesus Christ*, intended for the abbey of Saint-Denis; at the same time, Larry was working on unidentified tapestries for the Duchess of Guise. The name of Pierre de Larry recurs in several contracts, of dates between 1547 and 1568, which have been published by J.-J. Guiffrey. Other documents indicate the existence of Antoine de Larry, of Girard Laurent, whose descendants were to be prominent in the workshops of the Louvre and the Gobelins from the time of Henry IV to that of Louis XIV, and of Guillaume Torcheux or Tricheux, who was active from 1536 to 1570. There was also Pierre Blasse, to whom we must return shortly, as well as several other high-warp weavers of lesser note.

FRANCIS I AND TAPESTRY. Susceptible as he was to the attractions of the arts, it was not likely that Francis I would neglect tapestry. Probably he endeavoured to support French weavers, but for a considerable period it was the workshops of Brussels and Antwerp that were favoured with his preference and his commissions. On occasions, they wove designs originating in France. Shortly after his arrival in Fontainebleau, in 1532, Primaticcio was given the task of going to Brussels with the small-scale design for a *Story of Scipio Africanus* and returning with 'the large design of the said story'. In the same year, Pierre de Pannemaker, the famous Brussels weaver, executed for Francis I a set enriched with silk, silver and gold threads; the designs of the six hangings were supplied by Matteo del Nassaro of Verona, best known as an engraver of gems, who also supervised their execution. Another Brussels merchant furnished the king with three sets in 1534; these were a *Story of Romulus and Remus*, a set of *Espaliers*, and a *Creation of the World* in five hangings. *Stories of Actaeon and Orpheus* 'in gold and silk with verdure and little figures' followed in 1538; the vendor on this occasion was Matteo del Nassaro, who had again made the journey to Brussels, but his true role in the transaction remains unclear. About the same time, there are records of several other acquisitions, likewise in Brussels.

Realizing perhaps the disadvantages of these purchases from abroad, or possibly for reasons of finance, Francis I finally established a tapestry-workshop at Fontainebleau. The only certain information concerning this is derived from a few references in the royal building accounts between 1540 and 1550. The date of its inauguration is unknown, but is presumed to have been about 1540; there are virtually no indications regarding the date of its closure.

THE FONTAINEBLEAU WORKSHOP. The existence of the Fontainebleau workshop is an indisputable fact. It appears to have been under the directions of the superintendant of the royal buildings, Philibert Babou de La Bourdaisière. Pierre and Jean Le Bries, who received the highest salaries, may have been in charge of the weaving.

As a result of a statement made by the historian Sauval, the Fontainebleau workshop was long considered to have been a genuine royal factory, and has often been referred to as a forerunner of the royal tapestry factories of the seventeenth century. In fact, it seems to have been formed on a temporary basis, and is therefore more properly classified with the itinerant workshops, and the 'house' workshops such as those — to cite two important seventeenth-century examples — of Cadillac, founded by the Duc d'Épernon, and of Vaux, formed by Nicolas Fouquet.

THE TAPESTRIES OF THE GALLERY OF FRANCIS I. Only one certain work of the Fontainebleau workshops is known. This is a set of hangings which reproduces part of the decoration of the gallery in the château of

Fontainebleau known as the Gallery of Francis I; designed and partially executed by Rosso, this decoration was completed by Primaticcio (1531–1540). Accurate copies of the original compositions were prepared by Claude Badouyn or Baudouin, a minor painter of the School of Fontainebleau, possibly with the assistance of other members of the same school.

The tapestries, which were still on the looms when the king died, in 1547, may have been presented to the Austrian Emperor by Charles IX, on the occasion of his marriage to Elizabeth of Austria. They are recorded in the 1690 inventory of the Austrian Imperial Wardrobe; not long afterwards Joseph I had the 'F' of Francis I altered to his own initial.

After a period of oblivion, the set, now in the Kunsthistorisches Museum, Vienna, proved a revelation when it was seen again after the first world war. Apart from its high quality, it is also valuable as showing the appearance of the Gallery of Francis I before the restorations of the eighteenth and nineteenth century. As Louis Dimier has shown, the side of the gallery reproduced is that towards the Court of the Fountain. The same authority suggests that the perfection and uniformity of the weaving indicates that it was carried out under the direction of a painter, perhaps Primaticcio himself.

ARABESQUES. Some decorative tapestries with arabesques and ornaments in the style of Androuet du Cerceau have also been attributed to the Fontainebleau workshop, but there is no evidence to support this. Their designs comprise a figure-subject in a small central cartouche, accompanied by slender colonnettes, arabesques, trophies, garlands, flowers and fruit. A *Death of Joab* is in the Musée des Gobelins, which also possesses the cut-down remains of two tapestries showing *Cybele* and *Flora*; the initials 'H' and 'D' and the crescents in the borders indicate a date in the reign of Henri II. The Musée des Arts Décoratifs at Lyon possesses two further pieces (*Bacchus* and *Neptune*, from the former E. Peyre collection). They may perhaps have formed, together with the Gobelins fragments, a set of *Seasons* or *Gods of Olympus*. It appears that no one has so far endeavoured to connect these tapestries with a contract of 4th August 1550, by which Pierre Blasse, master tapicer of Paris, agreed to weave a piece of high-warp tapestry with 'grotesques', for Charles de Pisseleu, Bishop of Condom.

PIERRE BLASSE I AND II AND THE 'STORY OF ST. MAMMÈS'. It would be rash to suppose that Pierre Blasse was the principal high-warp weaver of the middle of the sixteenth century. He must, however, have been among the most important of his time, and he is certainly the one about whom we have the most positive information, despite the existence of another man of the same name who, as appears from a legal document, was his father.

There were, in fact, two men called Pierre Blasse, both high-warp tapestry-weavers. The first, who was married to Marguerite Remy, died in 1550. The second worked between 1540 and 1550 on the tapestries of the Gallery of Francis I at Fontainebleau. The level of his salary, which was among the lowest, would be more in proportion with the work of a young man like Pierre II, than that of a craftsman at the height of his career, such as Pierre I. Yet it was Pierre II Blasse, husband of Mariette Presleau, who in January 1544 agreed to execute, together with Jacques Langlois, a *Life of St. Mammès*, which Cardinal de Givry, Bishop of Langres, proposed to give to his cathedral.

THE 'LIFE OF ST. MAMMÈS'. A contract dated July 1543 records that the author of the cartoons for this set was Jean Cousin the Elder. Well known for his participation in the decorations for the celebrated entry of Henri II into Paris in 1549, and for his *Livre de perspective* (1560), Jean Cousin the Elder had, as early as 1541, painted six episodes of a *Life of St. Geneviève* for tapestries ordered by the confraternity of Sainte-Geneviève-du-Mont.

Of the eight hangings of the *Life of St. Mammès*, three have survived. Two are in the cathedral of Langres; the third, *St. Mammès surrendering to the tribunal of the governor of Cappadocia*, was given to the Louvre in 1940. These tapestries still retain a link with the Gothic tradition in their presentation of several consecutive scenes in a single composition, but the classical buildings, and the wide borders ornamented with strapwork, grotesque masks, cherub-heads and fruit, show the dominance of the Renaissance style.

EMBLEMATIC TAPESTRIES. Prior to the signature of the 1544 contract for the *Story of St. Mammès*, Pierre II Blasse showed Cardinal de Givry a proof of his ability in the shape of a tapestry of 'fantasies and devices', which he had woven for a parliamentary official.

The description of this piece serves to direct attention to the numerous emblematic tapestries executed during the middle ages and, even more, in the sixteenth century. These showed initials, mottoes, isolated charges from the arms of the owners, or shields of arms, which might be represented in a landscape setting, hanging from trees, or accompanied by symbolic figures or heraldic animals; alternatively, the motifs might be simply repeated on a plain background. Most of these tapestries were destroyed at the Revolution, but drawings of a good many are preserved in the Gaignières collection (Paris, Bibliothèque Nationale). In his *La Tapisserie du XIIe à la fin du XVIe siècle* (1911), J.-J. Guiffrey illustrated a tapestry with the arms of François Miron, then in the Brauer collection, opposite one of the Gaignières drawings. A few other examples are known. A small fragment recently acquired by the Musée de Cluny has the ground formed of bands of two different colours, a treatment which is fairly common in this class; the ornament consists of cornucopiae, Greek letters, foliage and coats-of-arms. There is also the curious specimen bearing the arms of Charles d'Orléans, Count of Angoulême, and Louise of Savoy, the parents of Francis I, acquired by the Boston Museum about 1941, which has been attributed to a Touraine workshop.

These emblematic tapestries, although they were woven for members of the old and the new nobility and for the holders of various high offices, did not, perhaps, enjoy universal favour. At least, the Gaignières collection includes no example associated with several prominent personalities, such as Diane de Poitiers. It was for this lady, however, that one of the principal textile creations of the French Renaissance was woven — the *Story of Diana*.

THE 'STORY OF DIANA'. Until recent years, only five tapestries of the *Story of Diana* were known — four at the château of Anet, and one, *Diana imploring Jupiter for the gift of chastity*, in the Musée des Antiquités at Rouen. In 1943, a fragment of the *Triumph of Diana* appeared in the New York antique trade, and two further pieces, the *Taunting of Niobe* and the *Drowning of Britomartis* are now in the Metropolitan Museum (gift of the children of Mrs. Harry Payne Whitney, about 1943). Their side-borders seem to show some variants. Like the Rouen piece, they bear the arms of the Grillo family of Genoa, replacing the Greek delta and the combined initials of Henri II and Diane de Poitiers.

The scenes of the *Story of Diana*, which are explained in verse inscriptions of ten lines, are designed with a rare mastery. The rich borders, ornamented with arabesques, attributes of the chase, stags' heads and herms, produce, in conjunction with the sober harmony of the colouring and the delicacy of the weaving, an exceptionally beautiful effect.

The *Diana* set, which was probably woven for Diane de Poitiers and perhaps intended for the château of Anet, has been attributed to the Fontainebleau workshop. Since it was woven after the accession of Henri II, and since Philibert Delorme, who was appointed superintendent of the royal buildings in 1548, was presumably responsible for the Fontainebleau workshop at the time when it was woven, the rather hasty conclusion has been drawn that he was also the designer. It has even been claimed that the tapestries display 'the mark of his genius'. These assertions cannot be verified, especially since some of the evidence offered in support of them is erroneous; the same is true of the suggestions that the designs should be attributed to Jean Cousin the Elder, on the grounds of his authorship of the *Life of St. Mammès*. The attribution to the Fontainebleau workshop, since we do not know how long it lasted, is equally uncertain. It remains possible, but so does the execution of the set by a temporary workshop at Anet, or by a workshop in Paris.

THE WORKSHOP OF LA TRINITÉ. The lack of positive information concerning the fate of the Fontainebleau workshop should not be taken to imply that all interest in the textile arts was lost in the second half of the century, although the political troubles undoubtedly exercised an inhibiting effect.

Not long after the accession of Henri II, a tapestry workshop was organized at the hospital of La Trinité, in the Rue Saint-Denis (1551). La Trinité was a hospital and orphanage which included among its functions the instruction of orphans and abandoned children in various crafts. These included tapestry-weaving, as well as painting and the carding and spinning of wool. The tapestry-workshop of La Trinité continued to function down to the first half of the seventeenth century. Its last works were the tapestries of the *Story of St. Crispin and St. Crispinian*, executed in 1634–5 for the chapel of the cordwainers' guild, in Notre-Dame. Three of the hangings were destroyed in a fire started by the Commune in 1871; the surviving piece, at the Musée des Gobelins, is mediocre. It would give a poor impression of the capacities of the workshop, were it not that the latter receives a certain reflected glory from the reputation of some of the weavers which it trained.

MAURICE DUBOUT. The best known of these weavers was Maurice Dubout or Dubourg, who was working at La Trinité when, in 1584, he contracted with the churchwardens of Saint-Merry to supply a *Life of Christ*, after Henri Lerambert; twenty-seven designs for these hangings are preserved in the Cabinet des Estampes at the Bibliothèque Nationale. This set, which was woven by Dubout with the assistance of another high-warp weaver, Denis Lamy, and completed in 1594, has disappeared, with the exception of a head of St. Peter at the Musée de Cluny and some frag-

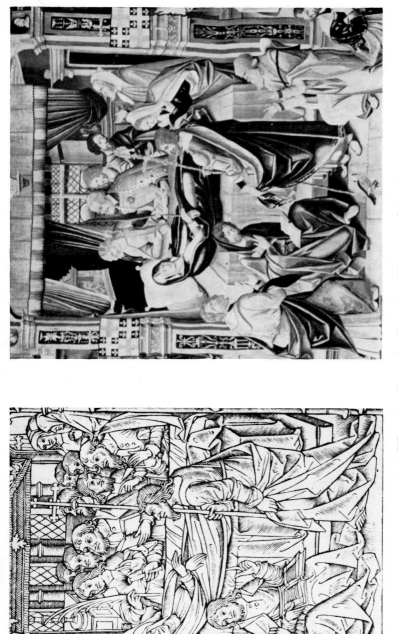

XXXIII. (A) Woodcut from the *Speculum Humanae Salvationis*
THE DEATH OF THE VIRGIN
(B) DEATH OF THE VIRGIN
Reims Cathedral

XXXIV. LIFE OF ST. REMI (detail)
Musée de Reims

XXXV. THE TRIUMPHS OF PETRARCH: THE TRIUMPH OF CHASTITY
Austrian State Collection, Vienna

XXXVI. TAPESTRY.
After the paintings of the Gallery of Francis I
Austrian State Collection, Vienna

PHOEBVS MARY QVE PHOEBE VOVLOIT TANT
S'ACCOMPAIGNER DORION LE CHASSEVR A
VEVX TV DIT IL FAIRE VN BEAV COVP MA SEVR
FRAPPE CELA QVI VA SVR MER FLOTTANT.
L'ARC ELLE ENFONCE ET SA VISEE ESTENT
SI DROIT QVE HELAS AMORT SANS Y PENSER
SON ORION LVY ADVINT D'OFFENSER
DONT LA DEESSE AVEC SES NYMPHES PLEVRE
MAIS IVPITER POVR DE RECOMPENSER
LVY DONE AV CIEL AVEC SÕ CHIEN DEMEVRE

XXXVII. STORY OF DIANA: THE DEATH OF ORION
Château of Anet

XXXVIII. LIFE OF ST. MAMMÈS

Musée du Louvre, Paris

XXXIX. EMBLEMATIC TAPESTRY WITH THE ARMS OF COLIGNY
Drawing in the Gaignières Collection, Cabinet des Estampes,
Bibliothèque nationale, Paris

XL. STORY OF ARTEMISIA: THE BOOTY

Mobilier national, Paris

CHAPTER VII

The Paris workshops in the seventeeenth century
The Gobelins Factory[1]:
1662–1793

Following this period of relative obscurity, tapestry-weaving in France burst, in the seventeenth and eighteenth centuries, into brilliant flower. The measures of economic reorganization decreed by kings and ministers included the formation of tapestry-workshops, which operated, not singly and in isolation as formerly, but grouped and combined in factories.

These factories did not exclude the possibility of individual initiatives in Paris and in the provinces, but, subsidized as they were by the Crown and working, now exclusively on royal commissions, now on private orders, they soon acquired a well-deserved reputation. They restored to tapestry a pre-eminent place among the luxury industries of the kingdom and, eventually, of Europe as a whole.

HENRI IV AND TAPESTRY. At a time when he was no more than King of Navarre, Henri IV showed interest in a project put forward about 1583 by one of his counsellors, Duplessis-Mornay. This scheme stressed the advantages which might accrue to the state from the establishment of a group of Flemish tapestry-weavers, selected from among those who had fled from religious persecution in their own country.

The King of Navarre was prevented from putting this plan into execution by the conflicts which arose between himself, Henri III, and the family of Guise, with its supporters in the Holy League — the so-called

---

[1] Tapestries made in the Paris workshops or in the Gobelins factory whose whereabouts are not specifically mentioned belong, in principle, to the Mobilier National. A number of them are exhibited in the châteaux of Pau and Versailles, or hang in official buildings in France, or French embassies abroad.

War of the Three Henrys. Having succeeded to the French throne as Henri IV, he had first to reconquer his kingdom, and it was only after the peace of Vervins (1598) that he can have had leisure to reconsider old projects and adapt them to his new responsibilities. In January 1601, the Sieur de Fourcy, the superintendent of the royal buildings, who had been in charge of 'high-warp manufacture' since January 1599, was appointed director of the 'tapestry-weavers employed by His Majesty'. Moreover, on 11th September 1601, the importation of foreign tapestries with 'forest-work' or verdure ornament was expressly forbidden.

These measures, like the introduction of the mulberry tree and the culture of silk-worms in Provence, were not taken by chance. They were the results of a considered programme, devised to protect the early stages of a national industry which was considered to be of value for the economy of the country.

THE WORKSHOP OF THE HOUSE OF THE JESUITS IN THE FAUBOURG SAINT-ANTOINE. Having paid a visit, several years before, to the tapestry-workshop of the hospital of La Trinité, founded by Henri II, Henri IV had been so well satisfied with the hangings which he had seen that he resolved, says the historian Sauval, not without some inaccuracies, to re-establish in Paris 'the tapestry-factories which had been discontinued as a result of the disorders of the preceding reigns'. For this purpose, adds Sauval, 'the king summoned Du Bourg [or Dubout] and Laurent, another excellent tapestry-weaver, to Fontainebleau; but as Du Bourg was robbed in the forest and unable to present himself, the king chose the other, whom he established in 1597 in the house of the Jesuits [the present Lycée Charlemagne], which had remained untenanted since the parricide of Jean Chatel, and along with him the famous painter Du Breuil, and Tremblai, an excellent sculptor. He [Laurent] was the director of this factory, with a salary of 1 *écu* and 100 *francs*, and as he had four apprentices their pay was fixed at 10 *sols* per day for each. As for the craftsmen who worked under him, some earned 25 *sols*, others 30, and others 40. After a time, Dubout joined him, and they remained there until the Jesuits were recalled, when they were transferred to the galleries.'

THE LOUVRE WORKSHOPS. The 'galleries' signify the Grande Galerie of the Louvre, beneath which Henri IV, who was equally concerned to foster all the industrial arts, had granted accommodation to a number of the most highly considered French and foreign craftsmen. This distinction carried with it various privileges and exemptions.

GIRARD LAURENT AND MAURICE DUBOUT. By a warrant of 4th January 1608, Henri IV granted accommodation beneath the Grande Galerie of the Louvre, then recently completed, to the high-warp weaver Girard Laurent, a former apprentice of the workshop of La Trinité. By letters patent of 22nd January following, the king made a similar grant to Maurice Dubout or Dubourg, likewise a former pupil of La Trinité, and Laurent's associate at the house of the Jesuits in the Rue Saint-Antoine.

In 1613, however, Girard Laurent surrendered to his son his appointment as royal tapestry-weaver and his accommodation in the Louvre. Dubout, on the other hand, probably continued to work for many years. The date of his death, however, is not known; it appears, moreover, that recent writers have confused the Maurice Dubout who was trained at La Trinité, with a second Maurice Dubout, his son, who disappears from the records about 1657.

PIERRE LEFEBVRE. A few years before this last date, Mazarin summoned another weaver of French origin, Pierre Lefebvre, from Florence, where he was directing a tapestry workshop. Lefebvre was established beneath the Grande Galerie of the Louvre by letters patent of 25th January 1655; his premises were near those of Laurent and Dubout, and of Pierre Dupont, manufacturerer of knotted carpets and founder of the Savonnerie. His sojourn in the Louvre, however, was destined to be brief. Three years later he returned to Tuscany, leaving behind him in Paris his son Jean Lefebvre, the future director of weaving at the Gobelins.

INVITATION TO FLEMISH WEAVERS. The documents and inventories of the period commonly employ the designation 'Paris workshop' without further specification. The uncertainty arising from this is made worse by the use of the same mark, a 'P' with a fleur-de-lis, in at least three separate workshops, and by the fact that different workshops wove the same designs.

As has been mentioned above, Henri IV had envisaged at an early date the idea of welcoming foreign craftsmen to his dominions. His aim in this was they should train pupils and found a tradition in France, thus liberating the country from the burden of heavy annual payments going abroad in return for manufactured articles.

With regard to tapestries, the workshop of Laurent and Dubout, which was at that time installed in the house of the Jesuits, was clearly inadequate to compete with the flourishing industry which constituted one of the principal sources of the wealth of Flanders. Thus Henri IV determined to return to the idea propounded by Duplessis-Mornay. In 1601, his agents succeeded in inducing a Flemish weaver, Francois Vernier or Versier, to come to France. We hear nothing further of this man, but several of his compatriots must have arrived at about the same period, including Francis van den Plancken (François de La Planche) of Oudenarde, and his brother-in-law, Marc de Comans, a native of Antwerp.

FRANÇOIS DE LA PLANCHE AND MARC DE COMANS. The brothers-in-law, who had formed a partnership in 1601, received letters patent permitting them to establish a factory in January 1607. A reading of this document shows how skilfully its essential clauses reconciled the aims of Henri IV with the interests of the parties concerned. In the first place, the king recognizes their social ambitions by commanding that they should be considered as noblemen, attached to and serving the royal household; they were thus able to enjoy all the prerogatives attached to this status. They were granted an exclusive privilege for fifteen years, with an absolute prohibition on the founding of any similar factory by any competitor; in addition, the ban on imports of all 'forest-work or verdure' tapestries was maintained, with contraventions punishable by confiscation and fines. The partners were guaranteed free accommodation, not only in Paris, but also in other towns in the kingdom where they might desire to open a workshop. Their workmen were to be exempt from escheatage, poll-tax and other obligations, and their raw materials were to be free of tax and excise-payments; tapestries sold in France or abroad could also be exempted from tax. Finally, the king guaranteed a pension of fifteen hundred *livres* to each partner, plus a sum of one hundred thousand *livres* to defray the expenses of setting up their first factory. A special clause authorized them to brew beer for themselves and their workers, a concession which must have been more valuable than might appear at first sight.

In return for these many advantages, the two Flemings agreed to maintain eighty looms in operation, including sixty in Paris and twenty in Amiens or in another town of their choice. In the first year they promised to instruct twenty-five apprentices, a number which was to be reduced to twenty in subsequent years. Finally, they agreed that the selling-price of their productions should not be in excess of that of the banned Flemish tapestries. Although supported by subsidies from the crown, the factory nevertheless remained a private enterprise, with absolute freedom to execute orders from private individuals on the same terms as orders from the king.

The Paris Workshops in the Seventeenth Century

THE FIRST GOBELINS FACTORY. The looms of La Planche and Comans, at first rather inconveniently installed in the outbuildings of the Tournelles palace, soon had to be removed elsewhere.

The problem of a suitable location, with adequate lighting, and close to running water, was solved thanks to a Parisian family to which La Planche seems to have been related — that of the Gobelins.

About 1440, a scarlet-dyeing workshop had been founded by a member of the family in the Faubourg Saint-Marcel. According to Rabelais, it owed part of its success to the properties of the Bièvre, a tributary of the Seine which flowed near by. The business of the Gobelins family and their associates, the Italian family of Canaye, eventually became an extremely important one, enabling them, after a period of a century and a half, to attain high office and to acquire titles of nobility. There could be no question of their retaining any longer the old workshop founded by Jean Gobelin between the mill of Croulebarbe and the Rue de la Reine Blanche, now Rue des Gobelins. Thus it was that La Planche and Comans were able to establish themselves there, and hence arose the name which, thanks to the second factory founded by Colbert at the same place, was to become, like Arras at an earlier period, a synonym for tapestry in several European languages.

The enterprise of François de La Planche and Marc de Comans was successful, despite inevitable financial difficulties and the obstacles raised by the magistrates of Paris.

When their privilege expired, the two Flemings were granted, on 18th April 1625, a renewal for a further period of eight years.

THE WORKSHOP IN THE FAUBOURG SAINT-GERMAIN. The harmonious relations existing between the two families deteriorated after the death of François de La Planche in 1627. The partnership contracted in 1601 was dissolved in 1638. The workshop of Marc de Comans remained in the Faubourg Saint-Marcel; in 1628, had he relinquished his position in favour of his son Charles (died 1634), who was succeeded first by his brother Alexandre (died 1650) and later by a second brother, Hippolyte. Raphaël de La Planche, the son of François, opened a new factory in the Faubourg Saint-Germain, which he relinquished to his son, Sebastien-François in 1661. The workshops finally closed down in 1667–8. The reputation of the Faubourg Saint-Germain factory stood higher than that of any other Paris workshop. The inventory of 21st September 1661, after the death of the wife of Raphaël de La Planche, and the inventory of the property of François de La Planche, taken after his death in 1627, offer some valuable information on this point.

THE DESIGNS. Based as they were on a common style, and reproducing designs by the same artists, generally within wide ornamental borders, the productions of the various Paris workshops are virtually indistinguishable. Unless documentary evidence is available, in inventories or contracts, it is often impossible to attribute them to one workshop rather than another.

HENRI LERAMBERT. Realizing that fine tapestries could not be produced by skilful weavers alone, and that good designers were also necessary, Henri IV granted to the painter Henri Lerambert the position of 'painter of the royal tapestries'.

Lerambert had shown his worth in his designs for the *Life of Christ*, woven at the workshop of La Trinité for the church of Saint-Merry (1584 — about 1594; the designs are in the Cabinet des Estampes of the Bibliothèque Nationale, and fragments of the tapestries in the museums of Cluny and the Gobelins).

To Lerambert are attributed the cartoons for the *Story of Artemisia*, based on a manuscript written by the apothecary Nicolas Houel about 1562 and illustrated by Antoine Caron (Bibliothèque Nationale, Cabinet des Estampes, and at the Louvre).

The *Artemisia* set, depicting the funeral honours rendered by the Queen of Caria to the memory of her husband, Mausolus, constituted an obvious allusion to widowhood, firstly that of Catherine de Médicis, and subsequently those of Marie de Médicis and Anne of Austria. Thus it could well have been woven repeatedly over a period of seventy-five years. It remains to be proved, however, whether it was in fact woven as early as the second half of the sixteenth century.

LERAMBERT'S SUCCESSORS. After Lerambert's death, in 1609, a competition was held between the various artists thought to be capable of taking his place. Guillaume Dumée and Laurent Guyot were judged to be the best; by a warrant of 2nd January 1610, they were jointly nominated to the vacant position, sharing between them the salary attached to it. An inventory attributes to them the designs for a set of *Kings of France*, now lost, and for a set of twenty-six pieces of *Pastor Fido*, derived from the extremely fashionable tale by the Italian Guarini.

Laurent Guyot was perhaps more active than his collaborator, who also became his brother-in-law. He is said to have been responsible for a *Story of Coriolanus*, which has also been attributed to Lerambert, for the *Hunts of King Francis*, after designs of the sixteenth century, and especially for the popular *Story of Gombault and Macée*. Inspired by woodcuts published in 1589 by Jean Le Clerc, this set had an extraordinary vogue, of which a distant echo is heard in Molière's *L'Avare*. The set in the museum of Saint-Lô, which was long considered one of the most complete French sets of the *Story of Gombault and Macée*, is now considered to have been woven in the workshops of Bruges.

In spite of these new designs, and the adaptation of older designs such as the *Story of Psyche*, after Michel Coxcie and Raphael, the *Story of Theagenes and Chariclaea*, painted by Ambroise Dubois at Fontainebleau, and the *Story of Diana* after Toussaint Dubreuil, most of the cartoons utilized by the Paris workshops were not particularly attractive. It was for this reason that Louis XIII, in 1622, commissioned from Rubens a *Story of Constantine*, to be woven in the workshop of the Faubourg Saint-Marcel.

SIMON VOUET. The return to France of Simon Vouet (1627), which is a milestone in the history of painting, exercised a no less salutary influence on tapestry-style.

Vouet, like his pupil Charles Le Brun at the Gobelins at a later period, employed numerous French and Flemish assistants, who were experienced in producing cartoons from his drawings.

The tapestries woven after designs by Simon Vouet are distinguished by the breadth and airiness of their composition and by the liveliness and gaiety of their colouring. Their decorative value is enhanced by superb borders, overflowing with the riches of the artist's abundant invention; executed in monochrome, they are said to have been inspired by the stucco sculpture of Jacques Sarrazin.

These qualities appear in the *Trials of Ulysses* (château of Cheverny), as well as in the *Story of Rinaldo and Armida*, after the paintings in the town-house of M. de Bullion, the superintendent of finances, in the Rue Plastrière. Among the examples of the *Story of Rinaldo and Armida* are those from Le Haras du Pin, exhibited in Paris for the first time in 1946.

The set of *Loves of the Gods*, woven by La Planche and Comans at Paris and Amiens (château of Champchevrier; château of Châteaudun) likewise reproduces paintings executed by Vouet for various châteaux, which were engraved by the artist's sons-in-law, Michel Dorigny and François Tortebat.

Lastly, an engraving of 1639 by Dorigny, and five others, dated 1665, by François Tortebat, show the *Scenes from the Old Testament* which were designed by Vouet, on the orders of Louis XIII, for the tapestries of the Louvre. Of these hangings, we may mention the *Saving of Moses* (Louvre) and the *Jephtha* (Mobilier National, at present at Rambouillet).

A contract of 20th April 1637, between Simon Vouet and Maurice Dubout, underlines the fact that the same designs by Vouet were woven by different Paris workshops; it shows, in addition, that the Louvre workshop was still active at this period. Possibly for this workshop, possibly for the factory of the Faubourg Saint-Germain, Poussin was asked, at the time of his visit to Paris (1641–2), to prepare the cartoons for a set of *Sacraments* after his paintings for Cassiano del Pozzo. He had no time to undertake this work, but it is not impossible that these compositions were reproduced in tapestry, perhaps at a later date.

THE 'STORY OF ST. GERVAIS AND ST. PROTAIS'. The principal set executed at the Louvre about the middle of the seventeenth century was the *Story of St. Gervais and St. Protais*. Although the initial contract for its execution, between Girard Laurent and the churchwardens of Saint-Gervais, was signed in 1652, it was not until 1661, when four of the hangings had already been woven, that the last cartoons became available. Of a serener gravity than Vouet's compositions, and less brilliant in colouring, the designs were the work of Philippe de Champaigne, Sébastien Bourdon, Eustache le Sueur, and Goussé. Five of the six pieces of the set belong to the Paris municipal collections and were formerly at the Musée Galliéra; fragments of the sixth piece belong to the Musée des Gobelins.

THE 'LIFE OF THE VIRGIN' SET. The continuing vitality of the Paris workshops was shown once more by the *Life of the Virgin*, designed by Philippe de Champaigne, Charles Poerson and Jacques Stella; some of the hangings, at least, were made by an independent weaver, Pierre Damour, who was formerly attached to the workshop of Daniel Pepersack, at Reims.

The fourteen pieces of this set, of which at least one bears the Brussels mark, are somewhat uneven in design and colouring and the borders are rather clumsily arranged. Most of them show the coats-of-arms of the Cardinal de Richelieu and of the Abbé Michel Le Masle, prior of Les Roches, chanter and canon of Notre-Dame, secretary and confidential agent of the minister of Louis XIII; it was Le Masle who commissioned the set for the cathedral-church of Paris. Begun in 1635 and finished in 1657, it was sold by the chapter, in 1735, to the cathedral of Strasbourg, where it still remains.

DECADENCE OF THE PARIS WORKSHOPS AND FOUNDATION OF THE GOBELINS. The troubles of the Fronde inevitably hampered still further the waning activity of these 'Paris workshops', directed by ageing craftsmen who had been brought up in the methods of an earlier generation. The skill which they transmitted was put to good use in the Maincy factory, founded by Nicolas Fouquet. After the arrest of the latter, Colbert prevented Louis XIV from ordering the dispersal of the Maincy looms. Instead, he had them removed to a building bought for the purpose in Paris, to which he also shifted the looms from the Louvre. There they were joined by those of the last members of the Comans family; those of the last La Planche retained their independence for only a little longer. Thus the royal factory of the Gobelins came to birth, fortified by the lessons of the past.

MAINCY. In order to further the decoration of his château of Vaux-le-Vicomte, Fouquet hit on the idea of establishing a tapestry-workshop in the village of Maincy, at about half a league from the splendid estate which was the theatre of his triumph and his fall.

By 1658 a number of high-warp weavers, some French, some Flemish, were established at Maincy and had commenced operations. Two years later, in May 1660, Fouquet obtained letters patent from Louis XIV, conferring on Maincy the status of a privileged factory for the weaving of high-warp tapestries.

Apart from a few variations this document reproduced the essential clauses of the letters patent which were granted to François de La Planche and Marc de Comans in 1607.

The Maincy factory was placed under the artistic direction of the painter Charles Le Brun, the future court painter of Louis XIV. While showing his exceptional gifts as decorator and organizer at the château of Vaux, Le Brun was unwittingly preparing himself for the vital role which he was to play at Versailles and at the Gobelins.

A number of *portières*, or door-hangings, with Fouquet's arms, were woven at Maincy after designs by Le Brun: the *portière* of the *Fames*, which was rewoven eleven times, and those of *Mars* and of the *Triumphal Car*. These were later woven again on the looms of the Gobelins. After a set of eight tapestries, intended to hang beneath the windows at Vaux, a set of verdures, and a set of *Muses*, based on one of the ceilings of the château, a start was made on a *Story of Constantine*, after Raphael and Le Brun. A set of *Meleager*, comprising eight low-warp tapestries, was also begun.

Other cartoons, prepared from Le Brun's designs by the painters Lefebvre, Valdor, Courant and Baudrin Yvart, were ready for weaving, when Fouquet fell from power in 1661.

Not long afterwards, the looms, the designs and the tapestries were transferred to the Gobelins, and the work continued, without interruption, on behalf of Louis XIV.

THE GOBELINS

The creation of the Gobelins by Colbert was not a chance occurrence. No doubt it was hastened by the fall of Fouquet and the necessity of finding useful employment for the craftsmen gathered at Maincy, but it was none the less the result of a carefully considered programme.

In a memorandum dated 1663, prepared on the eve of his appointment as superintendent of buildings, Colbert put forward the view that the age of private patrons was past. Thenceforward, no one but the king could aspire to stimulate the intellectual and artistic life of the kingdom.

THE ROYAL FACTORY FOR THE FURNISHINGS OF THE CROWN. Parallel to his efforts to reorganize the major arts by giving new statutes to the royal academy of painting and sculpture (1663) and by creating an academy of architecture (1671), Colbert established at the Gobelins a royal factory for the furnishings of the Crown (1667). Open to the best craftsmen, to the most highly qualified 'painters, master weavers of high-warp tapestry, founders, engravers, gem-cutters, joiners in oak and other woods, dyers, and other skilled workers in all sorts of arts and crafts', this factory was intended to contribute to the decoration and furnishing of the royal palaces. In addition to the economic motives which had inspired the comparable initiative of Henri IV, there was also on this occasion an imperative practical consideration — the necessity of obliging the tapestry-weavers, who had been established at the Gobelins since 1662, to submit to the tutelage of Charles Le Brun, first painter of the king, and director of the royal factory for Crown furnishings.

FORMATION OF THE GOBELINS WORKSHOPS. The tapestry-workshops installed at the Gobelins in 1662 were four in number. The origins of these indicate clearly enough the sources from which the new factory derived its experience. The three workshops producing high-warp tapestries were directed by Jean Jans the elder, a native of Bruges or Oudenarde, who was succeeded by his son in 1668, and by Jean Lefebvre, and Henri Laurent, all from the Louvre workshops. The fourth workshop, for low-warp tapestries, was directed by Jean de La Croix, from the workshop in the

Faubourg Saint-Marcel. It was another fugitive from the Faubourg Saint-Marcel, Jean-Baptiste Mozin, who took over the direction of a second low-warp workshop which was set up in 1667. He was replaced towards the end of the century by Dominique de La Croix; at about the same time a third low-warp workshops was founded, directed initially by Jean Souet and De La Fraye, and later by Souet alone.

THE WEAVERS. Like their superiors, some of the weavers, who numbered about two hundred and fifty, also came from the workshops of the Louvre, the Faubourg Saint-Marcel and the Faubourg Saint-Germain, as well as from Maincy. They included native Parisians, such as Mathurin Texier, Jean Souet and Jean Vavoque, who specialized in the most difficult tasks, and whose last descendant died, at the Gobelins, in 1823. Among the foreigners, there were natives of Brussels (Jacques Ostende, Ambroise van den Busch, Barthélemy Benoist) and of Antwerp (Jacques Benseman, Guillaume Duchesne, and Gabriel Dumontel and his two sons, who arrived about 1673).

ORGANIZATION OF THE WORK. The weavers and their families were housed within the enclosure of the new seminary of the arts; they had the use of little gardens, which were withdrawn from their successors only in the twentieth century. Their privileges and exemptions were the same as those granted by Henri IV to the Flemish weavers whom he established in France. The newcomers were maintained at the king's expense and could become master-craftsmen, with the right to set up independently, after six years apprenticeship and four years service.

The heads of the workshops, again in accordance with the arrangements made by Henri IV, operated independently. Their raw materials (wool, silk, and gold and silver threads) were supplied by the king, who deducted the value from the price of the tapestries which he bought, but they remained free to accept orders from private persons. The salaries of their workmen were calculated by the 'stick' and varied according to the type of work (flesh, faces and hands, draperies, landscapes, accessories), which was allocated according to individual capacity.

The essential innovation which resulted from bringing together the workshops at the Gobelins was their subordination to a director, who was to furnish them with designs and ensure that these were 'correctly executed'. The director, appointed in 1663, who bore the responsibility for the policy and organization of the whole factory, was Charles Le Brun.

LE BRUN. A pupil of Simon Vouet, Charles Le Brun, as a young man, succeeded in spending three years in Italy. The contact with the great masters of that country developed to the full his assimilative powers and his exceptional gift for the arts of decoration. On his return to Paris, Le Brun gave evident proofs of his talent, which led to his being selected by Fouquet to direct the decoration of the château of Vaux. When Fouquet fell from power, Le Brun passed into the service of Louis XIV and embarked on a most remarkable career.

A variety of official posts allowed him to extend his authority to every aspect of the fine arts. The result of this centralization, this unanimous deference to his taste, was the emergence of a homogeneous national style which reached its zenith in the creation of Versailles.

GREATER ELABORATION OF TAPESTRY CARTOONS. The extent and variety of his responsibilities forced Le Brun to assemble a large group of collaborators who executed his ideas and directions. Thanks to a well-drilled team, he was able to carry this method of work to a high degree of perfection in the preparation of cartoons for the Gobelins.

Contrary to the long-established tradition of cartoons painted in tempera, with summary indications of colour, the cartoons for the Gobelins were completely finished oil-paintings, which were cut up into fairly narrow strips to facilitate handling. In accordance with the practice which had long been followed in Flemish workshops, the weavers were expected to reproduce the design exactly. But in spite of the strict discipline which he established, Le Brun did not insist on precise matching of the painted colours. While demanding higher standards of drawing and modelling, he allowed the weavers to retain their traditional methods of colour-interpretation and their existing range of shades.

COMPLETION OF THE PRODUCTIONS OF THE MAINCY WORKSHOP. The work of the Gobelins factory began with the continuation and completion of the tapestries which had been started at Maincy for Nicolas Fouquet.

Among these were the *portières* of the *Fames*, of *Mars*, and of the *Triumphal Car*, verdure tapestries, and a set of the *Story of Constantine*, by Raphael and Le Brun, after the *Stanze* of the Vatican. There was also a *Story of Meleager* after Le Brun, comprising eight hangings and two *entre-fenêtres* (narrow pieces for hanging between windows). Lastly, there were the three pieces of a *Story of Moses*, after Le Brun, and the *Muses*, based on a ceiling painted by Le Brun at Vaux.

The Paris Workshops in the Seventeenth Century

THE 'ELEMENTS' AND THE 'SEASONS'. The first designs which Le Brun produced expressly for the Gobelins, in 1664, were for two separate, but complementary, sets, each comprising four hangings, plus *entrefenêtres*.

The *Elements* show allegorical figures in landscape settings. Each of the four *Seasons* depicts a pair of divinities in front of the royal château best fitted for the characteristic pleasures of the season represented.

The *entrefenêtres* of the *Seasons* were adapted for the set of *Infant gardeners*, in six pieces.

The main scenes of the *Elements* and *Seasons* are less striking than their ornamental borders, which include mottoes and inscriptions. The latter, devoted to the merits and virtues of Louis XIV, were reproduced in gouache in an album painted by the miniaturist Jacques Bailly (Bibliothèque Nationale) and engraved for the collection of the Cabinet du Roi; they were composed by the members of the Little Academy, the ancestor of the present Académie des Inscriptions et Belles-Lettres. This institution was designed to provide, by means of allegory or examples derived from antiquity, an iconographical and intellectual basis for the commemoration of the acts and exploits of the sovereign.

After the discreet evocation of the palaces of Louis XIV in the *Seasons*, Le Brun's designs for Gobelins tapestries soon turned to more overt flattery in the *Story of Alexander*. Later, abandoning such pretexts and allusions, they celebrate Louis' own military prowess in the *Story of the King*, and his pleasures and amusements in the guise of the *Months* or *Royal Residences*.

THE 'STORY OF ALEXANDER'. The originals of the five principal subjects of the *Story of Alexander* (1664–80), which were reproduced or engraved by the Audran family, Edelinck and Sébastien Le Clerc, are preserved at the Louvre. With their furious mêlées and their triumphal processions, organized and balanced without a trace of confusion, they represent the perfected type of Le Brun's historical pieces or 'great machines', transcribed in wool and silk. The high-warp hangings of this series have borders with herms; similar herms served for *entrefenêtres*. The *Story of Alexander* was rewoven no less than eight times by the high-warp and low-warp workshops, both with and without gold thread. There are also copies woven at Aubusson, Brussels and Munich.

THE 'STORY OF THE KING'. Charles Le Brun envisaged a set of tapestries depicting the *Story of the King* as early as 1662, but it was not until 1665 that weaving commenced. From then until 1678 fourteen designs were woven. One complete high-warp set is known, and several low-warp sets, as well as *entrefenêtres*.

A synthesis of the grandeur of the reign, an exaltation of its military and civil pomp as embodied in the person of Louis XIV, the *Story of the King* is one of the most accomplished series produced at the Gobelins.

The faithful rendering of the settings, the realism and interest of the landscape, depicted by Van der Meulen, who followed Louis XIV on his campaigns for this purpose, and the accuracy of the portraiture and costumes, combine to give the set unique value as a topographical and iconographical chronicle of the reign. Its incomparable elegance is set off by borders comprising Raphaelesque ornament, figures, coats-of-arms and initials; these borders vary in design, and in the low-warp examples they are less elaborate.

THE 'MONTHS' OR 'ROYAL RESIDENCES'. In contrast to the majestic pageantry of the *Story of the King*, the *Months* or *Royal Residences*, devised by Le Brun and his team of designers working in close collaboration, are concerned with the diversions and unpremeditated amusements of the court. The novel and original element in this rehandling of the ancient theme of the months lies in the manner in which the royal houses are pushed into the distant background of a landscape which is framed by a sumptuous architectural motif, a colonnaded portico garlanded with flowers. Below, on a balustrade, draperies, Persian carpets, vases of precious metals, bouquets of flowers and musical instruments are displayed with studied negligence. In front of this, as if on a shallow stage, appear small animals, birds, and all the inmates of the Versailles menagerie.

The charm and grace of this deft juxtaposition of nature and symbols of a most sophisticated civilization were acknowledged by the weaving of seven repetitions of the set between 1668 and 1694; eight *entrefenêtres* were also made.

TAPESTRIES AFTER RAPHAEL: THE 'ACTS OF THE APOSTLES' AND THE 'STANZE'. While these sets after Le Brun were in course of execution, other designs were also being woven at the Gobelins. A set of the *Acts of the Apostles* was begun in 1667, based on tapestries in the royal collection; the ten hangings reproduced the compositions of the original sixteenth-century set, woven in Brussels after designs by Raphael.

Twenty years later, another set after Raphael was put on the looms at the Gobelins; this was the *Stanze* or *Chambres du Vatican*, in ten hangings, after cartoons painted in Rome by the pupils of the French Academy there.

LE BRUN DISGRACED. In the interval of twenty years between the execution of the *Acts of the Apostles* and that of the *Stanze*, a number of events took place which were not without influence on the evolution of the Gobelins.

On the death of Colbert, in 1683, his successor, Louvois, had determined to keep Le Brun at a distance. His principal quarrel with him was that he had been Colbert's protégé.

Although Le Brun remained titular director of the royal factory for Crown furnishings, his period of absolute power was at an end.

THE 'STORY OF MOSES'. In the seven years of life which remained to him, the Gobelins workshops executed only two more tapestries after his designs: the *Brazen Serpent* and the *Burning Bush*. These were intended to complete a *Story of Moses* of which the remainder was based on masterpieces by Poussin in the royal collection.

COPIES OF FLEMISH DESIGNS. Unwilling to provoke a scandal, or unable, perhaps, to discover anyone with the talent and authority to take the place of Le Brun, Louvois fell back on the idea of copying old designs, which had been initiated at the Gobelins with the *Acts of the Apostles*. He gave orders that copies should be made of the finest Flemish sets in the royal collections.

In accordance with his instructions, low-warp copies were made of the *Fruits of War*, in ten pieces (1685–6), after Giulio Romano, the *Story of Scipio*, in ten pieces (1686–90), after the same artist, the *Hunts of the Emperor Maximilian*, known as the *Beautiful Hunts of Guise*, in twelve pieces (1685–7; museum of Chartres), after Bernard van Orley, and the *Months* after Lucas van Leyden, known as the *Lucas Months*, in twelve pieces (1688–9; ten pieces with the arms of the Comte de Toulouse were given by John D. Rockefeller to the Metropolitan Museum, New York).

Further sets inspired by Flemish tapestries of the sixteenth century and other sources gave evidence of a tentative movement towards a change of style. These tendencies appeared in the *Triumphs of the Gods*, the *Arabesque Months*, the *Fables* and the set of the *Indies*. Like the preceding sets, they were woven more than once.

THE 'TRIUMPHS OF THE GODS' (1686–7). The *Triumphs of the Gods* were also known as the *Arabesques of Raphael*. They comprise seven designs of Brussels origin, modernized by Noël Coypel, and an eighth, the *Triumph of Philosophy*, by Coypel himself.

This set marks a reaction away from scenes of **contemporary history** and magniloquent allegory towards a purely decorative type of composition which had been out of favour in the immediately preceding period; the *Arabesque Months* exemplify the same tendency.

THE 'ARABESQUE MONTHS' (1687–8). The *Arabesque Months*, woven for the Trianon after the designs of a Flemish set, modernized by Noël Coypel, show figures of gods beneath arcades, surrounded by attributes appropriate to the various months. They confirmed the trend towards themes unencumbered by intellectual or historical programmes.

'MYTHOLOGICAL SUBJECTS'. This movement was reinforced by the *Mythological Subjects*, in eight pieces (1686), after Giulio Romano, and by the *Mythological Subjects* after Raphael, woven at the same time. The two sets, based on drawings in the royal collection, breathe a spirit of pagan joy in their depiction of beautiful women, disposed in harmonious groups, or frolicking in the golden sunlight. The offended modesty of Mme. de Maintenon was responsible for the dresses and draperies which clothe the figures. The tapestries are enhanced by witty borders on a ground of simulated gold mosaic. The decorative artist Jean Le Moyne ('le Lorrain'), assisted by Boullongne and Hallé, was responsible for these lively compositions of 'grotesques', animals, birds, and monkeys driving goats. Here, as usual, fauna and flora have subordinate roles; in the next set, however, they come into their own.

THE 'INDIES' (1687). The dearth of cartoons available for the low-warp workshops suggested the utilization for this purpose of eight large pictures by the Dutch painter Albert Eckhout, which had been given to Louis XIV by Prince Maurice of Nassau. Their novel subjects, luxuriant vegetation, and 'Indian' figures introduced a new and exotic note in the late seventeenth-century production of the Gobelins. This was so favourably received that, in 1692–3, the painter François Desportes was given the task of retouching the originals for use on the high-warp looms. Forty years later, Desportes had occasion to paint new versions of Eckhout's designs, which served in their turn for the *New Indies* set, likewise woven at the Gobelins, which will be discussed in due course.

THE 'GALLERY OF SAINT-CLOUD'. The last set of new designs woven at the Gobelins in the seventeenth century was the so-called *Gallery of Saint-Cloud*. This reproduced the paintings executed by Mignard in 1677 in the château of the Duc d'Orléans, brother of Louis XIV, which were destroyed in the fire at Saint-Cloud in 1870.

XLI. RINALDO AND ARMIDA

After Simon Vouet

Le Haras du Pin

XLII. THE FLIGHT INTO EGYPT
Strasbourg Cathedral

XLIII. PORTIÈRE OF THE TRIUMPHAL CAR
After Charles Le Brun
Mobilier national, Paris. Gobelins

XLIV. STORY OF THE KING: LOUIS XIV ENTERING DUNKIRK
After Charles Le Brun
Mobilier national, Paris. Gobelins

XLV. THE MONTHS OR ROYAL RESIDENCES: CHÂTEAU OF CHAMBORD
Mobilier national, Paris. Gobelins

XLVI. MYTHOLOGICAL SUBJECTS
After Raphael and Giulio Romano, with borders by Jean
Le Moyne le Lorrain
THE DANCE OF THE NYMPHS
Mobilier national, Paris. Gobelins

XLVII. THE PORTIÈRES OF THE GODS: BACCHUS
After Claude III Audran
Mobilier national, Paris. Gobelins

XLVIII. THE GROTESQUE MONTHS IN BANDS
After Claude III Audran
Mobilier national, Paris. Gobelins

The set, comprising five hangings, was begun in 1686 in the private workshop of Jans, and was financed from the personal funds of Louvois. It was continued officially, on behalf of the king, in 1689, at the time of Le Brun's last illness, and marked the official abandonment of the latter's style.

DIRECTORSHIP OF MIGNARD. The advanced age of Mignard, whom Louvois appointed director of the royal factory for Crown furnishings after the death of Le Brun, made it impossible for him to bring about any real innovations in the organization of the Gobelins. He restricted himself to the supervision of the sets in course of execution and to the creation of an academy of drawing from the antique and the living model.

CLOSURE OF THE GOBELINS WORKSHOPS. The death of Louvois in 1691, and the exhaustion of the royal exchequer as a result of the war of the League of Augsburg brought to a halt the productive activity which had occupied the royal factory for Crown furnishings over a period of thirty years. The tapestry-looms shared the fate of the rest. Their activity slackened, and eventually stopped. In 1694, the workshops were forced to close. The weavers received orders to disperse. They enlisted in the armies, departed to offer their services to the Brussels workshops, found a temporary refuge at the Beauvais factory, or resigned themselves to waiting for better times.

THE GOBELINS IN THE EIGHTEENTH CENTURY

After remaining closed for four years, the Gobelins factory reopened its doors in 1699. It required complete reorganization. The royal factory for Crown furnishings had practically ceased to exist, and the high-warp and low-warp looms were alone, or almost alone, in resuming the old rhythm of production.

Ultimate responsibility for the factory was transferred back to the superintendent of buildings, a post which the architect Jules Hardouin-Mansard took over from Colbert de Villacerf. Mansard's successor, from 1708 to 1736, was the Duc d'Antin, a son of Mme. de Montespan. After him came Philippe Orry (1736–45), Le Normant de Tournehem, an uncle by marriage of Mme. de Pompadour, the Marquis de Marigny (1745–73), the same lady's brother, and the Comte d'Angivillier (1773–93). For the greater part of the century the titular directors of the factory were no longer painters like Le Brun and Mignard (died 1695), but architects. These were Desgodets (1699–1706), Jules Robert de Cotte (1735–47), Garnier d'Isle (1747–53), and Soufflot (1775–80). These were succeeded by the king's principal painter, J.-B. Pierre (1781–9), the architect Ch.-A. Guillaumot (1789–92), and the tapestry-contractor Jean Audran (1792–3).

Since the authority of the director of the factory was generally confined to administrative matters, he was seconded by an artistic director. This post was held from 1699 to 1735 by the king's principal architect, Robert de Cotte. He was succeeded by the well-known painters Jean-Baptiste Oudry (1733–55) and François Boucher (1755–70), both of whom exercised a more readily definable influence than Noël Hallé (1771–6).

Other painters were also attached to the factory. These included the history-painters Joseph Yvart (1699–1727) and Charles Chastelain (1720–1729), and the painters of ornament Michel Anguier (1699–1708), Claude III Audran (1699–1734), Philippe Meunier (1710–34) and Pierre-Josse Perrot (1715–49). Among specialists in flower-painting were J.-B. Blain de Fontenay (1699–1715), his son (1715–30), and Jean-Marc Ladey (1734–1749). None of these, however, acquired a reputation comparable with that of Louis Tessier (1749–84) or Maurice Jacques (1737–84).

As in the seventeenth century, the actual weaving was in the hands of contractors, who retained a relative independence, including the right to undertake private commissions, while remaining subject to the same obligations as their predecessors.

The first high-warp workshop remained in the hands of Jean Jans the younger until 1723; it then passed to his son, Jean-Jacques Jans (1723–31) and eventually to the Audran family (Michel, 1732–71, and Jean, 1771–94). Jean Lefèvre, who directed the second high-warp workshop from 1699 to 1736, was succeeded by Mathieu Monmerqué (1736–44) and Pierre-François Cozette (1749–96). A third high-warp workshop, formed in 1703 under Louis Ovis de La Tour, was suppressed in 1734.

The four low-warp workshops, those of Jean de La Croix (1662–1712), Dominique de La Croix (1693–1712), Jean Souet (1699–1722) and Jean de La Fraye (1699–1730), were joined by a fifth, that of Étienne Le Blond, in 1701; later, they were successively amalgamated into a single workshop, directed by Jacques Neilson (1751–88).

Neilson, who was succeeded by Cozette the younger on the eve of the Revolution, introduced many useful innovations in low-warp technique. It was also at his instigation that Vaucanson devised a mechanism which allowed the low-warp weaver to verify the correctness of his work (1757).

Neilson concerned himself no less effectively with the dye-workshop.

Under his supervision, the chemist Quemizet endeavoured to curtail certain abuses arising from the excessive multiplication of colours, but his example was not much followed.

Aberrations of this kind were responsible for a certain amount of trouble in the factory about the middle of the century. Operations were also hampered by the low state of the royal exchequer. Moreover, the factory suffered from the lack of firm administrative and artistic authority, such as had been exercised by Charles Le Brun.

THE PORTIÈRES OF THE 'GODS'. The first set to be put on the looms after the reopening of the Gobelins was that of the *portières* of the *Gods*, after Claude III Audran.

The transformation which was taking place in architecture, and the new style of interior decoration, with its lighter, slimmer ornament, could not long go unregarded in tapestries. The latter, in their turn, offered an important contribution of their own to the style which was being formulated, a contribution marked by the increasing importance of purely ornamental forms.

Hardly fifteen years had elapsed since Noël Coypel's adaptation of the *Triumphs of the Gods*, or the Beauvais *Grotesques* of Jean I Berain and J.-B. Monnoyer, when the *portières* of the *Gods*, by Claude III Audran, one of Watteau's masters, made their contribution to the renewal of tapestry style. The new manner was to win over a fresh generation, too young to have felt the effects of the dictatorship which Le Brun had exercised over the fine arts.

The eight *portières* of the *Gods*, of which four symbolize the seasons, and four the elements, show light and fragile porticoes, garlanded or surrounded with flowers and fruit. The general composition, the ornament, and the accessories are the work of Claude III Audran; he prepared the designs in great detail, as can be seen from his sketches, preserved in the Cronstedt collection of the Nationalmuseum in Stockholm. The figures of the gods themselves, and of the children who appear below, were designed by Louis de Boullongne and Corneille. The animals and birds were probably the work of François Desportes.

The hangings of this set were rewoven, with variants, a great many times. Two hundred and thirty-five specimens are known, showing the three different types of borders used for high-warp and low-warp sets.

THE 'GROTESQUE MONTHS' IN BANDS (1709). Claude III Audran had a second opportunity of adapting his diverse talents to the requirements of tapestry in the *Grotesque Months* in bands, made for the château of the Grand Dauphin at Meudon. This series, woven by the low-warp workshops of La Croix and Le Blond, and exceptionally rich in gold and silver, was never repeated, at least at the Gobelins. The designs, which were engraved by Jean Audran in 1726, are in many respects a kind of condensed version of those of the *portières* of the *Gods*. The three hangings are divided into bands about two feet wide, which are separated by borders ornamented with lozenges, shells, dolphins and the initials of the Grand Dauphin. Claude III Audran was to give still further proofs of his inventive imagination in his designs for the *Chancelleries*.

THE 'CHANCELLERIES'. The *Chancelleries*, often woven at the Gobelins or Beauvais, were sets of tapestries adorned with fleurs-de-lis, the royal arms, and the attributes of justice, which were traditionally presented by the sovereign to the Lord Chancellor of France. They were saved from monotony by the imagination and inventiveness displayed in the designs of the borders or central groups.

NEW PORTIÈRES OF 'DIANA' AND THE 'ARMS OF FRANCE'. Among other work, there is mention of two new *portières*, that of *Diana*, and that of the *Arms of France*, after Pierre Josse Perrot (1737), now in the Louvre. These are composed in the manner of Audran, but with reminiscences of late seventeenth-century style.

THE 'ALENTOURS'. Another innovation adopted at the Gobelins in the eighteenth century, even more important than the charming style of the *portières* of the *Gods* or the *Grotesque Months*, was the type of tapestry with ornamental surrounds known as *alentours*.

The *alentours* were one of two standard methods employed at the factory in the eighteenth century for framing the main subject of the tapestry; the other was the picture-frame border, simulating carved and gilded wood. In tapestries with *alentours*, the main subject was reduced to a relatively small framed picture in the centre of the field, while the remainder of the tapestry was given up to the *alentours*, consisting of simulated damask, cartouches, attributes, trophies, flowers, human figures or animals. This device was first employed in the *Story of Don Quixote*.

THE 'STORY OF DON QUIXOTE'. The *Story of Don Quixote* is mentioned for the first time in the accounts for 1714, and thereafter is referred to repeatedly in the Gobelins archives, down to 1794.

In the course of these eighty years nine sets were woven, whose varying compositions were based on the numerous designs painted, with a lively and entertaining sense of the picturesque, by Charles-Antoine Coypel.

The prolonged success of the *Don Quixote* set was due not so much to the popularity of the subject as to the decorative merit of its *alentours*, of which six different versions were produced. From the first, by Blain de Fontenay and Claude III Audran, to the sixth, by Louis Tessier, these show the same care in the arrangement of the motifs, and the same ingenuity in devising the details of trophies, animals and flowers.

THE 'SCENES OF OPERA, TRAGEDY AND COMEDY'. After the *Story of Don Quixote* and the four hangings of *Daphnis and Chloe*, which were woven at the Gobelins, as unofficial work, after the paintings of the future Regent (1715; more probably by Charles-Antoine Coypel) for his château of Bagnolet, *alentours* appeared once more in the *Scenes of Opera, Tragedy and Comedy*. The designs, painted by Charles-Antoine Coypel from 1744 to 1752, were first woven for the Queen of Poland, mother of the Dauphine Marie-Josèphe of Saxony (former royal palace at Dresden; five pieces in the royal palace at Stockholm). To the original scenes derived from Molière, Corneille, Racine and Quinault, some other subjects were later added, borrowed in part from the *Operatic Fragments* (1733–44) after Charles-Antoine Coypel.

The *alentours* were designed by Jean-Marc Ladey, Chevillon and Tessier; these were later replaced by narrow borders simulating picture-frames. Tapestries intended to be set in panelling and framed with a beading of gilt wood were woven without borders.

Charming as are the *alentours* in this and the preceding sets, it was in the set of the *Gods*, after Francois Boucher and Maurice Jacques, that they attained their greatest perfection.

THE SET OF THE 'GODS'. The complete success achieved here, which marks the zenith of the eighteenth-century production of the Gobelins, makes us forget the oddity of the conception of these *alentours*, with their simulated pictures, in simulated frames, hanging by simulated ribbons, and throwing simulated shadows on simulated damasks.

Designed by Maurice Jacques about 1758, the *alentours* of the tapestries of the *Gods* served as a foil to scenes depicting the loves of the gods, the designs for which were painted by François Boucher between 1762 and 1764, though based in part on ideas which the artist had already utilized at an earlier date. The *alentours* were modified on several occasions. Changes in certain motifs and the addition of various 'ornaments in the Greek manner' coincided with the earliest manifestations of the Louis XVI style. After 1770, Louis Tessier was given the task of progressively eliminating certain forms of cartouche, which appeared 'dated'.

Charmed, like Louis XV, by the elegance and refinement of these designs, several English noblemen ordered sets of the *Gods*. At their request, additional pieces were woven to form overdoors, frames for windows and mirrors, and panels to fill other small spaces, so as to provide a complete covering for the walls. Some of these sets remain in the rooms for which they were made. The set at Osterley Park is accompanied by a matching set of tapestry furniture covers, which was repeated several times at the Gobelins.

RELIGIOUS AND MYTHOLOGICAL TAPESTRIES. The charm of the *Gods*, the *Story of Don Quixote*, or the *portières* of Claude III Audran, must not be allowed to obscure the fact that the production of the Gobelins, during the first half of the eighteenth century, also included belated manifestations of the tradition of Charles Le Brun. These appeared in a number of religious or mythological sets, sometimes of large dimensions, designed in accordance with the rules of classicism, as codified by the French Royal Academy of Painting.

A set of the *Old Testament*, comprising eight hangings after Charles-Antoine Coypel, was begun in 1710. As a complement to this a *New Testament* set was woven, to designs by Jean Jouvenet and Jean Restout, between 1711 and a date after 1755.

Meantime a succession of mythological, allegorical and historical sets had been made on the high-warp and low-warp looms. They included an *Iliad*, in five pieces (1713–30), after Charles-Antoine Coypel, the *Arts*, in two pieces (1740–55), after Jean Restout, the *Story of Mark Antony*, in three pieces (1741), after Charles Natoire, and the *Story of Theseus* (1744), one piece, after Carle van Loo.

THE 'STORY OF ESTHER' AND THE 'STORY OF JASON', AFTER JEAN-FRANÇOIS DE TROY. The designs of François de Troy were characterized by reminiscences, not of Le Brun, but of the splendour and magnificence of the Venetian painters. His *Story of Esther* (1737–40) has settings worthy of the most luxuriant imaginations of Venice, an overflowing wealth of accessories and draperies, and superb costumes suggestive of the enchantments of the opera. The seven hangings of the set were rewoven on fifteen occasions (Compiègne, Fontainebleau, Uffizi gallery in Florence, Buckingham Palace and Windsor). Their success brought Jean-François de Troy the commission for a *Story of Jason*, in seven pieces (1743–6).

C. THE NEW INDIES: THE INDIAN HUNTER

The borders of the *Esther* and *Jason* sets take the form of simulated carved and gilt frames. These recur in the *New Indies* set, and in two sets with contemporary subjects: the *Turkish Embassy* and the *Hunts of Louis XV*.

THE 'NEW INDIES'. The uninterrupted production of tapestries after the *Indies* paintings given to Louis XIV by Prince Maurice of Nassau in 1687, in the versions prepared by François Desportes for the high-warp looms in 1692, eventually rendered the old cartoons unfit for further use. In 1735, François Desportes was commissioned to produce eight new cartoons, which were exhibited at various Salons from 1737 to 1741. Although based on the old designs, they presented a more lively and realistic vision of nature than did the originals (Vienna; Quirinal palace, Rome).

THE 'TURKISH EMBASSY' (1731–4), AFTER CHARLES PARROCEL. The dynamic quality, which distinguishes the *New Indies* from the static effects of their seventeenth-century predecessors, may also be discerned, though in a different form, in the *Turkish Embassy*, the first of two sets with contemporary subjects woven at the Gobelins in the eighteenth century.

THE 'HUNTS OF LOUIS XV'. A similar absence of pomposity and ostentation characterizes the *Hunts of Louis XV*, in eight pieces (1734–45), by Jean-Baptiste Oudry (Compiègne; Pitti palace, Florence). In spite of its title, the set is concerned much more with nature than with the king. The scenes represented are so many pretexts for illustrating the varied landscape of the forests of Compiègne and Fontainebleau.

OUDRY AND THE GOBELINS. With their faithful rendering of landscape, of the portraits of Louis XV and his companions, of the horses and dogs, and with their simulated carved and gilt frames, the *Hunts of Louis XV* are exact reproductions of paintings. They are conceived in the manner of, and on the scale of, pictures; their dispersed centres of interest are ill-adapted and alien to the tapestry technique.

These observations go some way to explain the controversy which arose at the Gobelins at the end of the first half of the eighteenth century. The details of this, with the disputes between Jean-Baptiste Oudry and the weavers, would be more than a little comic, were it not that they had grave consequences for the future of tapestry in France.

Since 1726, Oudry had been painter to the Beauvais factory, and his cartoons had been instrumental in saving it from ruin. Coming to the

Gobelins to prepare and supervise the weaving of the *Hunts of Louis XV*, he was appointed superintendent in 1733, and took over the artistic direction of the factory.

Oudry's insistence on exact reproduction of his cartoons had already given rise to certain difficulties at Beauvais. The renewal of these demands at the Gobelins brought on him the enmity of the contractors directing the workshops, who were anxious to preserve their own prerogatives.

The dispute, however, was concerned not so much with aims as with means. The contractors at the Gobelins, like Oudry himself, wished to make tapestries which were imitations of paintings. They showed this clearly at a later stage by exhibiting their works at the Salon, thus competing with the painters on their own ground. The point at issue was simply this: was the painter justified in insisting that his colouring and his effects of light and shade should be exactly reproduced in the tapestry, or should these details be left to the discretion of the weavers, who knew from experience the resources and practical possibilities of their craft?

The death of Jean-Baptiste Oudry (1755), though it made the dispute less bitter, could hardly modify the basic conflict of views.

Among the unfortunate consequences of the controversy, the most regrettable was the multiplication of dyes, without which the palette and colour-shading of the painter could not be reproduced. Dye-chemistry permitted an infinite variety of colour-scales, but some of the tints obtained were inevitably ephemeral, and have faded irreparably, with disastrous effects to the colour-balance of the tapestries in which they were used.

BOUCHER. Having been transformed, first by imperceptible shifts of taste, and subsequently by deliberate policy, into imitations of painting, Gobelins tapestries henceforward depended more and more on borrowings from the latter art.

As on several other occasions in the history of the factory, a need was felt, about 1750, of renewing and bringing up to date the stock of cartoons. Michel Audran, in charge of the high-warp workshop, asked the painter Etienne Jeaurat to supply him, as a private commission, with designs for a set of *Daphnis and Chloe* (1738–41), in the manner of Boucher's pastoral subjects, as well as for the *Village Festivals* (1750–3).

In 1747, and again in 1751, the contractors at the Gobelins complained of the 'want of designs', and the ill-effects of this scarcity on private orders.

The appointment of François Boucher as superintendent of the factory, after Oudry's death, offered some prospect of stabilizing a situation which, owing to serious financial difficulties, was becoming menacing.

Boucher's artistic directorship at the Gobelins justified the hopes raised by his successful contributions to the work of the Beauvais factory. After *Sunrise* and *Sunset*, woven before his appointment (1752–3), he collaborated with Carle van Loo, Pierre and Vien on a set of the *Loves of the Gods*, for which he supplied cartoons remarkably like his designs for Beauvais. Lastly, from 1758 onwards, Boucher began work on the cartoons for the set of the *Gods*, whose *alentours* have been mentioned above.

Well before 1770, however, it had to be admitted that the changes which had taken place 'in the last few years in the taste and arrangement of apartments necessitated alterations in the type and normal dimensions of tapestries'.

FURNITURE AND PORTRAITS. While awaiting these expected alterations, the factory rapidly extended its production of tapestry furniture-covers, some in conjunction with sets of wall-hangings, some with independent designs. In competition with Beauvais, the Gobelins multiplied pastoral scenes, chubby children and plump Cupids, after Boucher, and bouquets of flowers, tied with blue or pink ribbons, after Maurice Jacques; these were adapted to the shapes and dimensions of sofas, armchairs, folding screens and fire-screens.

At the same time, the looms were busy with replicas of easel-pictures and portraits.

Among portraits woven and exhibited at the Salon from 1763 onwards were those of *Louis XV, the Queen,* the future *Louis XVI, Marie-Antoinette* (Bordeaux Chamber of Commerce), the *Empress Maria-Theresa* and *Joseph II* (château of Versailles). A chorus of delighted exclamations was heard also before the *Little girl with a cat* (Marie-Amélie de Silvestre) and its companion-piece, the *Young Artist,* after Drouais (Louvre, and museum of Tours), and before the copies after Boucher, Van Loo, or even Rembrandt. No one perceived that these works were, in fact, artistic aberrations, utterly opposed to the true potentialities of the craft of tapestry.

GOBELINS TAPESTRIES FROM 1770 TO 1794. Nevertheless, it was these same disastrous principles which were invoked to effect the desired 'alterations' in tapestry style. The remaining sets woven at the Gobelins before the Revolution forced the closure of the factory were nothing more than reproductions of pictures. To make matters worse, the pictures chosen were generally of indifferent quality.

The Paris Workshops in the Seventeenth Century

The four pieces of *Turkish Costume* (1772–5), after Amédée van Loo, contributed a last touch of exoticism, which is not without charm. The *Story of Henri IV*, in six pieces (1782–7), after François-André Vincent, is an interesting example of the utilization of the cult of that popular king to stimulate patriotic sentiment.

With the five pieces of the *Seasons* (1773–91), after Callot, neo-classicism made its appearance — not unexpectedly, since objects and ornaments 'in the Greek manner' were the current craze. But the nadir of dullness was not yet reached. To attain this it was necessary to weave the *Scenes from French History* (1784–7), in nine pieces, after Brenet, Durameau, Vincent, Barthélemy, Ménageot, Le Barbier the elder and Suvée. One hundred and thirty years of incessant research, of intense activity, had brought the Gobelins factory to the miserable torpor of the *Continence of Bayard* or the *Partisans of the Fronde arresting President Molé*.

D. THE GODS. AFTER FRANÇOIS BOUCHER

CHAPTER VIII

The Beauvais Factory in the seventeenth and eighteenth centuries

The Beauvais factory, like the Gobelins, was created by Colbert. But whereas the Gobelins existed primarily to execute royal commissions, the Beauvais factory, though under the protection of the king, remained a private enterprise. Successive directors found, however, that their independence was bought at the price of recurrent financial difficulties, despite the subsidies received from the Direction of Buildings.

Beauvais specialized in low-warp weaving. The work executed there, though rarely in the van of fashion, followed fairly closely the current trends of taste and the evolution of decorative style.

HINARD. On the 5th August 1664, letters patent were issued, dated from Vincennes, in favour of the 'royal factories of high-warp and low-warp weaving established in the town of Beauvais and other places in Picardy'. By these letters, the direction of the workshops was entrusted to Louis Hinard, merchant tapestry-weaver, a native of Beauvais, established in Paris. Hinard undertook to give employment to one hundred weavers in the first year, of French or other nationalities, and this number was to be increased up to six hundred after six years. He also agreed to maintain fifty apprentices. In return, Hinard and his eventual successors were granted subsidies, and a privilege of thirty years duration.

WORK OF HINARD. The loss — intentional or otherwise — of the archives of the factory prior to the first quarter of the eighteenth century makes it impossible to compile a complete list of the works of Louis Hinard. We know, however, thanks to the *Accounts of Buildings* and the *General Inventory of Crown Furnishings* that he supplied, for the decoration of the royal châteaux, various verdures of 'fine' or 'ordinary' quality, with flower-beds, fountains and orange-trees; he also supplied landscape tapestries, sometimes enlivened with small figures, animals and birds. Some of these hangings are said to have been woven after designs by Fouquières, a pupil of Rubens. In addition to the foregoing, Hinard also produced at least two more ambitious sets of tapestries: one, in eight pieces, with details in gold, showed *Children's Games*, after Corneille; the other, in six pieces, depicted a *Picard Wedding*.

HINARD'S EMBARASSMENT AND RUIN. Unfortunately for Hinard, his expenses eventually outran his receipts. On several occasions, he petitioned for, and obtained, subsidies. They did not suffice to save him. Was he an ineffective administrator, unable to control a dangerous situation? Were his tapestries too expensive? Did he neglect Beauvais in favour of the private workshop which he continued to maintain in Paris? These suggestions are probably not far from the truth. But it is also possible that Louis Hinard was the victim of intrigue. Whatever may be the truth of the matter, it is certain that, having come to the end of his resources and his credit, he was forced to withdraw from the factory in 1684. His ruin was complete and final.

PHILIPPE BEHAGLE. His successor was Philippe Behaegel or Behaghel, known as Behagle, a merchant tapestry-weaver of Oudenarde, who had subsequently worked at Tournai. The directorship of Behagle, which lasted twenty-one years, was a fruitful one from the artistic point of view. He founded a school of design and succeeded in inspiring the workshops with new vigour. Louis XIV paid them a visit in 1686 in order to express to Behagle his interest and satisfaction.

Behagle's privilege 'for the re-establishment of tapestry in the town of Beauvais' was signed on the 21st February 1684. In broad outline, it was a repetition of the privilege granted to Hinard twenty years before, except for the omission of certain financial guarantees. On the other hand, it contained certain additional concessions, which gave Behagle greater liberty of action.

BAERT AND BLOMAERT. The privilege of the 21st February 1684, refers more than once to Behagle's 'partner'. He had, in fact, two partners. A legal document of 13th June 1684, which has come to light recently, provides some important information on this point.

The first partner, Jean Baert, came from a family settled in Oudenarde and had been a childhood companion of Behagle; he obtained letters of naturalization in 1674. Much later, in 1711, he was to receive a privilege of thirty years' duration for the manufacture of tapestries in the town of Torcy-en-Brie, a lordship which had been raised to a marquisate for the benefit of a nephew of Colbert. The conditions of operation of the factory were to have been the same as those of Beauvais; Baert, however, did not make use of the privilege.

The second partner, Georges Blomaert, belonged to a family of master tapestry-weavers who worked at Oudenarde, Ghent 'and elsewhere'. In 1677, he had been given permission to set up at Lille 'a factory similar to that of Brussels' and he was busy with this project down to the time of his agreement with Behagle.

By the deed of 13th June 1684, the three partners, Behagle, Baert and Blomaert, sought primarily to define their respective responsibilities in Beauvais and in Paris, where Baert had a shop in the 'Rue du Petit-Lyon'. In 1692, however, there is a reference to another shop 'for the tapestries of Beauvais' in the Rue de Richelieu. This may perhaps be due to a confusion with the old shop of Hinard. Nevertheless, it does suggest certain doubts regarding the duration of the Behagle-Baert-Blomaert partnership, notwithstanding the fact that, about 1695, the Swedish envoy mentions a dispute between Behagle and his 'partner' which was threatening to 'disrupt' the Beauvais factory.

THE FIRST WORKS OF BEHAGLE AT BEAUVAIS. The situation which Behagle had to face, at the outset of his operations at Beauvais, was difficult in several respects.

While continuing to weave verdures, especially verdures with birds, four specimens of which are in the Musée de Mon-Repos at Lausanne, he also undertook designs of rather higher artistic pretensions. These early works presumably included the set of *Conquests of Louis XIV*, which was begun not later than 1690. It was the sequel to another set on the same theme, with allegorical adjuncts, which Behagle had woven at Tournai.

THE 'CONQUESTS OF LOUIS XIV'. The Beauvais set of the *Conquests of Louis XIV*, after cartoons by the battle-painter Jean-Baptiste Martin which are clearly based on the engravings of the *Great Conquests of the King* by Sébastien Le Clerc, is obviously not to be compared with the Gobelins set of the *Story of the King*. Nevertheless, it merits some consideration for the correctness of its workmanship, the breadth of the scenes represented, and its strict regard for historical accuracy. To the several specimens of the main subjects in private collections we may add the *Battle of Cassel*, at the château of Maisons-Laffitte.

THE 'ACTS OF THE APOSTLES'. With the same facility, Behagle under-took the weaving of the *Acts of the Apostles* after Raphael. These hangings, which are now in the cathedral of Beauvais, while the cartoons are said to be in the cathedral of Meaux, are distinguished by their floral borders. They are supposed to be the work of weavers from the Gobelins, to whom Behagle gave shelter at Beauvais during the temporary closure, from 1694 to 1698, of the royal factory for Crown furnishings.

THE 'TENIERS TAPESTRIES' AND THE 'SEAPORTS'. Among other works executed by Behagle at Beauvais were *Teniers tapestries* (village scenes in-spired by the paintings of Teniers), a *Story of Achilles*, *Chancelleries* for the Lord Chancellor Boucherat, after a design by Bonnemer, with borders by Jean Le Moyne, and a complete set of furnishings for the parliament of Rouen. Prior to 1693 he had also completed a set of *Seaports*, which must have been identical with the *Seaports* after Kerchove and Campion, which are commonly but erroneously assigned to the first half of the eighteenth century. A set in Sweden, at the castle of Björnstorp (Skåne), has bold borders with a design of shells.

THE 'GROTESQUES' OF JEAN I BERAIN AND J.-B. MONNOYER. None of these sets, however, achieved a success comparable with that of the *Grotesques* on a yellow or 'Spanish tobacco' ground, which are among the happiest of the late seventeenth-century creations of Beauvais. They are often called the *Berain Grotesques*, with reference to the supposed colla-boration of the king's designer. But it would be more appropriate to call them the *Berain-Monnoyer Grotesques*, for, if the former inspired the designs, the actual cartoons were the work of the well-known flower-painter Monnoyer, who also worked for the Gobelins.

Although they were conceived prior to 1689, some time before the death of Le Brun, the style of the *Grotesques* clearly belongs to a new artistic period, quite unlike that which the great dictator of the arts had moulded to his taste.

Based on the classical *grotteschi* of Raphael, as adapted by Berain, the *Grotesques* show leafy arches and fragile architectural constructions resting on slender colonnettes of lapis-lazuli. The vacant spaces of the composi-tion are filled with bouquets and baskets of flowers, with large birds perched on the marble entablatures, and various other motifs. The fore-grounds are enlivened by figures in costumes of many hues, animal-tamers, dancers and characters from the Commedia dell'Arte.

The *Grotesques* enjoyed an extraordinary success, and were woven many times, with a considerable number of variants, down to 1725 or later. The existence of this vogue is confirmed by some hundred and fifty surviving hangings, of varying quality, corresponding to the designations of 'fine' and 'ordinary' *Grotesques*, which appear in the archives of the factory (examples in the Louvre and Musée des Arts Décoratifs, Paris; Musée de Tapisseries, Aix-en-Provence; Stockholm Town Hall; Schloss Bruchsal, Baden; in Czechoslovakia, etc., etc.). The designs were also imitated by Aubusson weavers working at Berlin in the eighteenth century, as well as being reproduced in embroidery.

BERAIN. Berain made a more personal contribution to some other sets than he did to the *Grotesques*. This is not true of the set of *Great Gods*, which, though it has been much discussed in connection with Beauvais, was in fact woven in the Paris workshop of Bacor; but it can be said of the *Conquests of Charles XI of Sweden* and the *Marine Triumphs with the arms of the Comte de Toulouse*. These also were largely executed outside the factory itself, in Behagle's private workshop in Paris, in the Faubourg Saint Martin.

THE 'CONQUESTS OF THE KING OF SWEDEN'. This set comprises four hangings: the *Battle of Landskrona*, two episodes of the *Battle of Lund*, and the *Battle of Malmö*. Two further pieces were projected but were never commenced. The cartoons for the set, which hung for many years in the castle of Drottningholm and is now in the royal palace in Stockholm, were painted by Jean-Baptiste Martin after designs by the Swedish artist Lemke. Berain's participation was limited to the designs for the borders, the cartoons for which were prepared by Louis-Guy de Vernansal. Only the *Battle of Landskrona* was executed at Beauvais, in 1699. The *Second Day of Lund* was evidently completed by Dominique Lacroix, a weaver from the Gobelins, who signed it. The other two pieces were woven, as has been mentioned, in Behagle's workshop in Paris.

THE 'MARINE TRIUMPHS'. The *Marine Triumphs with the arms of the Comte de Toulouse*, now the property of the Bank of France, were also woven, according to the indirect testimony of the Swedish envoy in Paris, in Behagle's private workshop. Like the *Conquests of Charles XI*, they were originally ordered from Jean-Baptiste Hinard, the son of Louis Hinard, and both commissions passed into Behagle's hands when Hinard was arrested for debt — a contretemps for which Behagle was probably not entirely without responsibility.

The four hangings, enriched with silver thread, were based on designs by Berain, completed and adapted by some artist more familiar than the king's designer with the techniques of painting. Their sumptuousness is reminiscent of the settings which Berain devised for the operas of Lulli, in his capacity as designer to the Royal Academy of Music.

THE PRELUDE TO THE STYLE OF THE EIGHTEENTH CENTURY. The *Grotesques* and the *Marine Triumphs* foreshadow the eighteenth-century emphasis on purely ornamental compositions, which had been too much neglected during the preceding thirty years. Much of the credit for the introduction of the new style at Beauvais and in Behagle's Paris workshop must be given to Berain. But some is also due to Behagle himself. Working at a time when a long-established stylistic hegemony was beginning to break up, he was astute enough to realize that it was essential to strike out a new line. In Berain, he found the right man at the decisive moment. He did not succeed in avoiding, and it was probably impossible to avoid, serious financial difficulties, but he ensured the functioning of the Beauvais factory and established its reputation as second only to the Gobelins.

FOREIGN CLIENTS OF BEAUVAIS. In addition, Behagle attracted to the factory large numbers of customers not only from France, but also from abroad. On his death, in 1705, he was succeeded by his widow and his sons, but they were unable to maintain their heavy financial responsibilities and were forced to give way, in 1711, to the brothers Filleul.

DIRECTORSHIPS OF THE FILLEUL BROTHERS AND OF M. DE MÉROU. The directorship of the brothers Filleul, coinciding as it did with the difficult period of the end of the reign of Louis XIV and the beginning of the Regency, was one of continual harassment. Their management of affairs was not above reproach. The details of their production are not entirely clear. Among noteworthy sets are the *Story of Telemachus*, in six hangings, after Arnauld, *Animal Combats*, by the Fleming Souef, and the *Metamorphoses*, in six hangings, after Houasse. The *Chinese Hangings*, by Vernansal and Blain de Fontenay, are assigned by a number of writers to the period of the Filleul brothers, but it is not impossible that it may have been initiated by Behagle at an earlier period (about 1688).

In spite of some clumsiness in the design, and a certain incoherence in the composition of the principal pieces, the *Chinese Hangings* are a skilful essay in the *chinoiserie* style which was so fashionable in the second half of the seventeenth century. A large number of repetitions exist. There are

XLIX. STORY OF DON QUIXOTE
After Charles-Antoine Coypel
Mobilier national, Paris. Gobelins

L. THE NEW INDIES: THE INDIAN HUNTER
After François Desportes
Mobilier national, Paris. Gobelins

LI. STORY OF JASON: THE GOLDEN FLEECE
After Jean-François de Troy
Stockholm, Royal Palace

LII. THE HUNTS OF LOUIS XV: THE KING HOLDING THE BLOODHOUND
After J.-B. Oudry
Mobilier national, Paris. Gobelins

LIII. (A) THE DAUPHIN, LATER
LOUIS XVI
After M. Van Loo

(B) MARIE-ANTOINETTE
AS DAUPHINE
After Drouais
Chambre de commerce,
Bordeaux. Gobelins

LIV. SEAPORTS
Björnstorp Castle, Skåne, Sweden. Beauvais

LV. GROTESQUES ON A YELLOW GROUND: THE MUSICIANS
After Jean I Berain and Jean-Baptiste Monnoyer
Schloss Bruchsal, Baden. Beauvais

LVI. CHINESE HANGINGS
After Vernansal and Blain de Fontenay
Beauvais

three pieces in the Louvre; their incomplete borders reproduce the *chinoiserie* borders of the Berain-Monnoyer *Grotesques*.

After being reduced, like Behagle before them, to such expedients as the organization of a lottery, the Filleul brothers were obliged, in 1722, to abandon Beauvais to M. de Mérou. Prior to their departure, they had engaged the painter Jacques Duplessis as designer to the factory, on the understanding that he would direct the design-school and provide, each year, pictures of three to four feet in height, to serve as designs for tapestries of fifteen French ells. He does not appear to have respected the clauses of this agreement. In five years, apart from minor works, Duplessis seems to have produced little more than the designs for a set of *Gipsies* and for an *Isle of Cythera*, in six pieces. These, with the *Fair of Bezons*, after Martin, *Cephalus and Procris*, by Damoiselet, and *Verdure and Birds*, by Firens, represent virtually the entire production of the early years of Mérou's directorship; they are mentioned, along with other sets dating from the time of his predecessors, in the inventories of the shops or warehouses which the factory maintained in this period at Paris, Leipzig and Ratisbon.

OUDRY. The appointment of the painter Jean-Baptiste Oudry in place of Duplessis, on 22nd July 1726, was an important event in the history of Beauvais, for it saved the workshops from ruin, and initiated their finest period. For an annual salary of 3,500 *livres*, Oudry undertook to furnish every three years 'six pictures three to four feet in height, newly composed and completely finished, to serve as designs for tapestries of eighteen ells'. The dominating position which he rapidly acquired in the factory was reinforced in 1734 when, after Mérou had been dismissed for falsification of the accounts, Oudry entered into partnership with Mérou's successor, Nicolas Besnier, a goldsmith and former alderman of Paris. Thenceforward, Beauvais became, in Voltaire's phrase, 'the kingdom of Oudry.'

This 'kingdom' was ruled with a firm hand. According to tradition, Oudry suppressed the high-warp looms, which had continued to work alongside the low-warp looms down to this time. He endeavoured to improve the professional training of the weavers. With this in view, he carried through a reorganization of the existing design-school, and, in 1750, he founded a second school which was to be free and open to all.

At Beauvais, as at the Gobelins, where he was appointed inspector of the works in 1730, Oudry demanded of the weavers an exact reproduction of both the design and the colouring of the cartoons. Nor did his zeal stop at this point; his principal merit lay in his renewal of the stock of designs.

OUDRY'S TAPESTRIES. As a private enterprise, obliged both to attract and to keep its customers, Beauvais was in a better position than the Gobelins to adapt itself rapidly to public demand, to changes of taste and to modifications of architectural style. Oudry realized this better than anyone, and acted in consequence.

Oudry, a pupil of Largillière, and an academician since 1719, had begun as a portraitist and history-painter, but had come to devote himself principally, though not exclusively, to the painting of landscapes and animals, in a direct and naturalistic vein. Most of his work for Beauvais was of this kind.

In 1727, he designed the six compositions of the *New Hunts*, which were followed, in 1730, by the eight pieces of *Country Pleasures*. In 1732, he hit on the idea of presenting four scenes from the works of Molière; three tapestries of this series, with Rococo surrounds including flower-garlands, shrubs and leaf-scrolls on a yellow ground, are in the Metropolitan Museum, New York. The *Metamorphoses* followed, in 1734. After these sets, which demonstrate the diversity of his inspiration, Oudry returned to more familiar subjects in the *Fine Verdures* of 1736. This set, originally comprising ten hangings, was augmented until it finally included twenty-one designs. Its success was so great that it was rewoven many times at Beauvais, and there are innumerable versions made in other French and foreign factories.

At the same time, sets of furniture-covers were being woven which enjoyed an ever-increasing success.

THE 'DON QUIXOTE' SET, AFTER NATOIRE. Oudry not only poured out the treasures of his own imagination for the benefit of Beauvais, but he also requested cartoons from other painters of merit.

In 1735, a set relating the *Story of Don Quixote* was commissioned from Charles Natoire (nine out of ten hangings, Aix-en-Provence; the cartoons at Compiègne).

But although Natoire shows admirable qualities in these designs, he was far from rivalling the superlative gifts of another painter whom Oudry summoned to Beauvais — François Boucher.

BOUCHER. Boucher, a recent recruit to the Academy, was at this time only on the threshold of a career which was to bring him eventually to the position of principal painter to the king. But he was already displaying the brilliant talents which made him supreme among the decorative artists of the period.

In the space of twenty years, Boucher designed no less than forty-five tapestries for Beauvais, forming six different sets. These are not only some of the most successful works of the artist; they are also among the most characteristic examples of French art in the eighteenth century.

THE 'VILLAGE FESTIVALS'. The fourteen tapestries of *Village Festivals*, in Italian settings, were begun in 1736. These subjects, like those of the *Noble Pastoral*, begun in 1756, offered little scope for dramatic narration, but they were quite enough to stimulate the lively imagination of Boucher, and the weaver's shuttle, guided by his ingenious pencil, has produced the characteristic effects of sumptuousness and decorative abundance which are present in most of his tapestries. These qualities are seen to no less advantage in the *Chinese Hangings*, which are quite unrelated to the set of the same name by Blain de Fontenay and Vernansal.

THE 'CHINESE HANGINGS'. The designs for the *Chinese Hangings*, which Boucher exhibited at the Salon in 1742, have been identified as the little pictures in the Besançon museum; there is apparently another in a private collection. The cartoons, prepared by the painter Dumont, were six in number.

The compositions were repeated, in an altered and simplified form, by the Aubusson workshops.

THE 'STORY OF PSYCHE' AND THE 'LOVES OF THE GODS'. The *Story of Psyche*, slightly earlier in date than the *Chinese Hangings*, were no less admired by the public of the time. Begun in 1741, it comprises five hangings (Swedish royal collections; four pieces at the Quirinal; Tuck gift at the Petit Palais, the property of the Musée des Beaux-Arts de la Ville de Paris). Like the *Loves of the Gods*, in nine hangings, inspired by Ovid, which were woven on the Beauvais looms from 1749 onwards, the episodes of the *Story of Psyche* are no more than a pretext for representing the rosy or nacreous flesh of lovely women who, adorned with pearls and luxurious draperies, form harmonious groups in enchanting settings.

THE 'OPERATIC FRAGMENTS'. The inhabitants of this charming and elegant Olympus made a last appearance at Beauvais in the *Operatic Fragments* (1752); thereafter, they transferred their allegiance to the Gobelins factory, for which Boucher also prepared numerous designs.

ANDRÉ-CHARLEMAGNE CHARRON. The partnership of Besnier and Oudry, which had produced such excellent results, came to an end in 1753.

In January 1754, the direction of the royal factory of Beauvais passed into the hands of André-Charlemagne Charron, a relation of the principal tax-gatherer for the Paris region. He appears to have been the first director to obtain from the Treasury an annual grant of three thousand *livres* for the purpose of commissioning new designs. It was also stipulated that a complete set of hangings, with furniture-covers, was to be delivered to the Garde-Meuble or the Foreign Ministry for presentation to favoured courtiers, ambassadors or foreign sovereigns. These diplomatic presents, which travelled as far afield as China, did much to enhance the international reputation of Beauvais.

Charron, finding it difficult to dispense with Oudry's collaboration, signed an agreement with him on 1st February 1754. As before, Oudry was to be responsible for supplying designs for hangings, for supervising the execution of these and of the designs chosen for furniture-covers, for examining the wools and silks supplied by a dyer at the Gobelins, and, lastly, for directing the design-school.

The death of Oudry, on 30th April 1755, allowed the new partnership no time to bear fruit. His successor, the landscape-painter Juliard, gave little time to his duties and soon resigned the position to the painter Jean-Jacques Du Mons, who had previously been inspector at Aubusson. Juliard and Du Mons continued to utilize the designs of Oudry and Boucher.

BEAUVAIS PRODUCTION AFTER 1750. The trend towards neo-classicism, however, was already making itself felt in the fine arts. It seemed inevitable that the pastoral and rustic scenes and the charming mythological subjects must be put aside in favour of the heroic themes, more in keeping with the 'grand style' of antiquity, which were favoured by the new generation of painters. In 1761, Charron applied to sell or transfer to Aubusson a certain number of Oudry's cartoons which were considered to be 'of no further use'. In the same year, Boucher's son-in-law Deshays sent to Beauvais the designs for the *Iliad of Homer*, in seven pieces, accompanied by designs for furniture-covers 'with animals in landscapes, representing fables, and chestnut-coloured surrounds with flowers and ornament'. In 1763, the same artist produced a series of designs based on the *Astrée* of Honoré d'Urfé. Only three of the six scenes were executed and they seem to have enjoyed no great success. Nevertheless, the choice of subject is not without interest, since it seems to show that, despite the current stylistic trends, there were still some diehard partisans of bucolic themes and amorous eclogues. Even more significant is the persistent influence of Boucher, which is clearly apparent in the *Russian Sports* of Jean-Baptiste Le Prince, woven from 1769 onwards, and which still remains lively in the *Pastorals with blue drapery* of Jean-Baptiste Huet, about 1780.

THE 'RUSSIAN SPORTS'. Le Prince, returning from a stay of five years in northern Europe, had brought back with him innumerable sketches, which he utilized for the rest of his life for the creation of a pseudo-Russian style, on the lines of the popular pseudo-Chinese and pseudo-Turkish styles; for a short time, this had a certain vogue. Apart from a few costumes and accessories, there is nothing Russian about the six tapestries of the *Russian Sports* (examples in the Tuck collection at the Petit Palais). They remain charming rural gatherings with 'no other purpose than to beguile the eye in domestic settings'.

Single figures appear on the chair-backs of the matching series of furniture-covers.

FRANÇOIS CASANOVA. Large numbers of furniture-covers also accompanied the sets designed by François Casanova, brother of the memoirist. These included, in 1772, the eight tapestries of the *Country Pastimes*, and in 1777, the six pieces of the *Gipsies*. In the choice of subjects, there is a manifest desire to escape from a powdered and beribboned world and to renounce the heritage of Boucher.

THE 'PASTORALS WITH BLUE DRAPERIES'. Before its final extinction, the era of 'Smiles and Graces' knew one last triumph in the *Pastorals with blue draperies and arabesques*, comprising ten hangings, by Jean-Baptiste Huet (1780). These include, among others, *Fishing*, the *Swing*, the *Offering to Cupid*, the *Dance* and *May-day* (at the *sous-préfecture*, Pontoise; Camondo collection in the Louvre; Inveraray Castle, Argyll).

RETURN TO THE ACADEMIC STYLE. The *Conquest of the Indies* by Lavallée Poussin, in three pieces (1785), and the *Military Convoys* by François Casanova, in six pieces (1787), marked the beginning of a period of transition. This evolved rapidly towards the only conclusion which the style of the period allowed, a rigid academism of very limited appeal. The milestones on this road are the *Arts and Sciences*, after Lagrenée, in four pieces (1788), the *Four Continents* (1790; Osterley Park), the *Story of Alexander* (1792) after Lavallée Poussin, the two scenes of *Achilles* (1792), designed by Desoria, and lastly *Aristotle and Aspasia surprised by Alexander* and *Alcibiades surprised by Socrates* (1793), after Monsiau.

ORGANIZATION OF BEAUVAIS FROM 1780 TO THE END OF THE CENTURY. In 1780, De Menou, a tapestry-weaver from Aubusson, had replaced Charron as head of the factory. At the time of his arrival, the number of workers had fallen to about fifty, but it increased to a hundred and twenty about 1789. Menou obtained permission to supplement tapestry-weaving with the production of knotted carpets of the Savonnerie type, and this continued until 1792. It was resumed in 1800 in a separate organization, distinct from the tapestry-factory, but was abandoned in 1819.

At the beginning of the Revolution, the Beauvais looms continued to function normally. After being closed down in year II (1793), as a result of a dispute between Menou and the weavers, they were reopened by a decree of the Committee for Agriculture and the Arts, dated 13th Prairial, year III (1794). The factory ceased to be a private concern; henceforward, it was guaranteed by the state, under the supervision of a director, assisted by a keeper of stores.

CHAPTER IX

Aubusson and other factories in the seventeenth and eighteenth centuries

The history of the great development of tapestry-weaving in France in the seventeenth and eighteenth century is not limited to royal factories, such as the Gobelins, or factories enjoying official privileges and state subsidies, such as Beauvais, and the Paris workshops of the first half of the seventeenth century.

The work of the main centres was followed or imitated in others of less importance. The private workshops of La Marche were granted certain privileges by the Crown; other workshops, established in Paris or in provincial towns, were dependent on their own resources or on subsidies from the local authorities.

As will be seen, there were many connections and influences which linked these various centres.

FELLETIN AND AUBUSSON

ORIGINS. We do not know the circumstances which led to the foundation of tapestry-workshops in the fief of Aubusson, which, created at the end of the ninth century, was attached to La Marche in the seventeenth. The tradition which attributes the introduction of the textile arts in the upper valley of the Creuse to Saracens who were settled there after the battle of Poitiers is of legendary origin. It was long considered probable that the first looms were set up by Flemish weavers about the beginning of the fourteenth century, when the county of La Marche belonged to Louis de Bourbon, husband of Marie de Hainault. Although this hypothesis cannot be excluded, it is simpler to suppose that the first looms in La Marche were indeed established by Flemings, as is indicated by the similarity of techniques and technical terms in the two centres, but not before the sixteenth century.

Other Factories in the Seventeenth and Eighteenth Centuries

FELLETIN. The earliest references mention only Felletin, a little town on the Bordeaux-Lyon road, to which several tapestries are attributed in the posthumous inventory of Charlotte d'Albret, Duchess of Valentinois, widow of Cesare Borgia (1514). The descriptions of these have been compared with a set of tapestries at the château of Talcy, bearing the initials of Robert Chabot and his wife, Antoinette d'Illiers, on vertical stripes of brown and red. It is also conceivable that a tapestry with 'foliage and beasts' in the inventory of Charlotte d'Albret may be identical with a small piece in the Musée de Cluny, acquired in 1942.

Sixteenth-century texts show clearly enough that the workshops of La Marche were beginning to experience a degree of prosperity.

TAPESTRIES OF LA MARCHE IN THE SIXTEENTH CENTURY. Although Felletin tapestries, in the time of Henri III, were worth less than the Flemish product, it does not follow that the weavers of La Marche were less skilful. Like the Flemings, they wove verdures, landscapes and biblical and mythological subjects in the sixteenth century. But, living far from the great urban centres, in an age of difficult communications, and operating small family workshops, grouped in a guild organization, they were obliged to seek their customers close at hand, among the local squires, or citizens of moderate means. It was necessary, therefore, to sell cheaply, and for this reason they concentrated on the type of work which could be executed rapidly, utilizing the low-warp technique. Their production included, at one end of the scale, the coarse 'menu-verd' of Bellegarde (a place near Aubusson), which was woven by the countryfolk during the winter season, but they were also capable of showing the skill and care necessary for more important commissions, from churches, bishops, rich abbeys and noblemen. To obtain such orders, the weavers became travellers, ranging far and wide, alone or in groups, to show samples of their capabilities. If they did not set up their looms on the spot, they often had the satisfaction of returning home with a contract for a *Story of Ahasuerus*, a life of a patron saint, of *St. Martial* or *St. Peter*, or for a set of *Heroes*. The weaving was carried out in family workshops where generation after generation became masters of their craft.

PREPARATION OF DESIGNS. The designs used by the Aubusson weavers were often borrowed from engravings. For cartoons, they had drawings executed in grisaille on stout paper, in five shades, normally prepared by mixing soot and water, with small details in bistre and white. The weaver himself, sometimes guided by a painter, selected his own colours, generally within a rather limited range.

Other Factories in the Seventeenth and Eighteenth Centuries

FIRST HALF OF THE SEVENTEENTH CENTURY. After the great expansion of their trade in the first two-thirds of the sixteenth century, the wars of religion ushered in a period which was all the more bitter since most of the inhabitants of the region had adhered to Calvinism. They were thus among the first to acknowledge Henri IV as king.

The latter, as soon as he was firmly seated on the throne, put into operation an ambitious economic programme designed to free the kingdom from the burden of foreign debts incurred through the importation of luxury goods. This programme, which has already been mentioned in connection with the Paris workshops, also conferred benefits on the industry of La Marche.

Later, an order-in-council of 15th February 1620 exempted the contractors of Aubusson 'and other neighbouring places from customs duties on tapestries made in their factories and sent to Paris. . . . As they had been privileged to do in former times'. This decision gave rise to complaints from the guild of tapestry-weavers of Paris, who were not pleased by this concession to their competitors in La Marche.

ICONOGRAPHY OF AUBUSSON TAPESTRIES IN THE FIRST HALF OF THE SEVENTEENTH CENTURY. Like their predecessors, the Aubusson weavers of the seventeenth century reproduced traditional patterns, or copied engravings, always with the same disregard for naturalism.

The 'forest-work', flowering plants and 'verdures' of the period of Henri II, with towns, woodlands and animals, as in the pieces at the presbytery of Anglards-de-Salers, gave place to verdures of the characteristic seventeenth-century type, in which plants with broad leaves or full-blown flowers spring up in landscapes adorned, on occasions, with bridges, cottages, a castle with battlemented towers, animals, small birds, herons and parrots.

HUNTING SCENES. Wolf-hunts, fox-hunts and falconry remained popular, as in the time of the Valois kings. The same may be said of religious subjects.

RELIGIOUS SUBJECTS. As examples of these, we may cite the *Assumption, Virgin and Child, St. Nicaise* and *St. Remy,* which the tapestry-weaver Lambert undertook, in 1625, to deliver within four months to the chapter of Reims cathedral. The order for the *Life of St. Saturnin,* in three hangings, for the collegiate church of Saint-Maimboeuf at Angers (now in the

Musée des Tapisseries, Angers), was carried out in 1649. A rather later example, among many other works, is the *Martyrdom of St. Barbara*, designed by François Finet and presented by the weavers, in 1678, to the church of Sainte-Croix at Aubusson (now Guéret museum). The *Story of Daniel*, the *Life of Samson*, the *Life of Joseph*, the *Virgin with the Rosary*, the *Life of Christ* (church of Notre-Dame-de-Nantilly, Saumur), *Christ among the Doctors*, and the *Ecce Homo*, mentioned in contracts and preserved in various church-treasuries and collections, were woven contemporaneously with large numbers of secular subjects.

SECULAR SUBJECTS. Mythological themes were not entirely absent from the repertory of Aubusson, but for the greater part of the seventeenth century they seem to have been less common than subjects derived from the history or literature of antiquity, such as the lives of *Paris* and *Helen*, *Achilles* or *Coriolanus*. Considerable use was made of the illustrations of popular modern works, such as the *Pastor Fido*, the *Gierusalemme Liberata*, the *Cyrus* of Mlle. de Scudéry and the *Marianne* of Tristan l'Hermite. Probably unwittingly, the painter Claude Vignon inspired a number of cartoons, through the engravings made by Abraham Bosse after his designs for the *Ariane* of Desmarets, published in 1639, and *La Pucelle ou la France delivrée*, by Chapelain, published in 1656.

With the same lack of ceremony, the Aubusson weavers copied successful tapestries produced in other French workshops. Among these imitations, which were generally somewhat simplified, were the *Loves of Gombault and Macée*, as modernized by Laurent Guyot for the workshops of Paris. The same procedure was followed with the *Children's Games*, after Corneille, and it became, indeed, an accepted practice, which persisted down to the middle of the eighteenth century. In 1666, the Crown purchased a Felletin tapestry representing *Earth*, with details in silk and gold thread, copied from the Gobelins set of the *Elements*, after Charles Le Brun. A little later, the *Story of Alexander*, after Le Brun, which was woven several times at the Gobelins between 1663 and 1668, was adapted for the workshops of La Marche by the painter François Finet, working either directly from the original tapestries or from the engravings by Gérard Audran and Sébastien Le Clerc (Pézenas museum). Further specimens were woven about 1744. The set of *Months* or *Royal Palaces*, which was begun at the Gobelins in 1669, also inspired a number of Aubusson tapestries. Four pieces, depicting Chambord, Fontainebleau, Versailles and Vincennes, have been noted in Denmark (formerly at Rosenholm, Jutland; now in a collection near Copenhagen).

Other Factories in the Seventeenth and Eighteenth Centuries

REORGANIZATION OF THE AUBUSSON AND FELLETIN FACTORIES BY COLBERT. In 1664, Colbert, in pursuance of his plans for aiding and re-organizing French industry, ordered an investigation into the requirements of the tapestry-weavers of La Marche. The latter did not fail to stress, among their other wishes, the necessity of procuring a 'good painter', and a dyer capable of initiating them into the secrets of his craft. Letters-patent issued in July 1665 gave a favourable reply to these two requests. Moreover, they bestowed on the private workshops of Aubusson the official charter which had hitherto been lacking. Liberty of management and the corporative character of the group remained unchanged; the status of royal factories was bestowed, not on individual workshops, and this should be emphasized, but on the group as a whole.

FACTORY-MARK AND GALLOON-BORDERS. The mark AUBUSSON, sometimes shortened to MRD or MRDB (Manufacture royale Daubusson or Du Buisson), followed by the initials of the manufacturer, was to be woven in each tapestry. This formality was not always respected, any more than was the regulation prescribing blue galloon-borders for the tapestries of Aubusson. Similar letters patent accorded to Felletin in 1689 prescribed brown galloon-borders for tapestries woven there. The favourable effects which should have resulted from these different measures were compromised by failure to implement the most important clauses, those relating to the provision of a painter and a dyer. Despite official promises, the Aubusson weavers waited in vain for their arrival. The results of this omission were unfortunate enough; to them were added the equally unhappy consequences of the revocation of the Edict of Nantes (1685).

THE WORKSHOPS OF LA MARCHE AND THE REVOCATION OF THE EDICT OF NANTES. Many families of La Marche, as has been mentioned above, had adopted the Calvinist reform. Deeply attached to their religious beliefs, they preferred to go into exile rather than renounce them. Nearly two hundred craftsmen left the area. Among these were the families of Barraband, Mercier, Peux, Claravaux and Deschazaux, some of the best and oldest established families of weavers in Aubusson. Abandoning homes and possessions, they found refuge in various foreign countries, where they resumed the practice of their profession.

DIFFICULTIES OF THE AUBUSSON WORKSHOPS. NEW LETTERS PATENT (1732–3). This defection was a rude blow to the Aubusson industry. Its effects were not materially diminished by the appointment of the famous collector Evrard Jabach to the position of 'director of the Aubusson factory', nor by his efforts to promote the production of woollen and hemp thread. The foundation of a workshop, about 1687, by the Duc de la Feuillade had no better results.

About the end of the seventeenth century and the beginning of the eighteenth, the economic position of the weavers became extremely precarious; it declined still further in the difficult years at the end of the reign of Louis XIV and during the minority of Louis XV. The authorities did not, however, lose interest in the weavers of La Marche. New letters patent in 1732 and 1733 renewed the most important provisions of those of 1665. They suppressed the Bellegarde looms, and prohibited women from engaging in tapestry-weaving.

ESTABLISHMENT OF WORKSHOPS FOR PILE CARPETS. With a view to employing the women who were thus excluded from the low-warp looms, workshops were founded at Aubusson in 1743, and at Felletin in 1768, for the production of pile carpets 'in the Turkish manner', of the type made at the Savonnerie factory. The manufacture both of these and of smooth-faced carpets was successfully developed, and has continued down to our own day.

OFFICIAL INITIATIVES. Thanks to the intervention of the Counsellor of State Louis Fagon, the long-awaited painter finally arrived in 1731. This was Jean-Jacques Du Mons. When he left for Beauvais, his functions were taken over by Nicolas-Jacques Juliard.

The arrival of Du Mons had been preceded by that of 'Mr. Firmazeau, dyer at the Gobelins', who had been invited to advise the interested parties and to train apprentices. The post of director of the factory, which had had only one incumbent since Jabach, was transformed into that of inspector, in which form it long remained the appanage of the Laborey family. Finally, as a result of a suggestion made by the commissioner for the administrative district of Moulins, two schools of design, each with a dozen pupils, were opened at Aubusson in 1742. The instructors were local artists, Gilbert Finet, son of a pupil of Jouvenet, François Roby and Pierre de Seiglière; they worked under the direction and control of the king's painter attached to the factory. An official responsible for the selection and matching of wools and silks was appointed in 1748.

ZENITH OF THE AUBUSSON INDUSTRY. These initiatives heralded Aubusson's most brilliant period. Alongside the small workshops, which remained numerous, a certain number were able to achieve a remarkable growth, thanks to the technical and commercial ability of certain families and individuals — Grellet, Picon, Vergne, Picqueaux, Furzaud, Roby. Most of them possessed warehouses or depots in Paris, in the neighbourhood of the Rue de la Huchette, the Pont Saint-Michel and the Rue de Buci. They succeeded in convincing the purchasing public of the quality of their products, and they found a steady market in the French capital and abroad.

AUBUSSON TAPESTRIES IN THE EIGHTEENTH CENTURY. In conformity with the changes in interior decoration and in public taste, the subjects of Aubusson tapestries of the eighteenth century were chosen solely for the sake of their visual grace and charm. Among the most favoured were country scenes, pastoral subjects, landscapes with animals, floral ornament, a *Story of Don Quixote*, and verdures described as having 'Flemish designs'. In addition to these compositions, which were the work of local artists, and of somewhat unequal quality, merging rapidly into the common Aubusson tradition, a certain number of designs by major artists were also utilized.

OUDRY AND BOUCHER. Oudry was the painter chiefly favoured by the Aubusson weavers. A free rendering of the *Hunts of Louis XV* was produced only a short time after the original set was woven at the Gobelins in 1733. This was followed by many hangings and furniture-covers based on the *Fables of La Fontaine*. In 1761, Aubusson received from the Beauvais factory the cartoons of the *Country Pastimes* and *Metamorphoses*, which had been painted thirty years earlier. These were utilized on several occasions. François Picqueaux completed seven tapestries of the *Metamorphoses* in 1771, and five more were woven by Pierre Grellet Du Montant in 1783.

Besides Oudry, Boucher occupied the Aubusson looms for a considerable period with his *Chinese scenes*. Some of these tapestries included only a small number of figures, borrowed from engravings by Aveline, Balechou and Ingam. The designs for the others, which were intended for Beauvais, were exhibited at the Salon in 1742. Copies must presumably have been sent to Aubusson, or perhaps the versions woven there were based on the engravings by Huquier.

About 1780, the persistent vogue for this imaginary Far Eastern world led to the production of the *Chinese landscapes*, inspired by Jean Pillement. These show trees of various more or less exotic species, kiosks with the upturned eaves characteristic of Chinese roofs, rocks, birds, and plants with luxuriant foliage.

OTHER WORKS OF THE EIGHTEENTH CENTURY. COPIES OF ENGRAVINGS. The works mentioned above did not prevent the Aubusson weavers from continuing their traditional practice of copying engravings. Among the many prints reproduced were the *Four Ages*, by Nicolas de Larmessin after Lancret, *Sea-pieces* after Vernet, and compositions by Baudouin and Lawrence. It is rather exceptional to find that some mythological pictures, exhibited by Lagrenée at the Salon of 1759, were described as 'designs for Aubusson'. Were these in fact woven? It is difficult to find any confirmation of this, and it is likely that novelties of this kind were less attractive to prospective purchasers than replicas of well-known sets such as the *Pastorals with blue draperies*, after Huet, first woven at Beauvais in 1780 under Menou, who had himself arrived from La Marche only a short time before. Other pieces (e.g. those of the old Segerhof at Basle, published by J.-J. Marquet de Vasselot) were more or less freely adapted from engraved originals.

RANSON. Though he never held the official position of king's painter at Aubusson, Ranson did a good deal of work for the tapestry-weavers there. His influence appears in sets of furniture-covers, which he endowed with a particularly attractive grace and charm.

ECONOMIC DIFFICULTIES OF THE LATE EIGHTEENTH CENTURY. The expansion in the production and sale of furniture-covers did not, however, succeed in averting the economic and social difficulties which threatened the industry in La Marche. In a memorandum composed at an assembly held in 1789 to select the delegates to the States-General, the members of the corporation of tapestry-weavers did not shrink from pronouncing the word 'decadence'. The principal reason was said to be the subjection of 'imported raw materials and exported manufactured goods to ruinous customs duties'. The ensuing events made it impossible to take any action in respect of these complaints. Within a short time, the Revolution forced the Aubusson workshops to close their doors.

PARIS AND THE PROVINCES

The encouragement given by Henri IV and his successors to the textile industries in general and to tapestry-weaving in particular produced conditions which favoured the establishment of workshops in the provinces. Apart from La Marche, and Amiens and Tours, where, according to their privilege, François de La Planche and Marc de Comans had their additional looms, most of these enterprises were the result of the initiatives of private individuals. In general, their existence was brief and of only transitory importance.

CALAIS AND AMIENS. In return for the privileges which were lavished on them by the letters patent of Henri IV (January 1607), the Flemish weavers François de La Planche and Marc de Comans undertook to maintain eighty tapestry-looms, including sixty in Paris and twenty at Amiens. This promise was kept; it may perhaps have been no more than a confirmation of an existing fact. The posthumous inventory of François de La Planche (1627) refers to the establishment of the Amiens factory in 1604; other documents mention factories at Calais and Amiens in 1614.

The existence of the Calais factory remains hypothetical. On the other hand there are a fairly considerable number of tapestries bearing the Amiens mark of an 'A' and fleur-de-lis, as used at the time of La Planche and Comans, with designs after Simon Vouet, similar to those woven in Paris (Musée des Gobelins; Palais de Justice, Riom; châteaux of Champchevrier and Châteaudun). Other Amiens tapestries are mentioned in old inventories and descriptions. We do not know the precise date at which the workshop of Comans and De La Planche came to an end, but tapestry-looms continued to operate in Amiens for some time thereafter.

TOURS. High-warp looms had existed at Tours in the sixteenth century, but the workshops had been ruined by the disasters of the period. François de La Planche and Marc de Comans endeavoured to resuscitate them. On the 23rd February they made an agreement for this purpose with Alexandre Motheron, a member of a family of merchant-tapicers of Tours, possibly of Aubusson origin, and with his partners. The agreement was ratified by letters patent of Louis XIII. The partnership was brougth to an end in 1628, since the death of François de La Planche made it difficult to continue. The Motheron family continued to operate the looms, but in spite of the eulogies of Cardinal Barberini (1630) and the encouragement given by Marie de Médicis and Cardinal Richelieu, the Tours 'factory' lapsed into comparative inactivity. It was no longer in existence when, at the beginning of the eighteenth century, the collected statutes of the community of master tapestry-weavers of Paris paid a last tribute to the quality of its productions. Among the latter were a set of the *Story of Coriolanus*, after Henri Lerambert (Mobilier National), and an uninspired *Life of St. Saturnin* (1640; Angers cathedral).

CHARLEVILLE AND REIMS. The Flemish weaver Daniel Pepersack, established at Charleville with the title of tapestry-weaver to the Duke of Mantua, was called to Reims in 1629 by the parishioners of Saint-Etienne-le-Vieil. This first commission was followed by others. Pepersack's workshop, which included weavers of Brussels origin, existed until 1647.

After the four hangings made for Saint-Pierre-le-Vieil, Pepersack wove tapestries for the convent of Saint-Etienne. In 1633, the Archbishop of Reims, Henri de Lorraine, ordered from him a set of the *Life of Jesus*, in twenty-nine pieces, after cartoons by the painter Mergallet. The partial preservation of these 'models and patterns', painted 'in distemper on good new hemp canvas' with only very general indications of colouring, permits some interesting comparisons with the seven tapestries of the set (seventeen prior to 1914) which are exhibited in the museum at Reims. The designs are completed by ornamental borders heavily laden with flowers and fruit. In 1638, Pepersack began a set of *Theagenes and Chariclaea*, in eight pieces, and in 1648 he undertook a last set, ordered by the chapter of Notre-Dame in Paris. There may be some connection between this and the tapestries of the *Life of the Virgin*, woven in the cloister of Notre-Dame by Pierre Damour, who worked in conjunction with Pepersack between 1638 and 1650.

CADILLAC. The tapestries woven at Cadillac were not commercial productions, but were made in the private workshop set up by the Duc d'Epernon, formerly a favourite of Henri III.

Claude de Lapierre, 'master tapicer of the town of Paris' and former head of a workshop in the Faubourg Saint-Marcel factory founded by Comans and De La Planche, was in the service of the Duc d'Epernon from 1632 until 1637. With the assistance of eight journeymen, he wove for the Duke a set of twenty-seven pieces representing the *Story of Henri III*. The only complete hanging remaining is the *Battle of Jarnac* (Louvre; formerly Baron Pichon collection); a fragment of the *Siege of La Rochelle by the Duc d'Anjou in 1572* has been noted in a private collection. The set, which has large borders, is uninspired in conception and design. A piece with a related subject, the *Death of Henri III* (Musée de Cluny, E. Sénart bequest), may be mentioned here, although it was woven at a slightly earlier date.

LVII. STORY OF DON QUIXOTE: THE MARKET

After Natoire

Musée des tapisseries, Aix-en-Provence. Beauvais

LVIII. CHINESE HANGINGS
After François Boucher
Beauvais

LIX. STORY OF PSYCHE
After François Boucher
Petit-Palais, Paris. Beauvais

LX. VENUS AND ADONIS
17th century
Guéret Museum. Aubusson

LXI. (A) ARRIVAL OF THE FARMER'S WIFE
Engraving by Jubier after J.-B. Huet
Cabinet des Estampes, Paris

(B) ARRIVAL OF THE FARMER'S WIFE
Aubusson workshops, second half 18th century
Historisches Museum, Basle

LXII. GROTESQUES

(After the Beauvais GROTESQUES ON A YELLOW GROUND)
woven at the Barraband workshop in Berlin

Chevening, Kent

LXIII. VEGETABLE UNIVERSE
By Lurçat
Aubusson workshops, 20th century

LXIV. SPRING IN PARIS
By Gromaire
Aubusson workshops, 20th century

Other Factories in the Seventeenth and Eighteenth Centuries

VALENCIENNES. There is no evidence for the existence of tapestry-workshops at Valenciennes during the first half of the seventeenth century, though a reference of 1643 to Pierre Regnier, a merchant or commission-agent, has been cited in this connection. Later in the century, Philippe de May (or Du Metz) was subsidized by the municipality in order to provide instruction in tapestry-weaving for poor children. His high-warp workshop, founded in 1681, was still in existence in 1690. He executed a *Story of St. Giles* in eight hangings for the chapel of Saint-Pierre, after cartoons by Jacques-Albert Gérin.

About 1728, Nicolas Billiet wove verdures after designs by the painter Dubois; specimens of his work show perspective views of gardens, with arbours and geometrically patterned flower-beds divided by box hedges.

LILLE. The Lille workshops of the fifteenth and sixteenth centuries were succeeded by others in the seventeenth century, but most of the latter had a relatively short life.

For half a century after the cession of the town to France (1667), weavers were continually presenting themselves to the magistrates with requests for grants of buildings, subsidies and various exemptions, to enable them to open workshops. Some of these craftsmen came from Audenarde, Ghent and Brussels; some had been employed in the Gobelins workshops.

Joris (later Georges) Blomaert, who presented a petition in 1677, opened a workshop in Lille about 1680, but abandoned it again in 1684 in order to undertake the direction of the Beauvais factory, in partnership with Philippe Behagle and Jean Baert; the latter also had interests in Lille (1684–92). The Pannemaker workshop operated at Lille for half a century, but was less highly thought of than that of Jean de Melter, of Brussels, which, thanks to his son-in-law Guillaume Warniers, acquired a considerable reputation.

After the death of Warniers (1738), the Lille industry was overtaken by a sluggishness from which it never recovered. Only François Boucher succeeded in maintaining his activity for a few years; he is said to have made a *Story of Psyche*. Etienne Deyrolles, son of a tapestry-weaver at the Gobelins, had an establishment at Lille in 1780; he attempted to revive the industry, utilizing the old technique of hatched shading.

The tapestries woven at Lille in the seventeenth century long remained subject to Flemish influences. The designs most favoured were those inspired by the paintings of Teniers; Guillaume Warniers produced particularly skilful and well woven tapestries of this type.

Other Factories in the Seventeenth and Eighteenth Centuries

PARIS. The workshops of the Louvre, of De La Planche and Comans, and of the Gobelins, were not the only ones producing tapestries in Paris in the seventeenth century. Documentary references and indications in various specialist studies permit us to draw attention for the first time to a number of private workshops established in the French capital.

Besides the looms of Pierre Damour, the independent weaver who, after being a pupil or associate of Daniel Pepersack, was given temporary accommodation in the cloister of Notre-Dame while weaving the tapestries of the *Life of the Virgin*, a number of independent workshops were operated by the contractors and former weavers of the Gobelins. In addition, there were the workshops of the contractors of the Beauvais factory. Lastly, the temporary workshops set up in private houses for the execution of specific orders give further proof of the vigour of the industry in Paris.

WORKSHOPS OF THE GOBELINS CONTRACTORS. The Gobelins factory was organized in such a way that the heads of workshops were, in effect, contractors, who remained free to work for private individuals. They made use of this concession, and a number of them established separate workshops of their own.

Jans the younger, who directed one of the principal high-warp workshops at the Gobelins from 1668 to 1723, also had looms outside the Gobelins 'in the house with the sign of Great Louis'. The posthumous inventory of Mathieu Monmerqué (1749), director of a low-warp workshop from 1730 to 1735, likewise mentions tapestries executed 'by the weavers who worked for the said deceased outside the Gobelins'. A little later, in 1751, an inventory of the chattels of a simple craftsman of the factory in his lodging 'on the third floor of a house in the Grande Rue of the Faubourg Saint-Antoine with the sign of the Great Monarch', includes a number of chair-covers in course of execution.

These three examples throw some light on the private production of the contractors and weavers of the Gobelins. They also help to explain why tapestries are found in which the designs used at the Gobelins are modified and altered, and why such tapestries do not figure in the official records of the factory.

Some tapestries, indeed, were begun in private workshops and completed on the Gobelins looms, a procedure which resulted in the introduction of new decorative ideas.

The set of the *Great Gods*, which was attributed in turn to the Gobelins and to Beauvais, is now known to have been woven in yet another private workshop in Paris, that of a member of the Bacor family, who had worked in Flanders, at Beauvais and at the Gobelins (another member subsequently directed the workshop of La Malgrange at Nancy).

THE BACOR WORKSHOP AND THE SET OF THE 'GREAT GODS' AFTER JEAN I BERAIN. This set, inspired by an engraving after Jean I Berain, exists in two or three examples, divided between public and private collections (Mobilier National, from the former Martin Le Roy collection, château of Alaincourt, Oise; Kunstindustrimuseum of Copenhagen; Stieglitz museum in Leningrad, etc.). Signed specimens, seen prior to 1939 at the château of Laversine, prove that the set of the *Great Gods* was the work of Bacor. Without going into complex genealogical details, it will suffice to say that in 1710 two members of the family, uncle and nephew, are known to have had a workshop of ten looms in the 'grande rue Mouffetard, près l'hostel des Gobelins'.

PARIS WORKSHOP OF LOUIS HINARD. During the period in which he was director of the Beauvais factory (1664–84), Louis Hinard, merchant and tapestry-contractor, retained his own workshop in Paris. He still continued to operate the latter, with the assistance of his son Jean-Baptiste, after he had been obliged to quit Beauvais. The productions of the Hinard workshop were of sufficiently high quality to gain the commission for the *Marine Triumphs*, after Jean I Berain, which were intended for the Comte de Toulouse, son of Louis XIV and Mme. de Montespan. The work came to an abrupt halt when Jean-Baptiste Hinard was arrested for debt. Indirect confirmation of this fact is provided by the Swedish envoy, Daniel Cronström, who, for his part, had entrusted to the Hinard workshop the *Conquests of Charles XI of Sweden*. After the bankruptcy of the two Hinards, Behagle took over their best workmen, and the two commissions into the bargain.

One set made in the Hinard workshop has survived. It shows *Naval Attributes*, in two hangings and four panels, originally with the arms of Colbert de Seignelay and Catherine-Thérèse Goyon de Matignon, and subsequently bearing the arms of Mme. de Seignelay and her second husband, the Comte de Marsan (private collection; reproduced by Fenaille as the work of the Gobelins).

PARIS WORKSHOP OF PHILIPPE BEHAGLE. Philippe Behagle, who succeeded Louis Hinard as director of the Beauvais factory, had a private workshop in Paris in the Faubourg Saint-Martin; this is apparent from the

Tessin-Cronström correspondence. The *Marine Triumphs with the arms of the Comte de Toulouse* were no doubt woven there (between 1694 and 1698), simultaneously with two hangings of the *Conquests of Charles XI of Sweden*.

WORKSHOPS IN PRIVATE HOUSES. In connection with the weaving of the *Conquests of Charles XI*, the Swedish envoy wrote, in 1698: '. . . the tapestry-weavers are unemployed; victuals are cheap. . . . It would be a good plan to set up a workshop, as many people are doing at present in their own houses. . . .' This was no novelty, but a survival of a procedure which was common in the middle ages and the Renaissance.

In 1688, the posthumous inventory of Louvois records tapestries 'made in the house'. The Duc d'Epernon had followed the same procedure in employing Claude de Lapierre to weave the *Story of Henri III* (1632–7) at Cadillac. The practice was sufficiently common to be mentioned in the letters patent by which Louis XIV raised the Maincy workshop, founded by Nicolas Fouquet, to the status of a factory.

GISORS. Adrien de Neusse, a native of Audenarde who had worked for some time at the Beauvais factory, was operating a high-warp workshop at Gisors in 1703. His only known work is a portrait of Louis XIV, which he presented to the magistrates of the town (1708; formerly in the museum at Gisors).

TORCY AND CAMBRAI. In 1703, Jean Baert of Audenarde, who worked successively at Paris, Beauvais, Tournai and Cambrai, obtained letters patent authorizing him to open a workshop at Torcy, with the status of a royal factory. There is no reason to suppose that this project was ever realized. Much later, in 1724, Jean Baert received permission to found a workshop at Cambrai, where an earlier attempt to resuscitate the tapestry industry, in 1682, had proved fruitless. Baert died in Cambrai, at an advanced age, in 1741. His descendants continued to operate the workshop, which survived, though not without difficulty, until the Revolution.

WORKSHOPS IN LORRAINE. Brussels weavers working at Nancy at the beginning of the seventeenth century included Herment l'Abbé (1604), Isaac de Hanele and Melchior van der Hagen (1613), and Bernard van der Hameiden (1616). The last-named wove several sets, among them a *Story of Holophernes*, a *Story of St. Paul* and a set of *Shepherds*.

The wars and invasions suffered by Lorraine in the seventeenth century prevented the ducal court from giving further encouragement to the industry.

Two tapestry workshops were set up after the peace of Ryswick (1697). The workshop of Charles Mitté, which was established about 1698 outside the town, at La Malgrange, a country-house of the dukes, produced more important works than that of the brothers Durand, assisted by Sigisbert Mathieu, which was accommodated in the attics above the Boucherie at Nancy.

Among Mitté's most notable works were two sets of the *Victories of Charles V, Duke of Lorraine*. The first set, in five hangings, was by Jean-Baptiste Martin, Jacques Guyon and Du Rup. The borders resemble the *entrefenêtres* with herms, woven at the Gobelins. A second set, in twenty-three pieces, after the painter Charles Herbel, was woven at La Malgrange in 1724 and 1725 (former Austrian Imperial collections at Vienna). The *Arabesque Months* on a blue ground, after Dieudonné Coclet, woven by Mitté from 1728 to 1736, are closer to the sixteenth-century Flemish designs on which they were based than to the easy elegance of the Gobelins set designed by Claude III Audran. There are ten pieces (Prague; one piece each at Schönbrunn and in the Episcopal Palace at Zagreb), of which four are said to have been executed at Poggio Imperiale, near Florence, after Duke François III had succeeded to the titles of the Medici.

Prior to 1720, the high-warp weaver F. Josse Bacor and his partner Sigisbert Mangin had established themselves at Lunéville; they subsequently removed to La Malgrange. Bacor, who had spent his apprenticeship at the Gobelins under the direction of Jean Lefebvre, was a member of the Flemish family of Bacor, whose representatives also worked at Beauvais, the Gobelins, and in a private workshop in Paris.

Two *Portraits of Duke Leopold* (died 1721), woven by Bacor in 1717, were succeeded by six *Portières with the arms of Duke Leopold and his wife*, Elisabeth-Charlotte d'Orléans (Austrian State collections); these were based on the same ornamental compositions, after Jean I Berain, as the *Naval attributes, with the arms of Seignelay and Matignon*, woven at Hinard's private workshop in Paris some thirty years before.

A guild of tapestry-weavers was constituted at Nancy in 1717. In 1734, Jean Bella, merchant, of Aubusson, received letters patent authorizing him to set up a factory for high-warp and low-warp weaving in the town.

Under the reign of Stanislas, the Durand workshop was practically the sole survivor; its production was by that time limited to low-grade tapestries with linen warp and woollen weft.

FRENCH WORKSHOPS ABROAD

French tapestry-weavers had been active in foreign countries since the middle ages. Master Nicolau, from France, was working in Barcelona in 1391. About 1429, Jean de France, and later, Nicolas de France, were working for the Gonzaga court at Mantua; Valentin d'Arras was active in Venice; Jacquart, son of Benoît d'Arras, worked at Siena. At Rome, during the pontificate of Nicholas V, Robert de Maincourt wove a *Creation of the World* (1455–6) which was still admired in the sixteenth century.

For the most part, however, these were isolated and transitory work-shops which were soon supplanted by Flemish establishments. They in-dicate the existence of an international interest in French tapestries at an early period. But an immeasurably wider influence was to be exercised by the French tapestry-weavers of the late seventeenth and eighteenth centuries.

The magnificence of Louis XIV provided a model which almost all the sovereigns of Europe aspired to imitate. The great development of tapestry-weaving in France, which had resulted from Colbert's initiative, persuaded foreign princes to set up tapestry workshops on their own terri-tories, in the hope of securing similar benefits for their national economies and, more especially, for their personal prestige. They gave orders to their agents to engage French tapestry-weavers who seemed capable of forming a school. In this way, tapestry-workshops were established through the length and breadth of the 'French Europe' of the eighteenth century. These workshops, directed at the outset by French craftsmen and generally producing tapestries inspired by French designs, formed a branch of French art, until, with the passage of time, they were gradually absorbed into the art of the country in which they were situated.

GERMANY

Among the families which emigrated to Germany following the revoca-tion of the Edict of Nantes (1685) there were many tapestry-weavers from the Aubusson area.

They quickly reassembled in three main centres — Berlin, Cleves and Schwabach — whence they gradually dispersed throughout Germany.

The newcomers, having emigrated together with their workmen and apprentices, continued to employ the traditional Aubusson methods. Their first works for their princely protectors were based on cartoons prepared, after a fashion, by local painters, but they were soon looking for compositions which would appeal to a wider circle of customers, and they did not hesitate to borrow extensively from the more successful sets woven in the French royal factories.

The original sets were not always reproduced in entirety. While the main elements would be retained, certain details might be suppressed, or others added from various sets of engravings, as convenience dictated.

INFLUENCE OF THE WORK OF JEAN I BERAIN. Among the engravings utilized in this way, those after Jean I Berain (1640–1711), designer to Louis XIV, occupied an important place. They were not, however, the original French engravings, but reversed replicas published, about the end of the seventeenth century, by Jeremias Wolf at Augsburg. Tapestries of this kind, though of rather inferior execution and dubious artistic value, are none the less interesting documents for the study of French artistic influence beyond the Rhine.

BERLIN. Following the revocation of the Edict of Nantes, the Protestant emigrants received a ready welcome in Brandenburg, thanks to the Edict of Potsdam (1686). The industries which the fugitives introduced were destined to play a considerable part in the economic rise of this area and, in particular, of Berlin. It was in Berlin that Jean Barraband of Aubusson established himself with his family, and set up a tapestry-workshop, in 1699. He was the brother-in-law of Pierre Mercier, another refugee from Aubusson, who, after short stays in a number of towns, and a period in Switzerland, had arrived in Berlin, where he was appointed tapestry-weaver to the Elector and was granted financial facilities enabling him to open a workshop with nine workmen. These grants were made in 1686; it is difficult, however, to reconcile this date with those of Mercier's sojourn in Berne. It appears, from accounts and payment-warrants, that the two workshops, that of Barraband and that of Mercier, remained entirely independent, or that they were united, if at all, only after Mercier's departure to Dresden. The latter event took place after the death, in 1713, of the Great Elector, who had become King of Prussia as Frederick I, and was due to the parsimony of his son and successor, Frederick William I.

Pierre Mercier was succeeded at the royal factory by his nephew, Jean II Barraband; the latter took Charles Vigne into partnership in 1720.

Pierre Mercier's principal work in Berlin was a *History of the Great*

Elector, of which one hanging bears the date 1693. Barraband's workshop wove reproductions with a skill which has led to some confusion in the past. Among these are two repetitions of the Beauvais set of *Grotesques on a yellow ground*, after Jean I Berain and Jean-Baptiste Monnoyer (Reichstag, Berlin; Chevening, Kent); some dispersed pieces must have belonged to a third set. Other Beauvais designs reproduced in Berlin were those of the *Chinese Hangings*, after Vernansal and Blain de Fontenay (specimens, in 1935, in the castles of Feldberg, Moravia, and Schlobitten, East Prussia).

Other works woven at Berlin were based on German designs and are not relevant to the present subject, but a set of the *Italian Comedy*, executed by Charles Vigne (died 1751), may be mentioned, since it shows figures or groups derived from engravings by B. Audran, Crépy the younger, Joullain, Larmessin, Moyreau and Thomassin, after Watteau and Lancret.

ERLANGEN. In 1686, members of the Deschazeaux family, one of the oldest families of Aubusson tapestry-weavers, sought refuge in the territory of the Margrave of Bayreuth. A little later, Jean Deschazeaux and his family set up a workshop at Erlangen, a little town outside Nuremberg, whose prosperity dates from the revocation of the Edict of Nantes.

Jean Deschazeaux the elder died in 1726; his son Jean II, born about 1700, lived until 1779.

The works of the Erlangen factory include the *Elements*, based on the Gobelins set of *Elements*, after Charles Le Brun, and *Water*, after Jean I Berain (prior to 1939, in the castle of L'Ermitage, near Bayreuth). Another set of five pieces after Berain must also have been made at Erlangen (Ratisbon, Thurn-und-Taxis collection; private collection, Paris).

SCHWABACH. By an edict of 4th January 1686, confirming a warrant of 25th October 1685, the Margrave John Frederick of Anspach granted religious freedom and material advantages to French refugees desiring to establish themselves in his territories.

The first tapestry-weaver who took advantage of this offer was Michel Claravaux, or de Claravaux, from Aubusson. He died, however, less than three years after he had established himself at Schwabach, in Franconia, between Anspach and Nuremberg. His workshop continued for a time, at first under the direction of his widow, and later under that of the guardian of their daughter Marie-Madeleine Claravaux.

Overwhelmed with debts, Marie-Madeleine Claravaux addressed a petition to the Margrave of Anspach in 1697, in which she is said to have 'taken refuge in Berlin'.

Other Factories in the Seventeenth and Eighteenth Centuries

In the eighteenth century, Jean Peux, a member of an Aubusson family, wove a number of tapestries at Schwabach after engraved designs of Jean I Berain (two pieces in the Veste, or fortress, at Coburg). Other tapestries, likewise after Jean I Berain, are in private collections, in the hands of dealers, or have passed through the sale-rooms.

DRESDEN. After the death of King Frederick I of Prussia in 1713, Pierre Mercier, the director of the royal factory at Berlin, removed to Dresden, where he died in 1729. His workshop there subsequently passed into the hands of Jacques Nermot, who wove various tapestries between 1735 and 1741.

Among the principal tapestries produced in the Dresden factory in the time of Pierre Mercier are *Prince Frederick Augustus of Saxony taking leave of his father, the Elector of Saxony and King of Poland* (1716) and the *Reception of Prince Frederick Augustus by Louis XIV at Fontainebleau* (1719), after Louis Silvestre, later known as Louis de Silvestre (until 1939, in the castle of Moritzburg, near Dresden). Another tapestry by Pierre Mercier, a *Still Life* (1715), is in the Musée des Gobelins.

In 1783, two weavers from the Gobelins made proposals for setting up a tapestry factory at Dresden, but the project was apparently not sanctioned.

MUNICH. A tapestry factory, established at Munich by Flemish craftsmen in the seventeenth century, maintained relations with the workshops of François de La Planche and Marc de Comans in Paris.

The arrival in Munich of nearly a dozen French tapestry-weavers led to the opening, about 1718, of another factory, which survived down to the beginning of the nineteenth century. Notable among its directors or principal craftsmen are François Carrée, Jean-Louis Vavoque, who was doubtless related to the Gobelins weavers of the same name, Chedeville, who had worked at the Gobelins after the cartoons of Boucher, and, above all, Santigny.

The tapestries of the Munich factory were generally woven after designs by German or Bavarian painters.

SWITZERLAND

BERNE. The Protestant weaver Pierre Mercier, of Aubusson, whose activities at Berlin and Dresden in the late seventeenth and early eighteenth century have already been mentioned, had also worked at Berne before going to Germany. It must be admitted that there are some obscurities in the chronology of his career, but they do not justify us in supposing that there were two weavers of this name. Mercier must have arrived in Berne about the time of the revocation of the Edict of Nantes. He may still have been there, as were two of his collaborators, Louis Mercier and Pierre 'Dixier' (Tixier or Tissier), in January 1689. The second of these two was in Magdeburg before the end of the year 1699. A tapestry table-carpet (Berne, Historisches Museum) provides a specimen of Mercier's work in Switzerland.

ITALY

FLORENCE. Although tapestry-workshops were relatively rare in Italy in the seventeenth and eighteenth centuries, French weavers were none the less well represented there.

Pierre Lefèvre is said to have entered the Florentine workshop, which had been founded by the Medici long before, in 1621. He was summoned to Paris by Cardinal Mazarin in 1647 and set up a workshop, together with his son Jean, beneath the Grande Galerie of the Louvre. Shortly afterwards, he returned alone to Florence. He made several more journeys to France, but from 1659 until his death in 1667 he remained continuously in Florence. His younger son, Jacques-Philippe, succeeded to his position there, but removed to Venice in 1677.

The list of tapestries executed under the direction of Pierre Lefèvre is a long one, including works after designs by Raphael, Andrea del Sarto, and other Italian artists, as well as by Rubens.

The workshop of Florence continued its operations down to the time when the house of Medici was succeeded by François III of Lorraine (1736), who immediately ordered its closure. Work was resumed about 1740 at Poggio Imperiale, where the Medici had also had workshops; the weavers were from Lorraine. Apart from repair-work, they also wove hangings, including some, such as the *Months*, after Dieudonné Coclet, which had probably been started at Nancy. The workshop was closed down finally in 1744.

ROME. Cardinal Barberini, nephew of Pope Urban VIII, pursued extensive enquiries in France and Flanders prior to establishing high-warp looms in Rome in 1635. The direction of these was entrusted to the Frenchman Jacques de La Rivière (Giacomo della Riviera), who was succeeded in 1639 by his son-in-law Gaspard Rocchi.

The death of Urban VIII (1644) and the banishment of his nephews halted the development of the Rome factory, without, however, entirely suppressing its activity. Most of its cartoons were based on designs by the painter Romanelli, but Nicolas Poussin is said to have supplied the designs for a *Story of Scipio.*

Early in the 18th century, Pope Clement IX founded a new tapestry factory at Rome and installed it in the convent of San Michele a Ripa (1710). The Frenchman Jean Simonet was in charge of the workshops until 1717.

TURIN AND NAPLES. It is uncertain whether or not the Demignot family of tapestry-weavers, who worked in Turin and several other Italian towns, were of French origin.

The weavers from the Florentine workshop, after its closure by François III of Lorraine, established themselves in Naples, where they copied Gobelins designs, notably the *Story of Don Quixote,* after Charles Coypel.

RUSSIA

A year before his visit to Paris, where he was to visit the Gobelins factory, Peter the Great of Russia had decided to establish a tapestry-workshop in St. Petersburg.

With the permission of the Regent, a team of weavers from the Gobelins left France for Russia in April 1716. They were followed six months later by a second group, including the merchant-tapicer Philippe Behagle, son of the former Beauvais contractor Philippe Behagle (died 1704), together with Jean Behagle, son of Philippe the younger, and two dyers, one for wool and one for silk.

The St. Petersburg factory, which was organized in the same lines as the Gobelins, copied the Gobelins set of the *Indies,* which the Tsar had brought back from Paris. In addition, the French painter Caravaque painted some new cartoons in honour of the Tsar. The craftsmen later dispersed without having trained pupils, and the factory remained more or less dormant in the two following reigns. It was revived, thanks to the arrival of new French weavers, in the time of Catherine the Great, and produced copies of the *New Indies,* after François Desportes.

Jean-Baptiste Rondet, one of the best 'face-makers' at the Gobelins factory, undertook the journey to Russia in 1757 and died there in 1764.

SPAIN AND PORTUGAL

It was a scion of France, King Philip V, who founded the Spanish national tapestry-factory in Madrid, near the Santa Barbara gate, in 1720. The original low-warp workshop, directed by Jacques van der Goten of Antwerp, was soon joined by a high-warp workshop. The latter was under the direction of the Frenchman Antoine Langer, who executed a copy of Raphael's *La Perla* in 1730. The Santa Barbara workshop also wove a *Story of Telemachus*, based on Fénelon, after designs by Michel-Ange Houasse or Procaccini, and scenes in the style of Teniers, designed by Louis-Michel van Loo. The workshop's principal claim to fame, however, lies in its tapestries after Goya (1776–91).

Contemporaneously with the weaving of the Goya tapestries, a tapestry workshop was set up in Portugal, as part of the financial and economic reorganization instigated by the Marquis of Pombal, minister of Joseph I.

As no Gobelins weaver was available, Pierre-Léonard Mergoux, from Aubusson, who had arrived in Portugal in 1774, was chosen to direct the looms, which were set up at Tavira, in the south. In association with a Portuguese, Pedro Theotonio Hector, Mergoux set to work to train apprentices. The death of Joseph I, and Pombal's disgrace and disappearance from the scene (1782), brought his work to an end in 1783. An episode from the *Story of Joseph*, woven at Tavira, is in the Museu de Arte Antiga in Lisbon; another piece woven at the factory is in the municipal museum at Figueira de Foz. Pedro Tavarès de Brito, a pupil of Mergoux, wove a carpet for the palace of Mafra in 1816.

DENMARK

About 1660, members of the Aubusson weaving-family of Barraband established themselves in Copenhagen, where Isaac maintained a tapestry-warehouse. At a later period, François Léger, who is supposed to have worked at the Gobelins and subsequently in Germany, was active in Denmark from 1736 until his death in 1744.

His arrival coincided with the decoration of the royal castle of Christianborg, and of Hirschholm, a house belonging to Queen Sophia Magdalena. His workshop was originally set up in a private house at Christianshav, a suburb of Copenhagen, but from 1738 to 1744, it was installed in the castle of Charlottenberg; it came to an end soon after the death of its founder. Specimens of Léger's work are preserved in the museum of popular art in Copenhagen and in the castle of Christianborg.

SWEDEN

Léger's workmen included Pierre-Louis Duru, who had been summoned from Cleves to Leipzig in 1736. He is probably identical with Pierre-Louis Daru, who wove various sets of furniture-covers in Stockholm after 1744.

ENGLAND

French tapestry-weavers, notably some from the Gobelins, are said to have worked in the Fulham factory, founded by an adventurous Capuchin monk, Père Norbert. After his flight, he was succeeded by another Frenchman, Passavant, who transferred the workshop to Exeter, but did not obtain any great success.

CHAPTER X

The nineteenth and twentieth centuries

The Revolution brought changes in the organization of the Gobelins and of Beauvais. It inaugurated a purge of their works; hangings adorned with fleurs-de-lis, royal ciphers and the former arms of France were burned at the foot of a tree of liberty in the courtyard of the establishment founded by Colbert (1793). But despite inevitable losses, and numerous administrative and financial vicissitudes, the two factories, which had come to be considered as important national institutions, were successfully preserved. Under the Directory and the Consulate, they resumed their activities, utilizing those of the old cartoons which were acceptable to the new orthodoxy, along with fresh designs which reinforced the idea that a tapestry was essentially a woven reproduction of a painting. Despite the reservations expressed by Chevreul, who succeeded Roard as head of the dye-workshop at the Gobelins in 1824, this conception held undisputed sway throughout the nineteenth century and persisted, indeed, down to the eve of the 1939–45 war. Although a few timid efforts were made to break away from the accepted routine, it was generally felt that the works which it produced represented the highest expression of the craft.

The private workshops of Aubusson suffered from similar vagaries of taste. But it was thanks to these workshops that modern ideas were eventually able to infiltrate into tapestry, to reinvigorate its exhausted tradition, and to open a way for it to resume its rightful place among the luxury industries of France, which still retain their world-wide reputation.

★　　★　　★　　★　　★

Lack of space makes it impossible to give here an adequate account of the tapestries of the nineteenth century. This is unfortunate, for, notwithstanding their questionable style and their absolute subjugation to the laws of painting, they are nevertheless characteristic of a specific period in the history of French tapestry.

From the first republic down to the second empire, successive governments tended to employ the Gobelins for political ends. Beauvais, however, continued to specialize to a great extent in furniture-covers.

The Beauvais factory was granted autonomy in 1926, was attached to the Mobilier National in 1936, and was compelled by the bombardment of 1940 to find shelter in the buildings of the Gobelins factory. It has made a successful contribution to the current revival of tapestry. This revival made its appearance at the Gobelins under the directorship of M. Guillaume Janneau (1935–45). The first steps towards a transformation of existing methods were the replacement of synthetic dyestuffs by natural products and the adoption of measures to restore the necessary independence to the weavers; this programme is being pursued and has already produced valuable results.

But the true source of the renewal of French tapestry was in the workshops of Aubusson, where the projects of Marius Martin, about 1920, were succeeded by the experiments undertaken by Madame Cuttoli between 1930 and 1938.

THE REVIVAL OF TAPESTRY. In a general survey of the work of the tapestry-weavers from their origins down to the present day, the present revival cannot properly be regarded either as a culmination or as a new beginning. To acclaim it as a renaissance would be as rash as to deny its importance and belittle the prestige which it has conferred on the decorative arts of France.

In the continuous sequence of styles which successive generations create for themselves, each generation condemns the contribution of its immediate predecessors, until time eventually succeeds in imposing its own impartial judgment. It will be wise not to forget this unalterable law. It may be difficult to believe that time will deliver a favourable judgment on the tapestry-pictures of the nineteenth and early twentieth centuries, but it is equally difficult to foresee the choice that will be made among the works of our contemporaries.

The modern movement in tapestry, when disentangled from the exaggerated and nonsensical praise which has too often been heaped upon it, is found to include one aim which had, sooner or later, to be pursued: the recreation of a decorative style in conformity with the fundamental laws, potentialities, aesthetics and usage of woven hangings, and the consequent liberation of the latter from the tyranny of painting.

LURÇAT. The artist chiefly responsible for the renewal of tapestry, both as a technique and as a means of expression, was, and still is, Jean Lurçat. A painter of pictures and frescoes, his painstaking researches, beginning with *Green Girls* and *Evening in Granada* (1917), brought him eventually to complete mastery. A number of works executed about 1927, using the system of colour-coded cartoons which has remained a favourite with him, foreshadowed a bold and personal conception of the art of the tapestry-weaver; they included the *Salon of M. Pierre David-Weill*, an ambitious design executed for a private patron.

From 1938 onwards, more frequent work for Aubusson, and the revelation which Lurçat received from the Apocalypse of Angers, enabled him to take a further step, which has been called a return to the traditions of the middle ages. This consists of the use of coarse textures and a colour-scale reduced to about a score of shades, thus restoring to tapestry an appearance of boldness and vigour. The symphony of colours, at once brilliant and subtle, which irradiates the tapestries of Lurçat, creates a fabulous world, animated by reminiscences of poetry and literature. Lines from Apollinaire, Aragon, Eluard, or Tzara provide the suggestion, if not the explanation, for panels in which dreams and symbols merge, evoking long-enduring echoes. A lyrical, humanist spirit breathes through the artist's favourite themes, in which the realistic, monstrous or gentle beasts, the flaming stars, the emblems of the seasons and the elements, give visual expression to the invisible forces of nature.

ASSOCIATION DES PEINTRES-CARTONNIERS DE TAPISSERIE. After the liberation of Paris, Jean Lurçat and Denise Majorel succeeded in bringing together the principal artists who had interested themselves in the problems of tapestry and who had had their cartoons woven. Realizing the importance of this initiative, Marc Saint-Saëns, Vincent Guignebert, Jean Picart Le Doux and Dom Robert quickly joined the group. Their first exhibition, at the Salon des Artistes Décorateurs in 1944, met with universal approval and support. The group, reinforced by Robert Vogenski, Jacques Lagrange and Robert Henry, continued its activities; exhibitions organized at Bordeaux, Dijon, Beaune, Lyon and in Belgium were no less favourably received. The exhibition of French tapestry from the middle ages to the present day, at the Musée d'Art Moderne in Paris, in 1946, gave a valuable opportunity for direct comparisons between the modern works and those of the past. It could not fail to encourage and stimulate the new movement. Strengthened by more new members, Denise Majorel's group was legally constituted in 1947 under the title of 'Association des peintres-cartonniers de tapisserie' (Association of painters of tapestry-cartoons). The Association, now endowed with official patronage and honorary committees, had as its president Jean Lurçat, as its vice-presidents Marc Saint-Saëns and Jean Picart Le Doux, and as its secretary-general Denise Majorel.

New exhibitions in North Africa and abroad continued to arouse considerable interest throughout the world — in Denmark, Sweden, Finland, Switzerland, Germany and Czechoslovakia, as well in North and South America, Egypt, Lebanon and Syria.

Young tapestry-designers, inspired by similar ideas and aims, planned comparable organizations in Scotland, Belgium and Switzerland. Meanwhile, the Association opened a permanent exhibition gallery in Paris, at 30, Rue Cambacères.

By 1955, the Association numbered twenty-four members, including, besides those already mentioned, Maurice André, Marcel Burtin, Georges Dayez, Marcel Dieulot, Oscar Dominguez, Emile Gilioli, Camille Hilaire, Claude Idoux, Louis-Marie Jullien, Le Moel, Albert Lenormand, Jacques Margerin, Mathieu Matégot, Mario Pressino, Gustave Singier, and Michel Tourlière.

COMPAGNIE DES ARTS FRANÇAIS. Jacques Adnet, artistic director of the Compagnie des Arts Français, also brought together a number of painters — Coutaud, Brianchon, Legueult, Roland Oudot and Planson — to take part in the revival of tapestry (1941–4). His appeal was also answered by Walch, Desnoyer, Despierre, Gruber, Héraut, André Marchand, Rohmer, Maurice Savin, Tal Coat, Terechkovitch. These were followed by the sculptors Couturier and Gilioli, and by the young artists Guillemart, Françoise Adnet, Pothier, Slavik, Cortot, Baumann, Darnat, Dany, Normand and Ipousteguy.

DIVERSITY OF MODERN TAPESTRIES. Much of the interest and charm of contemporary tapestries arise from the extraordinary variety of their styles. Hangings based on the styles of the middle ages, of pre-Columbian America, and of many other French and foreign models, all of them transformed by the personal inspiration and vision of the designers, provide an eloquent testimony to the vitality of the revival. The success of the movement and the welcome given to these works, which include representatives of every kind of art, from classicism to abstraction, is due, after Lurçat, to a number of other leading artists. The independence and power of Gromaire, the poise and balance of Coutaud, the subtlety of Picard Le Doux, the vehemence of Marc Saint-Saëns, the poetry of Dom Robert, the various characteristics of the other artists named — all these individual qualities are a continuing source of strength for the movement as a whole.

A living art is justified in seeking inspiration from the past only in so far as this can serve in the preparation of the future. No audacious novelty of thought, drawing, composition or colour can logically be denied to the art of tapestry. It is important, however, not to forget that the purpose of tapestry-hangings is to adorn large areas of wall and that they should therefore give the impression of an unbroken, decorative, coloured surface. Deep perspectives, distant backgrounds, and even patches of pale colour must be avoided, for they create 'holes' in the wall, which ruin the harmony and balance of the effect.

But even if, in the enthusiasm and joy of creation, some designers have occasionally, in recent years, overlooked these essential basic rules, no serious consequences need be feared. A craft which, after a continuous existence of more than five hundred years, succeeds in producing so fruitful a revival, is well able to sustain further development and change without suffering any fatal shock.

Biographical Notes on the Principal Weavers, Contractors and Designers

AUDRAN (Claude III), ornamental and decorative painter; Lyon, 1658–1734. He designed for the Gobelins the *portières* of the *Gods* (about 1699) and the *Grotesque Months* in bands (1707–8); drawings for these are in the Nationalmuseum, Stockholm. He also organized the 'manufacture of wall-hangings consisting of cut or powdered wool on waxed canvas'. According to Brice (1752 edition, IV, pp. 404–5) these were made of a 'prepared waxed canvas, to which were applied cut or crushed wools in different colours as required by the design. . . .' (See Weigert [R.-A.], *Catal. des dessins du Nationalmuseum de Stockholm exposés à la Bibliothèque nationale en 1950*) Cf. pp. 114–117, 149.

AUDRAN (Jean) the younger, weaver and contractor at the Gobelins factory, d. 1795. He directed a high-warp workshop from 1771 to 1794, and was director of the factory 1792–3.

AUDRAN (Michel), weaver and contractor at the Gobelins factory; Paris, 1701–71. He directed a high-warp workshop from 1732 until his death, and was succeeded by his son Jean.

BACOR, family of Flemish weavers, some of whom worked at Beauvais and the Gobelins. Two others, uncle and nephew, had a workshop in Paris, in the 'grande rue Mouffetard', in 1710. Lastly, F. Josse Bacor set up a workshop at Lunéville before 1720, in partnership with Sigisbert Mangin; he later moved to La Malgrange, just outside Nancy. (See Weigert [R.-A.], 'En marge des ateliers de tapisserie lorrains du XVIIIe siècle', in *Revue hist. de la Lorraine*, vol. 87, 1950, p. 9 ff.) Cf. pp. 127, 147, 149.

BAERT. Family of weavers and contractors. Jean-Baptiste Baert, weaver of Audenarde, naturalized French in 1674, had looms in Lille prior to becoming Philippe Behagle's partner at the Beauvais factory. In 1692, he went to Tournai, where he seems to have worked for about twenty years. In 1711, he received letters patent authorizing him to establish a factory at Torcy, but he does not seem to have made use of this privilege. He finally settled at Cambrai, where he died, in 1724, at a very advanced age. His son Jean-Jacques Baert (d. 1766) succeeded him, and was himself succeeded by his own son Jean-Baptiste Baert, who was born in 1726. The family workshop was ruined by the Revolution, and the last Baert died in poverty in 1812. (See Creteur [F.], 'L'art de la tapisserie à Cambrai; l'école des hautlissiers Baert . . .', in *Mém. Soc. d'émulation de Cambrai*, vol. LXXX, 1933.) Cf. pp. 124–125, 145, 148.

BANDOL (Jean de). See Bondolf.

BARRABAND. Family of weavers and painters of Aubusson. The founder of the family seems to have been Denys Barraband, merchant tapestry-weaver, one of the four consuls of Aubusson in 1578. About the middle of the seventeenth century, members of the Barraband family had a tapestry-warehouse in Denmark. The revocation of the Edict of Nantes led to the emigration of other members of the family, among them Jean Barraband, whose workshop in Berlin produced some important sets of tapestries. Jean III Barraband succeeded his father.

Among the members of the family who were converted to Catholicism and remained in La Marche were the ancestors of Jacques Barraband (1768–1809), one of the best-known painters of Aubusson. Cf. pp. 139, 151–152, 156.

BATAILLE (Nicolas), tapestry-manufacturer and merchant, d. 1400. Many works produced under his direction have disappeared, but the partial preservation of the *Apocalypse* set at Angers has made him the best-known tapestry-weaver or manufacturer of the middle ages. (See Guiffrey [J.-J.], 'Nicolas Bataille, tapissier parisien . . .', in *Mém. soc. nat. des antiquaires de France*, vol. XXVIII, 1877, and 'Nicolas Bataille . . .', in *Mém. Soc. hist. de Paris et de l'Ile-de-France*, vol. X, 1883.) Cf. pp. 33–40, 46.

BAUDUIN de BAILLEUL, painter, head of a workshop at Arras, who designed tapestry-cartoons from 1419 to before 1465. In 1449 he produced the cartoons for the *Story of Gideon*, which was woven at Tournai by Robert Dary and Jean de l'Ortie, and completed in 1453. (See Bibliography, under Chapter III.) Cf. pp. 44, 57, 61.

BAUMETZ or de BAUMETZ (Pierre), tapestry-contractor, merchant and possibly weaver, working in Paris in the late fourteenth century. His chief customer seems to have been the Duke of Burgundy, to whom he supplied many sets of pictorial tapestries, woven with 'fine Arras thread' (1385–99). In addition to very sumptuous work, he also sold hangings with figures of knights and ladies, and cushion-covers with 'white ewes under golden-yellow hawthorns on a green field'. Cf. p. 40.

BEHAGLE (Philippe BEHAGEL, known as), tapestry-contractor and weaver (d. 1704). A native of Audenarde, Behagle worked at Tournai before taking over the direction of the Beauvais factory from Louis Hinard in 1684. Despite grave financial difficulties, he extended the activities of the factory. He was succeeded by his wife and sons. Philippe Behagle also had a private workshop at Paris, in the Faubourg Saint-Martin. His son Jean, a dyer and tapestry-weaver, and his grandson Philippe left France to work at the St. Petersburg factory in 1716. (See Grouchy [Vicomte de], 'Vente de tapisseries par Philippe Behagle . . .', in *Rev. de l'art franç. anc. et moderne*, vol. VIII, 1892, pp. 62–4; Weigert [R.-A.], 'Remarques sur les *Conquêtes de Louis XIV*' [woven by Behagle at Tournai and Beauvais], in *Bull. de la Soc. de l'hist. de l'art franç.*, 1932, pp. 280–9, and 'La manufacture de Beauvais à la fin du XVIIe siècle. Deux documents relatifs à l'installation de Behagle à Beauvais', in *Hyphé*, 1949, pp. 219–24.) Cf. pp. 124–129, 145, 147, 155.

BELIN or BLAIN de FONTENAY, flower painter; Caen, 1653 — Paris, 1715. He was employed at the Gobelins factory from 1699 to 1715. Cf. pp. 114, 117, 128, 152.

BERAIN (Jean I), designer of ornament, '*dessinateur de la Chambre et du Cabinet*' of Louis XIV; Saint-Mihiel, 1640 — Paris, 1711. His designs were adapted for a number of sets of tapestries, of which the best known are the *Grotesques on a yellow ground*, woven at the Beauvais factory from cartoons painted by J.-B. Monnoyer, and the *Marine Triumphs with the arms of the Comte de Toulouse*. Replicas, published by Jeremias Wolf of Augsburg, of engravings after his ornamental compositions, were reproduced in tapestry by former Aubusson weavers working in Germany. (See Weigert [R.-A.], 'Les tapisseries d'après Jean Berain', in *Bull. musées de France*, 1934, pp. 165–7, fig.) Cf. pp. 115, 126–129, 147, 151–153.

BERNARD (Michel), high-warp weaver. A leading figure in Arras; 'prince of the wine' in 1402. Produced, or organized production of, the *Battle of Roosebecke*, completed in 1387. Wove many other sets, including the *Story* of Fierabras, *Story of Alexander* (1386), *Story of Octavian of Rome, Story of King Clovis, Story of Our Lady,* and the *Hunt of Gui de Roménie.* Cf. p. 47.

BLASSE (Pierre). There were two high-warp weavers of this name. The posthumous inventory of the workshop of the first (1550) has been published by J.-J. Guiffrey. The second, who worked in the Fontainebleau workshop, wove the *Story of St. Mammès* for Langres cathedral. (See Guiffrey [J.-J.], *Artistes parisiens du XVIe et du XVIIe siècle,* [1915]. Cf. pp. 92–93.

BLOMAERT (Joris, known as Georges), member of a Flemish weaving family. He set up a workshop in Lille about 1670; later, in 1684, he was in partnership with Philippe Behagle and Jean Baert at the Beauvais factory. This fact is at variance with J.-J. Guiffrey's statement that Blomaert set up a private workshop at Beauvais in 1684. Cf. pp. 125, 145.

BLOYART (Colart or Nicolas), tapestry-weaver of Tournai (d. before 1505). In 1501 he sold to Philip the Fair, Duke of Burgundy, four large hangings in wool and silk showing the *Story of the Condemnation of Banquet and Supper.* His widow and his son Henri carried on the workshop. Cf. p. 69.

BONDOLF (Jean de), known as Jean or Hennequin de Bruges, miniaturist, painter and *valet de chambre* to Charles V of France. Designer of the *Apocalypse* of Angers (1375–9). Cf. pp. 35, 36, 38.

BONNYN (Jacques), the oldest known weaver of Felletin, maker of coverlets and tapestries (1457). (See Thomas [A.], *Mém. Soc. sc. natur. et archéol. de la Creuse,* vol. XXI, 1919–21, pp. LXIII–IV.)

BOUCHER (François), painter and engraver; Paris, 1703–70. The hangings woven after his cartoons at Beauvais and the Gobelins constitute the most characteristic productions of French tapestry in the second third of the eighteenth century. His designs were also reproduced at Aubusson, generally after engravings. Boucher was artistic director of the Gobelins from 1755 to 1770. Cf. pp. 114, 117, 120–121, 130–133, 141.

BOURDON (Sébastien), painter and engraver; Montpellier, 1616 — Paris, 1671. He produced designs for the *Story of St. Gervais and St. Protais,* woven by the Louvre workshop. (See Brochard [Abbé Louis], *Les tapisseries de l'église Saint-Gervais et leurs cartons*, Aurillac, 1933.) Cf. p. 104.

BOURSETTE (Vincent), the earliest known high-warp weaver of Arras. In 1367 he executed tapestries ordered by the magistrate of Lille for Charles V and Charles de Trie, Comte d'Étampes; his customers also included Philip the Bold, Duke of Burgundy.

BRIANCHON (Maurice); Fresnay-sur-Sarthe, 1899. *Ballet*; *Opera* (Gobelins, 1944–5); *Diana Asleep*; *Aubade*; *Fauns* (Pinton workshops, Felletin, Aubusson, for the Compagnie française des arts). Cf. p. 161.

BRUGES (Jean or Hennequin de). See BONDOLF.

BURBURE or de BURBURE, tapestry weavers of Tournai. Colart or Nicolas (d. before 1518) sold a *Story of Banquet*, in eight hangings, which was intended for presentation to the Maréchal de Chastillon. Pasquier de Burbure is mentioned in 1537 and 1540. Cf. p. 67.

CAMOUSSE, painter. An inspector of the works at the Beauvais factory, Camousse was director of the factory from 1794 to 1800, before it became a state enterprise.

CAPARS (Jean), high-warp weaver of Arras, established at Tournai in 1352. He provides an additional example of the close relationship between the two great centres.

CARON (Antoine), painter and draughtsman; Beauvais, about 1520 — Paris, 1599. His drawings illustrating the *Story of Artemisia* are in the Bibliothèque Nationale (Cabinet des Estampes) and the Louvre (Cabinet des Dessins). No sixteenth-century specimens of the *Artemisia* tapestries have survived and it is, in fact, uncertain whether any were woven at that period. See Ehrmann [J.], *Antoine Caron, peintre de la cour des Valois*, Geneva-Lille, 1955. Cf. p. 102.

CASANOVA (François), painter; London, 1727–1802. He designed for the Beauvais factory the *Country Pastimes* in eight hangings (1772), and the *Gipsies* in six hangings (1777); these, like the *Military Convoys*, in six pieces (1787), were accompanied by furniture-covers. (See Dumonthier [Ernest], *Les Tapisseries de Beauvais d'après F. Casanova*, Paris, 1921.) Cf. p. 133.

CAUREE (Ysabeau), sometimes called De Halennes, merchant of high-warp tapestry at Arras (1313). Cf. p. 46.

CERIA (Edmond), painter; Evian-les-Bains (Haute-Savoie), 1884–1955. *The Hunt* (Beauvais, 1939), *The Route to the Indies* (Gobelins, 1941–3), *Still Life* (Beauvais, 1954).

CHAMPAIGNE (Philippe de), painter; Brussels, 1602 — Paris, 1674. He produced designs for the *Story of St. Gervais and St. Protais*, woven in the Louvre workshop during the first half of the seventeenth century, and for the *Story of the Virgin* (1635–57). (See note on BOURDON above.) Cf. p. 104.

CHARRON (André-Charlemagne), tapestry-contractor. He directed the royal factory at Beauvais from 1753 to 1780. Cf. pp. 132, 134.

CHEDEVILLE, weaver (second half of the eighteenth century). He worked at the Gobelins and was later associated with the direction of the Munich factory. Cf. p. 153.

CHÉRET (Jules), painter, draughtsman and engraver; Paris, 1836–1933. The Gobelins factory wove the *Four Seasons* (1909–14) after his designs, with matching furniture-covers.

CHIAZELLE. See SQUAZELLE.

CLARAVAUX. Family of weavers from Aubusson, several of whom emigrated after the revocation of the Edict of Nantes. They had a workshop at Schwabach, in the territory of the Margrave of Anspach; Michel Claravaux died there in 1689.

Other members of the family were converted to Catholicism and remained in France. In 1697, the widow of Jacques de Claravaux, Marthe Barraband, her son Jean, and two men, both named Pierre Mage, formed a partnership to carry on a tapestry business at the 'Aigle d'or', Rue de la Huchette, Paris. Cf. pp. 139, 152.

CLEMENT LE MAÇON, supplier of tapestries to John the Good of France. Cf. p. 32.

COMANS (Marc de), tapestry-contractor; Antwerp, 1563 — before 1650. He came to France with his brother-in-law, François de la Planche, and was his partner in a number of enterprises which forwarded the art of tapestry. The two Flemings received letters patent from Henry IV in 1607; their privilege was renewed in 1625. After the death of De La Planche, Comans continued to direct their joint workshop in the Faubourg Saint-Marcel, but Raphaël de la Planche, son of François, soon left to set up on his own. Marc de Comans was succeeded by his son Charles, who was succeeded in turn by his brothers, Alexandre (d. 1650) and Hippolyte. The last weavers of the Faubourg Saint-Marcel workshop ultimately found refuge in the Gobelins factory. Cf. pp. 19, 100–101, 103, 105, 143, 144, 146, 153.

COSSET (Jean), high-warp weaver of Arras. He sold many tapestries to Philip the Bold, Duke of Burgundy, 1384–1401. (See Lestocquoy [J.], *Les dynasties bourgeoises d'Arras du XIe au XVe siècle*, 1945, pp. 96 ff.) Cf. p. 47.

COTTE (Jules Robert de), architect, Paris; director of the Gobelins factory 1735–47. Cf. p. 114.

COTTE (Robert de), architect; Paris, 1656–1735. Principal architect to the king, 1708; director of the Gobelins factory, 1699. Cf. p. 114.

COULLANDON, family of weavers from Aubusson, several of whom, refusing to accept Catholicism, emigrated to Berlin. They were still active there in the eighteenth century, together with other craftsmen from La Marche.

COUSIN (Jean), the elder, master painter; d. 1560 or 1561. In 1541, he produced three designs, representing six scenes of the *Life of St. Geneviève*, for tapestries ordered by the confraternity of Sainte-Geneviève-du-Mont (no longer extant). In 1543, he executed for Cardinal de Givry the cartoons of the *Story of St. Mammès*, which were woven by Pierre Blasse and Jacques Langlois (Langres cathedral and Louvre). Cf. p. 93.

COUTAUD (Lucien); Meynes, near Nîmes (Gard), 1901. He frequented the independent academies and was introduced to tapestry by a commission from Mme. Cuttoli. After 1940, he began designing tapestries for the Compagnie des arts français, directed by Jacques Adnet. Among his principal tapestries are *Chamber Music, Rain and Shine* (1942), *The Harp of the Waters, The Piano of the Towns* (1943), *The Magic Hand* (1944), *Sleeping*

Girl, Green Afternoon (1945), *Palmistry, Snow and Rain* (1946, Pinton workshops, Felletin-Aubusson). Cf. p. 161.

COYPEL (Charles-Antoine), history- and genre-painter, and engraver; Paris, 1694–1752. He designed numerous tapestry-cartoons for the Gobelins: *Daphnis and Chloe* (1715), attributed to the Regent, *Operatic Fragments* (1733–44), and *Scenes from opera, tragedy and comedy* (1744–52). These designs had a great success; not so great, however, as the same artist's *Story of Don Quixote*, with its sumptuous *alentours*; this set is among the most distinguished works of French decorative art. Cf. pp. 117–118.

COYPEL (Noël), the elder, history-painter; Paris, 1628–1707. He adapted the old tapestry-designs of the *Triumphs of the Gods*, and added the *Triumph of Philosophy*. He also produced the cartoons of the *Arabesque Months*, which were likewise based on a set of Flemish tapestries. These two sets, executed at the Gobelins before the death of Charles Le Brun in 1690, heralded the decline of the latter's influence and style. Cf. pp. 111–112, 115.

COZETTE (Pierre-François), contractor and weaver at the Gobelins; Paris, 1714–1801. He studied painting under Charles Parrocel. His was one of the most important workshops at the Gobelins in the eighteenth century. He was also noted for weaving portraits and picture-tapestries. (See Leroy [G.], 'Le tapissier Cozette, peintre portraitiste au XVIIIe siècle', in *Réun. soc. B.-A. des déps.*, XXIII, 1890, pp. 137–44.) Cf. pp. 114, 172.

CROISETTES (Jean de), 'tapissier sarrasinois', who sold a gold-woven tapestry of the *Story of Charlemagne*, 1389.

DAMOUR (Pierre), weaver; Paris, about 1610–after 1657. Settled at Reims before 1638, he worked first in the workshop of Daniel Pepersack, and later on his own account. Between 1639 and 1650, he made many contracts with customers, most of whom were from Paris. In 1650, he settled in Paris, where he wove part of the set of the *Life of the Virgin*, which was given to the cathedral of Notre-Dame by Canon Michel Le Masle (at Strasbourg cathedral since the eighteenth century). Cf. pp. 104, 144, 146.

DARY (Robert), high-warp weaver at Tournai. Between 1449 and 1453, in collaboration with Jean de L'Ortie, he wove the *Gideon* tapestries, after designs by Bauduin de Bailleul. Cf. pp. 44, 57.

DESCHAZAULX or DESCHAZEAUX, family of weavers from Aubusson. François Deschazaulx is mentioned in 1580. After the revocation of the Edict of Nantes, some of his descendants emigrated and set up a workshop at Erlangen, near Nuremberg, under Jean Deschazeaux the elder (d. 1726) and his son Jean II (d. 1779). In 1755, Anne Coulloudon, widow of Jacques Deschazeaux, tapestry-merchant at Aubusson, died in Paris 'in the sentiments of the Protestant faith', and was buried 'at night, quietly, without pomp or scandal' in a timber-merchant's yard at the Port au Plâtre. Cf. pp. 139, 152.

DESGODETS (Antoine), architect, director of the Gobelins factory from 1699 to 1706; Paris, 1653–1728. Cf. p. 114.

DESHAYS (Jean-Baptiste), a son-in-law of François Boucher; Colleville, near Rouen, 1729 — Paris, 1765. The Beauvais factory wove the *Iliad* (1761) and the *Story of Astraea* (1763) after his designs. Cf. p. 132.

DESPORTES (François), portraitist and animal-painter. Champigneulles, 1661 — Paris, 1743. He worked for the Gobelins factory, and adapted for high-warp weaving (1692–4) the *Indies* paintings, which had been given to Louis XIV by Prince Maurice of Nassau in 1687. Forty years later, Desportes designed a new *Indies* set which was exhibited at various Salons between 1737 and 1741. (See Bodkin [Thomas], 'Les Nouvelles Tentures des *Indes*', in *Burlington Magazine*, vol. 84, 1944, pp. 65–6, fig.) Cf. pp. 112, 115, 119, 155.

DESREUMAULX (Willaume or Guillaume), tapestry-weaver with a workshop at Tournai (d. 1483). He made sales at the Antwerp fair and at Lille. Cf. p. 62.

DÉTROYAT (Hélène), painter; Paris, twentieth century. Tapestries after her designs include *The Meadows* (1942); *The Round* (1943); *The Castle, Moonlight* (1944, Goubely workshops, Aubusson); *Black Leaves*; *The Fairies* (1945); *The Pool, The Four Elements* (Braquegnié workshops, Aubusson); *The Garden* (Beauvais factory, 1954).

DOGER or DOGIER (Philippe) craftsman or supplier of King John the Good of France. Cf. p. 32.

DOURDIN (Jacques), tapestry-merchant in Paris, d. 1407. Associated with Nicolas Bataille in weaving the *Jousts of Saint-Denis*. Between 1386 and

1397, he executed at least seventeen sets of tapestries for Philip the Bold, Duke of Burgundy. Among his other customers were Ysabeau of Bavaria and the Duke of Orleans. He had been collector of the wine-duties at Arras. Cf. pp. 39–40.

DROUAIS (François-Hubert), portrait-painter; Paris, 1727–73. His contribution to tapestry was an indirect one; the fashion and taste of the second half of the eighteenth century led to several of his works being reproduced in tapestry. These reproductions are remarkable, but alien to the true spirit of the craft. (See Labat [Georges], *Nicolas Beaujon [1718/86] et les tableaux de la chambre de commerce de Bordeaux*, Bordeaux, 1913; Weigert [R.-A.] 'Un modèle de Drouais identifié; la *Petite Fille au chat*, tissée par Cozette', in *L'Amour de l'art*, September–October, 1932, p. 289.) Cf. p. 121.

DUBOIS (François), Flemish tapestry-weaver, established in Tours about 1575 (d. about 1596). He was not personally of great importance, but he provides an interesting example of the relationships, which require further elucidation, between Flanders and the workshops of Touraine, or even those of central France, in the sixteenth century. Cf. p. 86.

DUBOUT or DUBOURG (Maurice), tapestry-weaver and contractor; second half sixteenth century — first half seventeenth century. Trained in the workshop of the Hôpital de la Trinité, Rue Saint-Antoine. After 1594, he directed, in partnership with Laurent Girard, the workshop set up by Henry IV in the Jesuit house. In 1608, he obtained accommodation beneath the Great Gallery of the Louvre, with privileges and exemptions conferred by Henry IV. The date of his death is not known; he seems to have been confused with another Maurice Dubout, who died before April 1658. Cf. pp. 95–96, 98–99, 104.

DUBREUIL (Toussaint), painter; Paris, 1561–1602. He was chosen by Henry IV to execute cartoons for the workshop installed in the Jesuit house in the Faubourg Saint-Antoine. His *Story of Diana* was repeated several times by the Paris workshops during the first third of the seventeenth century. (See Weigert [R.-A.], 'Two Tapestries in the Ashmolean Museum', in *Burlington Magazine*, February 1950, pp. 193–4, fig.) Cf. pp. 98, 103.

DUFY (Raoul); Le Havre, 1877–1953. *Paris*, a set of furniture pieces, comprising screen, sofa, six armchairs and four chairs (Beauvais, 1929–

1930); *Collioure* (1941); *The Fine Summer* (1941–2; Aubusson, Tabard workshop); *Statue with two red vases* (1942); *The Music of Tintoretto*; *Music in the Country* (1948); *The Oise, the Seine and the Marne*; *The Black Frame* (1949).

DUMÉE (Guillaume), painter (d. about 1626). After the death of Henri Lerambert, he became painter 'for the tapestries of the king', in conjunction with Laurent Guyot. Cf. p. 102.

DUMONS (Jean-Joseph), history-painter; Tulle, 1687 — Paris, 1779. In 1731, he was appointed 'painter and designer of His Majesty for the tapestry factories established in the town and suburbs of Aubusson, and its environs'. In 1755, Dumons went to Beauvais to replace the painter Juliard, who took over Dumons' post at Aubusson. (See Gravier [L.], 'Instruction pour le sr. Du Mons, peintre du roy pour les manufactures d'Aubusson et de Felletin . . .', in *Réun. soc. B.-A. des dép.*, X, 1886, pp. 206–8.) Cf. pp. 132, 140.

DUMONTEIL or DUMONTEL, family of weavers from Aubusson, known from the beginning of the seventeenth century onwards. Several members of the family emigrated after the revocation of the Edict of Nantes; two brothers Dumonteil were weaving at Erlangen in 1734 and 1748. Pierre Dumonteil had the title of tapestry-weaver to the Court in 1748. Other members of the family remained in France and continued to work there down to the end of the eighteenth century.

DUPLESSIS (Jacques), painter. In 1721, he was attached to the Beauvais factory in the capacity of painter and designer. His most noteworthy designs were those for the *Island of Cythera* or *Temple of Venus*, 'where all the nations, of both sexes, gather together,' and for a set of *Gipsies*. He was succeeded, in 1726, by J.-B. Oudry. Cf. p. 129.

DU TREMBLAY (Jehan), craftsman or merchant, supplier of John the Good. Cf. p. 32.

DUVAL, family of weavers working at Tours in the sixteenth century, some members of which were well known. Cf. p. 86.

FERÉ (Pierre or Pierrot), high-warp weaver at Arras. In 1402, he wove the *Life of St. Piat and St. Eleuthère* (Tournai cathedral). Member of the corps of crossbowmen at Arras in 1423. (See Guesnon [A.], *Le haute lisseur Pierre Feré d'Arras*, Lille, 1910, offprint from *Revue du Nord*.) Cf. pp. 47–48.

FILLEUL (the brothers), contractors. Pierre, counsellor-secretary to the king; Etienne, counsellor-treasurer of naval veterans in the *département* of Le Havre. The brothers Filleul directed the royal factory of Beauvais from 1711 to 1722. Cf. pp. 128–129.

FINET, family of tapestry-weavers at Aubusson. Several members of the family produced designs or cartoons for tapestry in the seventeenth and eighteenth centuries. François I Finet (d. about 1690) was responsible for the design of the *Martyrdom of Saint Barbara*, the patron-saint of the Aubusson guild of tapestry-weavers, for which the hanging was woven (1678). Gilbert Finet (d. 1745) received the title of king's painter, and, with François Roby, gave instruction in drawing at the schools established at Aubusson in 1742. Another François Finet, born in 1729, also taught drawing to the future weavers of Aubusson from 1758 onwards. (See Pérathon [Cyprien], 'Les Finet, peintres de la manufacture de tapisserie d'Aubusson, XVIIe et XVIIIe siècle', in *Réun. soc. B.-A. des dép.*, XII, 1888, pp. 151–65.) Cf. pp. 138, 140.

FLAYMAL (Ryfflard), tapestry-weaver and wine-merchant at Arras. John the Fearless, Duke of Burgundy, ordered from him a *Battle of Liège*, in six hangings, which was completed three years after the date of the battle (1408). Cf. p. 51.

GARNIER D'ISLE (Jean-Charles), architect, director of the Gobelins factory from 1747 to 1753; 1697–1755. Cf. p. 114.

GRELLET, family of weavers at Aubusson, mentioned from about 1548 onwards. Seventeenth-century members of the family included Léonard Grellet, and Pierre Grellet, who executed a *Story of St. John the Baptist* (1685; Angers cathedral). François Grellet is mentioned between 1743 and 1750. Pierre Grellet Du Montant was contractor at the factory for silk hangings at Aubusson. (See the note on the Picon family, below.) Cf. p. 141.

GRENIER, family of tapestry-contractors and high-warp weavers at Tournai. Pasquier (d. 1493); Antoine; Jean (d. 1519). The works of Pasquier

Grenier were among the most important produced at Tournai during the second half of the fifteenth century; they have survived in fairly considerable numbers. Cf. pp. 54, 59–63, 67, 69, 70.

GROMAIRE (Marcel); Noyelles-sur-Sambre (Nord), 1892. Gromaire, though not a member of any particular group, has participated in the revival of tapestry since 1939. Among the principal pieces after his designs are *Spring in Paris* (1939, Pinton workshop, Felletin-Aubusson); *Summer, or Brittany* (1940, Desborderies workshop, Aubusson); *Autumn*; *Aubusson* (1940, Goubely workshops, Aubusson); *The Wood-cutters of Mormal*; *Winter, or the Mountain* (1941, Goubely workshops, Aubusson); *Water* (1942, Gobelins factory). Cf. p. 161.

GUIGNEBERT (Vincent), painter; Paris, 1921. Pupil of the École des arts décoratifs in Paris, 1937. In 1939, he met Jean Lurçat and worked with him until the outbreak of war. His first work to be woven, *The Fowler* (Goubely, workshop, Aubusson) dates from 1943. His production includes more than a score of tapestries, among which are *Tristan and Yseult* (1943, Goubely workshop, Aubusson); *The Hens* (1944, Berthaud workshop, Aubusson); *Our friends the birds*; *The Parade*; *The Flea-market* (1946, Goubely and Pinton workshop, Aubusson). Cf. p. 160.

GUILLAUMOT (Ch.-A.), architect, director of the Gobelins from 1789 to 1792; Stockholm, 1730 — Paris, 1807. Cf. p. 114.

GUYOT (Laurent), painter. In the competition which followed the death of Henri Lerambert he obtained the title of 'painter . . . to prepare the designs for tapestries to be made for the use of His Majesty', a position which he shared with his future brother-in-law, Toussaint Dumée. Among the tapestries designed by Laurent Guyot were *Astraea*, the *Kings of France*, the *Pastor Fido*, as well as the *Story of Gombaut and Macée*, which was woven in a number of different workshops, and whose principal scenes were based on engravings by Jean Le Clerc. As has been mentioned above (Chap. VI), the *Gombault and Macée* tapestries at the museum of Saint-Lô were in all probability woven in the workshops of Bruges. Among other examples of this set, which was woven in France as well as in Flanders, are the seven pieces at Broughton Castle, belonging to the Duke of Buccleuch, and the piece in the Musée Carnavalet. Cf. pp. 102, 138.

HINARD, family of tapestry-contractors and weavers. Louis Hinard (d. 1697) had private workshops in Paris, and was the first director of the royal factory of Beauvais (1664–84). His son Jean-Baptiste also had looms in Paris about the end of the seventeenth century. Philippe Behagle, Louis Hinard's successor as director of the Beauvais factory, raised difficulties for him which aggravated his financial embarassments. (See 'Apposition des scellés après le décès de Louis Hinart', in *Nouv. Arch. de l'art franç.*, 2nd series, vol. IV, 1885, pp. 175–90; Weigert [R.-A.] 'En marge de l'exposition des trésors de Vienne; deux compositions gravées d'après Jean Ier Berain', in *Gaʒ. des B.-A.*, 1948, pp. 152 ff.) Cf. pp. 123–125, 127, 147.

HOUASSE (René-Antoine), history-painter and portraitist; Paris, about 1645–1710. He worked at the Gobelins factory and collaborated on many cartoons after designs by Charles Le Brun. But was it the same Houasse whose *Metamorphoses* tapestries were woven at Beauvais during the administration of the Filleul brothers (1711–22)? Cf. p. 128.

HUET (Jean-Baptiste), painter of landscapes, animals and love-scenes; Paris, 1745–1811. His pastoral subjects were popular in the late eighteenth century. The principal set of tapestries woven after his designs were the *Pastorals with blue draperies and arabesques*, woven at the Beauvais factory (1780), with matching furniture-covers. Huet's designs were also reproduced, in modified form, by the Aubusson workshops. See Marquet de Vasselot [J.-J.], *Les tapisseries françaises du Segerhof, Historisches Museum Basel, Jahresberichte und Rechnungen*, Basle, 1925. Cf. pp. 133, 142.

JABACH (Evrard), financier and collector; Cologne; married 1648; d. 1675. After the sale of his collections to the king, he was appointed in 1670 'director of the royal tapestry factory of Aubusson'. Jabach was responsible for the introduction at Aubusson of silk-throwing and other processes in the preparation of silk. (See Pérathon [Cyprien], 'Evrard Jabach, directeur de la manufacture royale de tapisseries d'Aubusson', in *Réun. soc. B.-A. des dép.*, XXI, 1892, pp. 1063–78.) Cf. p. 140.

JACQUES (Maurice), painter of ornaments and flowers; Paris, about 1712–1784. Attached to the Gobelins factory from 1756 to 1784. His designs, especially those for the *alentours* for the tapestries of the *Gods* after François Boucher (about 1758), enjoyed a well deserved success. Cf. pp. 114, 117, 121.

JANDOYGNE (Jean de), master tapestry-restorer; fourteenth century.

JANS (Jean), tapestry-weaver and contractor; born at Audenarde. Appointed master tapestry-weaver to the king in 1654. After the foundation of the Gobelins, he directed the principal high-warp workshop there. He was succeeded by his son, also named Jean, who was director of a high-warp workshop at the Gobelins from 1691 to 1731. Sets of tapestries or individual hangings were also woven in the private workshops of the Jans family. Cf. pp. 106, 113, 114, 146.

JOUVENET (Jean), history-painter and portraitist; Rouen, 1664 — Paris, 1717. His work for the Gobelins prolonged into the seventeenth century the 'grand style' which Charles Le Brun had imposed on tapestry. Cf. p. 118.

JULIARD (Nicolas-Jacques), painter; Paris (?), about 1715–89. He succeeded Oudry as director of the schools and supervisor of work at Beauvais, and was responsible for providing new designs each year. In 1753, he was appointed to Aubusson in the place of Jean-Joseph Dumons, who succeeded him at Beauvais. Juliard is best known for seascape designs after Joseph Vernet. Cf. pp. 132, 140.

KERCHOVE. See VAN KERKHOVE.

LAGRANGE (Jacques), painter; Paris, 1917. The potentialities of the art of tapestry were revealed to him by seeing the *Apocalypse* of Angers in 1939. After his return from captivity, Jean Lurçat persuaded him to design cartoons for tapestry. *Suburb*; *Before the Wedding*; *Monsieur Tartine* (1946, Goubely workshop, Aubusson). Cf. p. 160.

LAPIERRE (Claude de), tapestry-weaver and contractor; Paris, about 1605 — Bordeaux, 1660. He is said to have been trained by and to have worked under François de La Planche and Marc de Comans. From 1632 to 1636, Claude de Lapierre directed the private workshop set up by the Duc d'Epernon in his château at Cadillac, near Bordeaux. He subsequently settled in Bordeaux and directed a tapestry-workshop there. Later he installed a factory for high-warp tapestries, Bergamo hangings and Turkey carpets in the Hôpital des Métiers (1658). (See Braquehaye, 'Lapierre, maître tapissier du duc d'Epernon, fondateur des manufactures de tapisseries de Cadillac et de Bordeaux', in *Réun. soc. B.-A. des dép.*, XVI, pp. 462–83.) Cf. pp. 144, 148.

LA PLANCHE (Franz VAN DEN PLANKEN, known as François de), tapestry-weaver and contractor. Audenarde, 1573 — Paris, 1627. Attracted by the offers and promises of Henry IV, he came to Paris with his brother-in-law and partner Marc de Comans about the end of the year 1600 or the beginning of 1601. Their workshop occupied a number of temporary homes, before being installed in the Faubourg Saint Marcel, where it was formally constituted and recognized by an edict of Henry IV in January 1607. Supplementary workshops were opened in the provinces, at Amiens and Tours, where La Planche and Comans entered into partnerships with the owners or directors of existing old-established workshops. In April 1625, they were granted a prolongation of their privilege for a further eighteen years, and in the following October La Planche requested that this should revert to his son Raphael after his death. (The posthumous inventory of François de La Planche, including the inventory of his workshop, was published in the first volume of M. Fenaille's work on the Gobelins factory.) Cf. pp. 19, 100–101, 103, 105, 143, 144, 146, 153.

LA PLANCHE (Raphael de), tapestry-contractor and weaver, younger son of François de La Planche. On the death of his father (1627), Raphael de La Planche entered into partnership with Charles de Comans, son and successor of Marc de Comans. The partnership was dissolved in 1633. Leaving Comans in the Faubourg Saint-Marcel, La Planche established himself in the Faubourg Saint-Germain, in the neighbourhood of the present Rue de la Chaise. (The buildings were on the even-numbered side of the Rue de la Chaise; La Planche had his house on the site of No. 11, Rue de Varennes, which was destroyed about 1910, when the Boulevard Raspail was constructed.) The Faubourg Saint-Germain workshop prospered and was noted for the perfection of its work. The posthumous inventory (published by M. Fenaille) of the wife of Raphael de La Planche (1661) provides useful information regarding the buildings and the work of the factory. In 1640, Raphael de La Planche was granted a prorogation of his privilege for nine years; a second prorogation, for twenty years, was granted in 1648. The Faubourg Saint-Germain workshop was finally closed down in 1667. Cf. p. 101.

LARRY (Pierre de), master weaver of high-warp tapestries, in Paris, about the middle of the sixteenth century. The text of a contract has survived in which he agrees to execute for Cardinal Louis de Bourbon a set of six hangings representing the six principal *Mysteries of the life of Jesus*; these were intended for the abbey of Saint-Denis. Other documents suggest that he was among the most important weavers of his time. There was also an Antoine de Larry, likewise a high-warp weaver. (See Guiffrey [J.-J.], *Artistes parisiens du XVIe et du XVIIe siècle*, 1915, pp. 254–7.) Cf. p. 90.

LAURENT (Girard). The first Girard Laurent was a 'merchant tapicer', of high-warp tapestries, in Paris, about the middle of the sixteenth century. His son, also named Girard, was trained at La Trinité, worked at the Jesuit house, and in 1608 received lodging and a workshop at the Louvre. He ceded his prerogatives to his son in 1613. Cf. pp. 90, 98–99, 104, 106.

LE BARBIER (Jean-Jacques-François), the elder, history-painter; Rouen, 1736 — Paris, 1826. He executed the cartoons of the set of *Four Continents* (1786), woven at the Beauvais factory. (See Digby [G.W.], 'A set of Beauvais tapestry alluding to the war of American independence', in *Burlington Magazine*, September 1950, pp. 251–5, fig.) Cf. pp. 122, 133.

LE BRUN (Charles), painter, designer and engraver; Paris, 1619–90. Principal painter to the king in 1662; director of the Royal Factory for Crown Furnishings at the Gobelins (1663, confirmed in 1667). His cartoons for tapestries, executed at the Gobelins, are the complete expression of the Louis XIV style in this medium. Cf. pp. 105–111, 113–115, 118, 138, 152.

LE CARDEUR (Thomas), merchant or weaver at Arras in 1342. Cf. p. 46.

LE CONTE (Pierre), six times alderman of Arras between 1392 and 1405; wine merchant. In 1385–6, sold the *Story of St. Anthony* to the Duke of Burgundy.

LEFEBVRE or LEFÈVRE, family of tapestry-weavers and contractors. Pierre Lefebvre went to Florence, where he directed, with the assistance of his four sons, the tapestry workshop founded by the Medici family. He was recalled to France by Mazarin and set up a workshop under the Great Gallery of the Louvre; he soon returned to Italy, leaving his son Jean Lefebvre in France. The latter, after a period in one of the workshops under the Great Gallery, was director of the factory created by N. Fouquet at Maincy, and was subsequently one of the two high-warp contractors at the Gobelins factory (1662–1700). He was succeeded by his son, Jean Lefebvre (1699–1736). Cf. pp. 99, 106, 154.

Léger (François), tapestry-weaver. He worked in Denmark from 1736 to 1744, after a period presumably spent in Germany. (See Sidenius [Mlle. M.-L.], 'Un tapissier français à la cour de Danemark au XVIIIe siècle', in *Bull. de la soc. de l'Hist. de l'art franç.*, 1920, pp. 16–36.). Cf. pp. 156–157.

Le Moyne (Jean), known as Le Lorrain, painter of ornament; not to be confused with his contemporary and namesake, Jean Le Moyne of Paris. His borders with grotesque ornament provided attractive accompaniments to the Gobelins tapestries of the late seventeenth century, such as the *Mythological Subjects* (1686), after Raphael and Giulio Romano. Cf. p. 112.

Le Prince (Jean-Baptiste), history- and genre-painter, and engraver; Metz, 1734 — Paris, 1781. His stay in Muscovy led him to specialize in pseudo-Russian subjects. Their success gained him a commission from the royal factory of Beauvais for the designs of the *Russian Sports* (1769), with matching furniture-covers. (See Delesalle [Hubert], 'Les tapisseries des *Jeux russiens*', in *Bull. de la soc. de l'Hist. de l'art franç.*, 1941–4, pp. 127–52.) Cf. p. 133.

Lerambert (Henri), 'painter in ordinary to the king' and 'painter for tapestries'; d. 1609. He produced the designs for the *Story of Coriolanus* and the *Story of Artemisia*. His designs for the *Life of Christ*, woven in the workshop of La Trinité about 1584 for the church of Saint-Merry, are preserved in the Cabinet des Estampes of the Bibliothèque Nationale (Ad. 104). Cf. pp. 95, 102.

Le Sueur (Eustache), history- and genre-painter; Paris, 1617–55. He collaborated in the execution of the cartoons for the *Story of St. Gervais and St. Protais*, woven in the Louvre workshops for the church of Saint-Gervais. (See Brochard [L.], *op. cit.*, above, under Bourdon.) Six hangings of the *Life of St. Bruno*, after Le Sueur, were woven at the Gobelins during the first half of the nineteenth century; under the second Empire, his *Muses*, painted for the Hôtel Lambert, were likewise copied in tapestry. Cf. p. 104.

L'Ortye (Jean de), high-warp weaver at Tournai. In 1449–53, he wove, with Robert Dary, the *Gideon* tapestries, after the cartoons of Bauduin de Bailleul. Cf. pp. 44, 57.

Lurçat (Jean), painter; Bruyère, 1892. Pupil of Victor Prouvé and Bernard Naudin. His interest in wall-painting dates from 1913, and in tapestry from 1915. Although continuing to work at easel-painting, he was to become the principal agent of the revival of tapestry. In 1947, with Denise Majorel, he founded the Association des peintres cartonniers de tapisserie, of which he is president. His tapestries are numerous. Among the most important are *The Garden of Cocks*; *Harvests* (1939, Tabard workshop, Aubusson); *Winter* (1940, idem); *It is the Truth*; *Liberty* (1942, Goubely workshop, Aubusson); *L'Apollinaire* (1943, Goubely workshop, Aubusson); *Man* (1945, Dumontet workshop, Aubusson); *Earth, Air, Water, Fire*; *Sly dogs* (1946, Tabard workshop, Aubusson). (The bibliography of Lurçat's work is extensive. See especially Courthion [P.], 'Les Tapisseries de Jean Lurçat', in *Art et décoration*, II, 1929, pp. 51–4, fig.; Hirsch [Pierre], *Jean Lurçat et la tapisserie*, Lille-Paris, 1948; *Jean Lurçat. Peintures, ceramiques, livres illustrés et tapisseries récentes, 1925/1952* [Catalogue of the exhibition at La Maison de la Pensée française, Paris, 1952].) Cf. pp. 159–161.

MAJOREL (Denise). See LURÇAT (Jean).

MANGIN (Sigisbert), tapestry-weaver. Established at Nancy at the beginning of the eighteenth century, in partnership with F. Josse Bacor. Cf. p. 149.

MATHERON or MOTHERON. Family of tapestry-weavers established at Tours, but probably of Aubusson origin. Alexandre I worked at Tours from 1550 onwards. Alexandre II was in partnership with François de La Planche and Marc de Comans as director of the Tours factory, which served as a subsidiary to the factory in the Faubourg Saint-Marcel, Paris. Cf. p. 143.

MENOU (Sieur de), contractor, director of the royal factory at Beauvais from 1780 to 1793. Under his direction, the Beauvais workshops began producing carpets of the Savonnerie type. Cf. pp. 134, 142.

MERCIER (Pierre), tapestry-weaver and contractor (d. 1729). It is probably his name which appears among the signatures appended to a set of regulations for the manufacture of tapestries at Aubusson in 1663. Pierre Mercier, who belonged to the reformed religion, left France at the time of the revocation of the Edict of Nantes. After working in Switzerland, at Berne, he settled at Berlin, where he was appointed tapestry-weaver to the Elector. After 1713, he opened a workshop in Dresden. His son was the painter, Philippe Mercier, who had a considerable success in England. (See Müntz [Eug.], 'Un tapissier français', in *Bull. de l'art*, 1899, pp. 11–12, 21–2.) Cf. pp. 139, 151, 153–154.

MERGOUX (Pierre-Léonard), tapestry-weaver, a native of Aubusson. From 1767 to 1773 he was responsible for the matching of the wools at Aubusson. In 1774 he went to Portugal, where he directed, until 1783, the Tavira workshop. (See Lacrocq [Louis], 'A propos des tapisseries de Tavira', in *Bull. de la soc. de l'Hist. de l'art franç.*, 1929, pp. 154–68.) Cf. p. 156.

MÉROU (Sieur de), contractor. He was contractor at the Boufflers factory, when his offer to undertake the direction of the royal factory at Beauvais was accepted. Mérou remained at Beauvais from 1722 to 1734. Cf. p. 129.

MIGNARD (Pierre), portraitist, history-painter and miniaturist. Troyes, 1610 — Paris, 1695. He became director of the Gobelins factory after the death of Charles Le Brun. The tapestries of the *Gallery of Saint-Cloud*, after paintings executed in 1677, were woven at the Gobelins between 1686 and 1689. Cf. pp. 112–114.

MITTÉ (Charles), tapestry-weaver. He set up a workshop at Nancy, about 1698. His principal works were the *Victories of Charles V, Duke of Lorraine*, and the *Arabesque Months on a blue ground*. Cf. p. 149.

MONCHY (André de), tapestry-weaver and merchant of Arras. Between 1390 and 1430, he received payments for a number of sets of tapestry: the *Story of Perceval the Welshman* (1390), the *Story of Ami and Amie*, the *Story of Pastime and Pleasure*, the *Story of Clinthe* (1396), the *Coronation of our Lady* and *The Entombment*.

MONMERQUÉ (Mathieu), weaver (d. 1749). He directed a low-warp workshop at the Gobelins (1730–5) in addition to his own private workshop. Cf. pp. 114, 146.

MONNOYER (Jean-Baptiste, known as Baptiste), flower-painter and engraver. Lille, 1634 — London, 1699. He was flower-painter to the Gobelins, but his major works for tapestry were the cartoons of the *Grotesques on a yellow ground*, inspired by Jean I Berain, woven at the Beauvais factory. (See Weigert [R.-A.], 'Les *Grotesques* de Beauvais', in *Hyphé*, No. 2, March–April 1946, pp. 67 ff., fig.) Cf. pp. 115, 126, 129, 152.

NATOIRE (Charles-Joseph). Nimes, 1700 — Castel Gandolfo, 1777. He designed for the Gobelins a *Story of Mark Antony*, in three pieces (1741), and for Beauvais the *Story of Don Quixote*. (See Boyer [F.], 'Cat. raisonné de l'oeuvre de Ch. Natoire', in *Arch. de l'art franç.*, new series, vol. XXI, 1949.) Cf. pp. 118, 130.

NEILSON (Jacques), tapestry-weaver (Paris, d. 1788). Contractor for the low-warp workshops of the Gobelins (1749–51; 1751–88); he was also responsible for various technical improvements in weaving. (See Curmer [A.], *Notice sur Jacques Neilson...*, Paris, 1878.) Cf. p. 114.

NERMOT (Jacques), tapestry-weaver and contractor (d. 1756). Succeeded Pierre Mercier as director of the Dresden factory. Cf. p. 153.

NEUSSE (Adrien de), tapestry-weaver; late seventeenth–early eighteenth century. He worked for several years at the Beauvais factory, before founding a workshop at Gisors, where he remained at least from 1703 to 1708. (See Davillier [Baron Ch.], *Une manufacture de tapisseries de haute lisse à Gisors sous le règne de Louis XIV ...*, Paris, 1876. The *Portrait of Louis XIV*, the only specimen of the work of Gisors, is said to have disappeared mysteriously from the museum of the town prior to 1939. Cf. p. 148.

OUDOT (Roland), painter and engraver; Paris, 1927. *Ceres and Pomona* (Pinton workshop, Felletin-Aubusson), *Ceres and the Seasons* (1953–4, Gobelins). Cf. p. 161.

OUDRY (Jean-Baptiste), painter; Paris, 1686–1755. Painter at the Beauvais factory (1726); director of the factory (1734). Artistic director of the Gobelins. He produced numerous designs: for the Gobelins, the *Hunts of Louis XV* (1733–46); for Beauvais, the *New Hunts* (1727), the *Country Pastimes* (1730), the *Comedies of Molière* (1732), the '*Metamorphoses*' of *Ovid* (1734), the *Fine Verdures* (1735), the '*Fables*' of *La Fontaine* (1736). (See Locquin [J.], 'Cat. raisonné de l'oeuvre de J.-B. Oudry', in *Arch. de l'art franç.*, 1912 [tapestry cartoons, pp. 91–100].) Cf. pp. 20, 114, 119–121, 129–132, 141.

PANNEMAKER, family of Brussels tapestry-weavers in the sixteenth century. Some later members of the family worked in France. François de Pannemaker and his son André, after a period at the Gobelins, had a workshop in Lille (1684), which, after the death of François, was directed by André and his brother-in-law, Jacques Delatombe or Destombes. In 1732, Guillaume Warniers or Wernier, the director of another well-known workshop in Lille, was in partnership with André's son, Pierre de Pannemaker. Cf. p. 145.

PARROCEL (Charles), painter and engraver; Paris, 1688–1752. He executed the cartoons of the *Turkish Embassy*, one of the few sets relating to contemporary history to be made at the Gobelins during the eighteenth century. Cf. p. 119.

PEPERSACK (Daniel). Of Flemish origin, Daniel Pepersack worked first at Charleville. In 1629 he was called to Reims, where he wove a large number of tapestries. His workshop continued down to 1647. Cf. pp. 104, 144, 146.

PEUX, family of Aubusson weavers, several members of which emigrated after the revocation of the Edict of Nantes. About 1716 they founded a workshop in Germany, at Schwabach, where the Claravaux family had preceded them. Cf. p. 153.

PICART LE DOUX (Jean); Paris, 1902. He began his career in bookbinding and publishing, which he abandoned in 1933 for publicity and graphic art. His first work to be woven was *The Harvest* (1944). He has produced large numbers of tapestry cartoons, including *The Fowler* (1946, Musée d'art moderne); *Snow* (1950, Mobilier National); *Paris* (1951, Chambre de Commerce); *The Dolphin* (1951, Mobilier National); *Still life with fountain* (1952, Gobelins, at the Mobilier National). (See Zahar [Marcel], 'Les tapisseries de Jean Picart Le Doux', in *Mobilier et Décoration*, 1948, pp. 3–71, fig.; Jean Picart Le Doux, *Tapisseries. Galerie de France*, 1950. Introduction by Georges Fontaine.) Cf. pp. 160, 161.

PICON, one of the principal families of Aubusson weavers. Jean-François Picon had a tapestry-warehouse at Lisbon. His son, Jean-Pierre Picon de Laubard, was one of the principal manufacturers of smooth-faced and pile carpets. With Pierre Grellet Du Montant he founded an establishment for throwing and dyeing silk which had the title of a royal factory. Cf. p. 141.

PICQUEAUX (François). From 1773 to 1786, he was responsible for the matching of wools and silks at Aubusson. This position had been created in 1748; it was originally held by the painter Jean Nouel. Cf. p. 141.

PINCON (Robert), tapestry-weaver and merchant. About 1377, he delivered a *Passion of Our Lord* for the chapel of the Duke of Anjou, and in 1386 he executed an *Apocalypse* set for Philip the Bold. According to J.-J. Guiffrey, he may have been responsible for introducing high-warp weaving at Lille (1398).

POISSONNIER (Arnould), high-warp weaver and contractor of Tournai (d. 1522). Other members of the same family are recorded in the Tournai archives: Jean the elder (d. before 1534), Hermès (1500 and 1534), Jean (d. about 1539), Jacques (d. 1540) and Pierre (a witness in 1544). Cf. pp. 67, 70.

POLASTRON (André). See SQUAZELLA (Andrea).

POUSSIN (Nicolas), painter and etcher; Les Andelys, 1594–1665. During his stay in Paris (1641–2) he was asked to prepare cartoons for the Faubourg Saint-Germain factory, after the series of *Sacraments* which he had painted for Cassiano del Pozzo. He had no time to do this. But the set is said to have been executed at a later date and to be still in existence. Other tapestries after paintings by Poussin were woven in the Paris workshops and at the Gobelins. (See Weigert [R.-A.], *Poussin et l'art de la tapisserie . . .*, Société Poussin, third issue, May 1950, pp. 79–85, fig.) Cf. pp. 104, 111, 155.

PRIMATICCIO (Francesco), known in France as Le Primatice or François de BOLOGNA; Bologna, 1504 or 1505–70. He arrived at Fontainebleau in 1532 and, after Rosso's death, was in sole charge of the decorative work there. In 1532, he was sent to Brussels by Francis I in connection with the weaving of a *Story of Scipio Africanus*. Becoming superintendent of the royal buildings after the death of Henry II, he was presumably responsible for the Fontainebleau tapestry workshop, if it was still in existence at that time. (See Dimier [L.], *Le Primatice*, 1900.) Cf. pp. 91–92.

RANSON, family of low-warp weavers at the Gobelins, one member of which was the designer of ornament, Pierre Ranson (1736–86). He published numerous collections of trophies, vases and the like. As successor of the painter Juliard at Aubusson, he exercised an influence which was by no means negligible. (See Clouzot [Henri], 'Documents inédits sur les Ranson', in *Bull. de la soc. de l'Hist. de l'art franç.*, 1915–17, pp. 124–161.) Cf. p. 142.

RAPHAEL (1483–1520). The weaving by the Brussels workshops, between 1515 and 1519, of Raphael's cartoons of the *Acts of the Apostles* marked the beginning of a new period in the history of tapestry. Other tapestries after his paintings were woven at Beauvais and the Gobelins. Cf. pp. 89, 103, 105, 108, 110–112, 154, 156.

RESTOUT (Jean), portraitist and history-painter. Rouen, 1692 — Paris, 1768. The style of his various cartoons for the Gobelins is comparable with that of Jouvenet, whose nephew and pupil he was. (See Messelet [J.], 'Jean Restout (1692–1768)', in *Arch. de l'art franç.*, new series, XIX, 1938; Weigert [R.-A.], 'Une tapisserie des Gobelins identifiée: *la Peinture* ou *Alexandre et Apelle* [1740–1742], d'après Jean Restout', in *Pro Arte*, 1949, No. 78, pp. 225 ff.) Cf. p. 118.

ROBERT (Dom), manuscript-illuminator and tapestry-designer. Born in 1907, he took holy orders in 1930 with the Benedictines of En-Calcat (Haute-Garonne). Jean Lurçat directed his attention to tapestry (1941), and his first work, *Summer*, was woven in 1942; this was followed by *The Poultry-yard* (1942); *The Visitation* (1945) and *The Creation of Man* (1946). Other works include *The Singing Tree*; *The Sweetness of Life*, and *The Virgin Terri Bilis, protectress of Dijon* (Beauvais). (See Barotte [René], 'Dom Robert, tapissier du paradis terrestre', in *Plaisirs de France*, February 1955, pp. 22–4, fig.) Cf. pp. 160, 161.

ROHMER (Georges), painter of still-life, etc.; Paris, 1913. His tapestries include *Autumn* (1943, Pinton workshop, Felletin-Aubusson), *The Storm* and *Concerto* (1955, Gobelins). Cf. p. 161.

RONDET (Jean-Baptiste), 'face-maker' at the Gobelins factory. In 1757 he left for Russia, where he died in 1764. Cf. p. 155.

RUBENS (1577–1640). The Paris workshops wove tapestries after his designs in the seventeenth century; at the period of the Restoration, the Gobelins wove a set of hangings after his *Story of Marie de Médicis*. Cf. p. 103.

SAINT-SAENS (Marc), wall-painter and tapestry-designer; Toulouse, 1903. His first tapestry, *The Foolish Virgins*, was woven in 1942. By 1953, he had completed fifty tapestry designs, including *Theseus and the Minotaur* (Musée d'art moderne). Other works are *Orpheus* (Gobelins factory; Mobilier National), *Midi* (Picaud workshop, Aubusson; Mobilier National) and *Song* (Tabard workshop, Aubusson; Mobilier National). Cf. pp. 160, 161.

SANTIGNY, tapestry-weaver (second half of the eighteenth century). He was one of the directors of the Munich factory. Cf. p. 153.

SARRASIN, family of tapestry-weavers and contractors of Tournai: Clément (d. 1514), Jacques (1514), Haquenet (1509), Jean (1520–66), Pierre (1508). Cf. pp. 44, 67.

SAVIN (Maurice), painter, sculptor, engraver; Mores (Drôme), 1894. Tapestries after his designs include *Country Works and Pleasures* (1941 onwards, Gobelins) in four hangings, *The Hunt* (this piece woven in 1943 at the Tabard workshop, Aubusson), *The Salamander, The Oxen, The Fair*.

SIMONET (Jean), tapestry-weaver, of Paris origin. From 1710 to 1717, he directed the tapestry-workshop established by Pope Clement XI at the hospital of San Michele a Ripa, Rome. Cf. p. 155.

SOUFFLOT (Joseph-Germain), architect; Irancy (Yonne), 1713–80). Director of the Gobelins factory (1755–80). (See Monval [J.], *Soufflot ...* (1713–1780), Paris, 1918, Chapter VI, 'Soufflot, directeur de la manufacture royale des Gobelins'.) Cf. p. 114.

SPICRE (Pierre), painter, d. 1478. Member of a family of Burgundian painters. He executed the cartoons of the *Life of the Virgin*, the weaving of which was not completed until about 1500; the tapestries are in the church of Notre-Dame at Beaune. (See Bacri [Jacques], 'La Tenture de la *Vie de la Vierge* de Notre-Dame de Beaune et son cartonnier ...', in *Bull. musées de France*, October 1933, pp. 125–6, fig.) Cf. p. 74.

SQUAZELLA (Andrea) or CHIAZELLA, painter. Pupil of Andrea del Sarto. He settled at Tours and designed the cartoons of the tapestries of *St. Saturnin*, which were given to the church of Saint-Saturnin at Tours in 1527. Cf. p. 86.

TESSIER (Louis), painter; Paris, about 1729–81. He was a flower-painter at the Gobelins factory. His designs for furniture-covers and for the *alentours* of several sets of hangings, including the *Story of Don Quixote* (sixth *alentour*), are among the most characteristic decorative works of the second half of the eighteenth century. (See Guiffrey [J.-J.], *Mobilier tissé à la manufacture des Gobelins . . ., d'après les modèles de Louis Tessier*.) Cf. pp. 114, 117–118.

THELU (Jean de), tapestry-contractor or merchant at Arras in 1328. Cf. p. 46.

TROY (Jean François de), history- and genre-painter. Paris, 1679 — Rome, 1752. The *Story of Esther* (1737 and 1740) and the *Story of Jason* (1743–6), woven at the Gobelins, had a great success. Cf. p. 118.

VAN DER MEULEN (Adam-François), painter of battles and landscapes; Brussels, 1634–90. He collaborated on various cartoons for the Gobelins, notably on those for the *Story of the King*. (See Gerspach, 'Les dessins de Van der Meulen aux Gobelins', in *Gaʒ. des B.-A.*, VIII, 1892, pp. 144 ff.; Brière [G.], 'Van der Meulen collaborateur de Le Brun', in *Bull. soc. Hist. de l'art français*, 1930, pp. 150–5.) Cf. p. 110.

VAN KERKHOVE or KERCHOVE (Josse), native of Flanders. 'Dyer at the house of the Gobelins'; from 1669, his title was 'dyer and tally-keeper of the works of the factory'. He directed the dye-shop until his death, and was succeeded by his son. Cf. p. 17.

VAN LOO (Amédée), painter of history, genre and portraits; Turin, 1715– about 1795. The four tapestries of his *Turkish Costume* were woven at the Gobelins from 1772 to 1775. Cf. p. 122.

VEBER (Jean), genre-painter and engraver; Paris, 1868–1928. His *Fairy Tales*, woven at the Gobelins from 1913 to 1923, stands out from other works of the period. He also provided designs for the Beauvais factory. (See Planes [Eugène], 'Les cartons modernes aux Gobelins d'aujourd'hui', in *La renaissance de l'art franç.*, March 1920, pp. 114–18.)

VERNANSAL (Guy-Louis), painter of historical and religious subjects; Fontainebleau, 1648 — Paris, 1729. He worked on cartoons for the Gobelins factory, and executed designs for Beauvais which were partly based on works of Jean I Berain. Cf. pp. 128, 152.

VERNET (Joseph), landscape- and sea-painter; Avignon, 1714 — Paris, 1786. The Aubusson workshops made considerable use of engravings after his compositions, made by local artists, including Nicolas-Jacques Juliard. Cf. p. 142.

VIGNE (Charles), tapestry-weaver (d. 1751). He succeeded the Barraband family at the head of the Berlin workshop. According to Cyprien Pérathon, he belonged to the Vignon family, tapestry-weavers of Aubusson. Cf. p. 152.

VINCENT (François-André), history-painter and engraver; Paris, 1746–1816. His set of the *Story of Henry IV*, woven at the Gobelins from 1782 to 1787, enjoyed renewed success under the Restoration, but it was a success which owed nothing to artistic merit. Vincent also collaborated on the cartoons for the *Story of France* (1784–7). Cf. p. 122.

VOGENSKI (Robert), painter; Paris, 1919. Autodidact, but subsequently worked with Jean Lurçat (1939 and 1944). Teacher at the École Nationale at Aubusson and later at the École Nationale des Beaux-Arts at Nancy. Since his first tapestry, *The Birds* (1945), he has designed many other cartoons. Cf. p. 160.

VOUET (Simon), history-painter and portraitist; Paris, 1590–1649. His return to France, in 1627, marked the beginning of a new period in the history of painting, and was of equal importance for the history and aesthetics of tapestry. Assisted by numerous pupils and collaborators, Vouet designed a number of sets of tapestries for the workshops at the Louvre and the Faubourg Saint-Marcel. Tapestries after his designs were also woven in the workshop in the Faubourg Saint-Germain and in the auxiliary workshop set up by François de la Planche and Marc de Comans at Amiens. (See Weigert [R.-A.], 'Une tenture tissée par l'atelier du Louvre pour Simon Vouet (1637)', in *Gaz. des B.-A.*, January 1949, pp. 11 ff.) Cf. pp. 103–104, 108, 143.

WALOIS, family of tapestry-weavers at Arras. Jean Walois delivered many tapestries to the Dukes of Burgundy between 1413 and 1445, including the *Seven Joys of the Virgin Mary*, the *Passion and Crucifixion of Our Lord*, the *Nativity*, the *Raising of Lazarus* and the *Last Judgment*. Cf. p. 49.

WARNIERS or WERNIER (Guillaume), tapestry-weaver and contractor (d. 1738). In 1700, he married the daughter of Jean de Melter of Brussels, the founder of a workshop in Lille. After the death of his father-in-law, Warniers greatly extended the activity of the workshop, which had twenty-one looms in 1713. Cf. p. 145.

WATTEAU (Antoine); Valenciennes, 1684–1721. He made no designs for tapestry and his work only rarely inspired the cartoon-painters. Several engravings after his designs were, however, reproduced by French tapestry-workshops active in Germany. Cf. p. 152.

WERNIER (Guillaume). See WARNIERS.

WUILLAUME au VAISSEL, citizen of Arras and high-warp weaver. In 1441–1442, he wove the *Resurrection* for the abbey of Saint-Vaast, after a cartoon by Jacques Daret. Cf. p. 44.

YVART (Baudrin), history-painter. Boulogne-sur-Mer, 1610 — Paris, 1690. He painted cartoons for the Maincy workshop, established by Nicolas Fouquet, and for the Gobelins factory. Cf. p. 105.

Bibliography[1]

GENERAL

Jubinal (Achille), *Les Anciennes Tapisseries historiées, ou collection des monuments les plus remarquables de ce genre qui nous soient restés du Moyen Age, à partir du XIe au XVIe siècle inclusivement* ... (2 vol., including one of pl., Paris, 1818–39); — Deville (J.), *Recueil de statuts et de documents relatifs à la corporation des tapissiers de 1258 a 1875* ... (Paris, 1875); — Guiffrey (Jules), *Histoire de la tapisserie depuis le Moyen Age jusqu'à nos jours* (Tours, 1886); — Havard (H.) et Vachon (M.), *Les manufactures nationales: les Gobelins, la Savonnerie, Sèvres, Beauvais* (Paris, 1889); — Migeon (Gaston), *Les arts du tissu* (Paris, 1909, 2nd ed., 1929); — Guiffrey (J.-J.), *Histoire générale des arts appliqués à l'industrie, du Ve à la fin du XVIe siècle* ... (Paris, n.d., [1913], pl.); — Baldass (Ludwig), *Die Wiener Gobelinssammlung* ... (3 vol., Vienna, 1920); — Hunter (Leland), *The practical book of tapestry* (1st ed., 1912; 2nd ed., Philadelphia, 1925); — Göbel (Heinrich), *Wandteppiche* (I Teil. 'Die Niederländer'. Band 1–2; II Teil. 'Die romanischen Länder'. Band 1–2; III Teil. 'Die germanischen und slawischen Länder ...'; Leipzig, 1923–34, many pl.); — Demotte (G.-J.), *La tapisserie gothique*, with preface by Salomon Reinach (Paris, 1924–6, pl.; publication incomplete); — Ackerman (Phyllis), *Tapestry, the mirror of civilization* (Oxford, 1933); — Verrier (Jean), *Notes sur l'histoire de la tapisserie*, in *Le dessin* (December 1933, etc.); — Janneau (Guillaume), *Évolution de la tapisserie* (Paris, 1947); — Niclausse (Juliette), *Tapisserie et Tapis de la Ville de Paris*, n.d. [1949]; — Planchenault (René), *Les tapisseries d'Angers* (Paris, 1955).

[1] For the period down to 1935, only the principal works are listed. For studies of special points, see Marquet De Vasselot (J.-J.) and Weigert (Roger-Armand), *Bibliographie de la tapisserie, des tapis et de la broderie, en France* (Paris, 1935). For the period since 1935, the present bibliography includes basic works and works which present new facts, and excludes works of vulgarization. See also the bibliographical notes appended to the brief biographies of the principal weavers, contractors and designers.

CHAPTER I

JANNEAU (G.), *La réhabilitation des colorants naturels dans la tapisserie* (in Revue des beaux-arts de France, 1942–3, p. 159); — REVERD (Lucien), *La manufacture des Gobelins et les colorants naturels* (in Hyphé No. 2, March–April 1946, etc.).

Exposition des tapisseries et tapis de la Chine, 7th–19th century. (Paris Musée des Gobelins, 1936); — *Exposition des tapisseries et tissus du Musée arabe du Caire, du VIIe au XVIIe siècle. Période musulmane.* (Paris, Musée des Gobelins, 1935); — ENGELSTAD (Helen), *Refil, Bunad, Tjeld; middelalderens Billedtepper i Norge. (Fortids Kunst i Norges bygder. Utgett av Kunstindustrimuseet i Oslo.* Oslo, 1952.)

CHAPTER II

LESPINASSE (R. de), *Les Métiers et Corporations de la Ville de Paris*, 3 vol. (Paris, 1879–97); *Tapissiers*, vol. II, pp. 687–721; — GUIFFREY (Jules), *La tapisserie aux XIVe et XVe siècles* (in Histoire de l'art, edited by A. Michel, vol. III, part I, 1907, pp. 343–74, fig.); — PLANÈS (E.), *La tapisserie gothique: Catalogue des pièces exposées au musée de la manufacture des Gobelins* (Paris, June 1928); — WEIGERT (R.-A.), *La tenture de l'*'Apocalypse' *d'Angers. Essai de mise au point* (in Bull. monumental, 1937, pp. 307 ff.); — PLANCHENAULT (René), *A propos d'un transport en Provence de l'*'Apocalypse' *d'Angers* (in Bull. de la Société nationale des antiquaires de France, 1941, pp. 136–42); *Le comput digital dans l'*'Apocalypse' *d'Angers* (in Bull. Soc. nat. antiquaires de France, 1942); *Les restaurations subies par la tenture de l'*'Apocalypse' (in Cahiers de Pincé et des musées de la ville d'Angers, January–December, 1943, pp. 173–88); *Des Y de l'*'Apocalypse' *d'Angers* (in Bull. Soc. nat. antiq. de France, 1943–4, p. 303); *L'*'Apocalypse' *d'Angers. Eléments pour un nouvel essai de restitution* (in Bull. monumental, CXI, 1953, p. 209); — PLANCHENAULT (René) et VITRY (Bernard), *La tenture de l'*'Apocalypse' *d'Angers. Sa présentation au château d'Angers* (in Monuments historiques de France, January–March 1955, pp. 27–38, fig.); — GRAHAM (Rose), *The 'Apocalypse' tapestries from Angers* (in Burlington Magazine, vol. 89, 1947, p. 229); — RORIMER (James) and FREEMAN (Margaret B.), *The Nine Heroes tapestries at the Cloisters. A picture book* (New York, Metropolitan Museum, 1953).

CHAPTER III

CRICK-KUNTZIGER (Marthe), *Les compléments de nos tapisseries gothiques.*
II. Un fragment inédit de la 'Bataille de Roncevaux' (in Bull. des musées
royaux d'art et d'histoire, Brussels, 1931, pp. 104–13, fig.); *Les complé-*
ments de nos tapisseries gothiques. III. Le pendant de notre 'Passion' (ibid.,
1931, pp. 157–66, fig.); *Remarques nouvelles au sujet de notre tapisserie de la*
'Passion' (ibid., 1933, pp. 31–8, fig.); — MARGERIN (Mlle.), *Les tapis-*
series de verdure, de leur origine au milieu du XIVe [for 16th] *siècle,*
dans les ateliers d'Arras, de Tournai et d'Audenarde (in Bull. des musées de
France, 1932, pp. 140–2, fig.); — LESTOCQUOY (Abbé J.), *Les financiers,*
courtiers et haute lisseurs d'Arras aux XIIIe et XIVe siècles (in Mém.
académie d'Arras, 1937–40, pp. 31–2); *Rôle des artistes tournaisiens à Arras*
au XVe siècle: Jacques Daret et Michel de Gand (in Revue belge d'arch. et
d'hist. de l'art, VII, July–September, 1937, pp. 211–27); *L'atelier de*
Bauduin de Bailleul et la tapisserie de 'Gédeon' (in Revue belge d'archéol.
et d'hist. de l'art, VIII, April–June, 1938, pp. 119–32); *Notes sur la tapis-*
serie à Arras (in Bull. de la comm. dép. des Monuments historiques du
Pas-de-Calais, VI, 1939); *Origine et décadence de la tapisserie à Arras* (in
Revue belge d'archéol. et d'art, X, 1940, I, pp. 27–34); *Praticiens du*
Moyen Age. Les dynasties bourgeoises d'Arras du XIe au XVIe siècle (Arras,
1945; pp. 45–9); — *L'art du Moyen Age en Artois, 15 avril–15 mai 1951.*
Tapisseries d'Arras, manuscrits à peintures, etc. Catalogue (Arras, 1951).

CHAPTER IV

SOIL (P.), *Les tapisseries de Tournai* (Tournai and Lille, 1892); — WEESE
(Dr. Arthur), *Die Caesar Teppiche im historischen Museum zu Bern* (Berne,
1911); — KURTH (Betty), *Die Blütezeit der Bildwirkerkunst zu Tournai*
und der Burgundische Hof (in Jahrb. der Kunstsammlungen der Allerh.
Kaiserhauses, XXXXIV, 1918, pp. 53–110, fig. and pl.); — ROLLAND
(P.), CRICK-KUNTZIGER (M.), MORELOWSKI (M.), *Le tapissier Pasquier*
Grenier et l'église Saint-Quentin à Tournai (in Revue belge d'arch. et
d'hist. de l'art, June–September 1936); — CRICK-KUNTZIGER (Marthe),
Note sur les tapisseries de l' 'Histoire d'Alexandre' du palais Doria à Rome
(in Bull. de l'Institut historique belge de Rome, XIX, 1938, pp. 273–6); —
TOWNSEND (Gertrude), *The Martyrdom of St. Paul: a fifteenth century*

tapestry (in Bull. of the Museum of Fine Arts, Boston, XXXVI, October 1938, pp. 64–72); — CRICK-KUNTZIGER (Marthe), *La tenture tournaisienne de l' 'Histoire de Judith et d'Holopherne'* (in Bull. des musées royaux d'art et d'histoire, March–April 1940, pp. 26–34, fig., pl.); — BURGER (D.), *Old tapestries representing the Seven Liberal Arts* (in Archives internationales des sciences, No. 13, 1950, pp. 859–73, fig.); — MAROT (P.), *Tapisseries du début du XVIe siècle* (in Bull. de la Soc. des antiquaires de France, Paris, 1945–7, pp. 61–2; on the 'Condemnation of Banquet' in the Musée Lorrain at Nancy); *La 'Condamnation de Banquet'. La moralité et les tapisseries* (in Mém. de la Société des antiquaires de France, 1955, pp. 293–311); — ERKELENS (Louise), *Drie fragmenten van een Hercules tapijt uit de laatste vijftien jaren van de XV eeuw* (in Bull. van het Rijksmuseum, 1951, No. 1, pp. 9–14); — VARAX (L.), *Les tapisseries du Cardinal de Clugny* (Lyon, 1926); — TOWNSEND (Gertrude), *Eight fragments of fifteenth century tapestry* (in Bull. of the Museum of Fine Arts, Boston, 1929; on the tapestries of the Cardinal de Clugny); — COMSTOCK (Helen), *A Tournai floral tapestry for Hawaii* (in The Connoisseur, vol. 119, 1947, pp. 107–8, fig.); — WYSS (Robert L.), *Die Berner Caesarteppiche und ihr ikonographische Verhältnis für Illustration des Faits des Romains im XIV. und XV. Jahrh.* (in Jahrbuch des Historischen Museums, Berne, 1955).

CHAPTER V

DESHAIRS (Léon), *La tapisserie au XVIe siècle* (in Histoire de l'art, ed. A. Michel, vol. V, part II, 1913, pp. 887–920, fig.); — SARTOR (M.), *Les tapisseries de Reims* (Reims, 1912; preface by Jules Guiffrey); — MARQUET DE VASSELOT (J.-J.), *Catalogue raisonné de la collection Martin Le Roy.* Fasc. IV: *Tapisserie et Broderie* (Paris, 1908); — *Musée de Cluny. Les tapisseries dites de la 'Dame à la Licorne'* (Paris, n.d. [1927], 2nd ed. 1949); — RUBINSTEIN-BLOCH (Stella), *Catalogue of the collection of George and Florence Blumenthal* (New York and Paris, n.d., vol. IV: *Tapestries and furniture, medieval and Renaissance*, 1927); — BACRI (Jacques), *La tenture de la 'Vie de la Vierge' de Notre-Dame de Beaune et son cartonnier Pierre Spicre, peintre bourguignon du XVe siècle* (in Bull. des musées de France, October 1933, pp. 125–6, fig.); *L' 'Histoire d'Hercule', tapisserie du musée des Gobelins* (in Gaz. des B.-A., XII, 1934, pp. 204–11, fig.); — MARQUAND (Eleanor C.), *Plant symbolism in the Unicorn tapestries* (in Parnassus, X, 1938, No. 5, pp. 3–8, fig.; on the Metropolitan Museum set); — TOWNSEND (Gertrude), *A French armorial tapestry* (in

Bull. Museum of Fine Arts, Boston, XXXIX, 1941, pp. 67–73, fig.; arms of Charles of Orleans and Louise of Savoy); — RORIMER (James J.), *The 'Triumphs of Fame and Time'* (in Bull. Metropolitan Museum of Arts. XXXV, 1940, pp. 242–4, fig.); *The 'Unicorn' tapestries were made for Anne of Brittany* (in Bull. Metropolitan Museum of Art, Summer 1942, pp. 7–20, fig.); — VERLET (Pierre), *La donation Dormeuil au département des objets d'art* (in Bull. des musées de France, XI, 1946, pp. 5–7, fig.); — KURTH (Betty), *A 'Tree of Jesse' tapestry* (in Connoisseur, vol. 122, 1948, pp 94–6, 3 fig.); — MARTIN (Paul), *La tapisserie royale des 'Cerfs volants'* (in Bulletin monumental, vol. 105, 1947, pp. 207–8); — VERLET (Pierre), *Les tapisseries de la donation Larcade* (in Revue des Arts, 1951, pp. 25–30; on the 'Noble Pastoral' in the Louvre); — CRICK-KUNTZIGER (Marthe), *Un chef-d'oeuvre inconnu du maître de la 'Dame à la Licorne'* (in Revue belge d'archéologie et d'histoire de l'art, XXIII, 1954); — PLANCHEN-AULT (René), *Sur quelques tapisseries de la cathédrale d'Angers. Les 'Instruments de la Passion'. La 'Dame à l'orgue'* (in Cahiers de Pincé et des musées de la ville d'Angers, 1954, pp. 1–12).

CHAPTER VI

Tapisseries de la Renaissance. Catalogue des pièces exposées au musée de la manufacture nationale des Gobelins, Paris, May–July 1929; — DIMIER (Louis), *La tenture de la galerie de Fontainebleau, à Vienne* (in Gaz. des B.-A., XV, 1927, pp. 166–70, fig.); — ROY (Maurice), *Les tapisseries de Saint-Mammès de Langres. Compositions authentiques de Jehan Cousin père* (in M. S. archéol., Sens, 1914); — PHILLIPS (J. G.), *Diane de Poitiers and Jean Cousin* (in Bull. of the Metropolitan Museum of Art, II, 1943, pp. 109 ff.; on the 'Story of Diana').

CHAPTER VII

DESHAIRS (Léon), *La tapisserie et les tapis au XVIIe siècle* (in Histoire de l'art, ed. A. Michel, vol. VI, part 2, 1922, pp. 885–910, fig., pl.); *La tapisserie au XVIIIe siècle* (in Histoire de l'art, ed. A. Michel, vol. VII, part 2, 1925, pp. 827–50, fig.); — GUIFFREY (Jules), *Les manufactures parisiennes de tapisseries au XVIIe siècle* (in Mém. de la Soc. de l'hist. de Paris et de l'Ile-de-France, vol. XIX); — *Artemisia tapestries from Barberini-Ffoulkes collection acquired by Art Institute* (in Bull. Minneapolis Institute of Arts, vol. 37, 1948, pp. 118–22, fig.); — WEIGERT (R.-A.), *La tenture de la 'Vie de la Vierge'. Un document inédit* (in Bull. Soc. hist. de l'art franç., 1938, pp. 247–9); — LEJEAUX (Jeanne), *La tenture de la 'Vie de la Vierge' de la cathédrale de Strasbourg* (in Bull. de la Soc. des amis de la cathédrale de Strasbourg, 2nd series, No. 6, 1951); — NICLAUSSE (J.), *Notes sur quelques tapisseries françaises conservées en Suisse* (in Hyphé, Nos. 5–6, September–December 1946, pp. 223–39; a 'Story of Roland' from a Paris workshop of the first half of the seventeenth century, 'Indies' sets from the workshop of J. Jans, and Beauvais verdures); — CORDEY (Jean), *La manufacture de Maincy* (in Bull. Soc. hist. de l'art français, 1922); — FENAILLE (Maurice), *État général de la manufacture des Gobelins depuis son origine jusqu'à nos jours* (Paris, 1903–23, 6 vol.; the nineteenth-century period, 1794–1900, was dealt with by F. Calmette, 1912); — WEIGERT (R.-A.), *Musée des Gobelins. Les belles tentures de la manufacture des Gobelins, 1662/1792.* Foreword by F. Carnot (Paris, 1937); — *Le Musée des Gobelins, 1938.* Critical notes by Juliette Niclausse. Foreword by Guillaume Janneau (Paris, 1938); — *Le Musée des Gobelins, 1939, De la tapisserie décor à la tapisserie peinture.* Critical notes by Juliette Niclausse. Foreword by Guillaume Janneau (Paris, 1939); — BENISOVICH (M.), *The history of the 'Tenture des Indes'* (in Burlington Magazine, vol. 83, 1943, pp. 216–25, fig., pl.); — WEIGERT (R.-A.), *Une tapisserie des Gobelins identifiée* (in Pro Arte, vol. VII, 1948–9, pp. 225–7, fig.; 'Painting' or 'Alexander and Apelles', from the set of 'Arts' after Jean Restout, 1740–55).

CHAPTER VIII

BADIN (J.), *La manufacture de tapisserie de Beauvais, depuis son origine jusqu'à nos jours.* Preface by J.-J. Guiffrey (Paris, 1909); — AJALBERT (Jean), *Beauvais, la manufacture nationale de tapisserie* (Paris, n.d. [1927]); — WEIGERT (R.-A.), *La manufacture de Beauvais à la fin du XVIIe siècle. Deux documents inédits relatifs à l'installation de Behagle* (in Pro Arte, VII, 1948–9, pp. 219–24, fig.); — WEIGERT (R.-A.), *La manufacture royale de tapisserie de Beauvais en 1754* (in Bull. Soc. hist. de l'art franç., 1933, pp. 226–42).

CHAPTER IX

PÉRATHON (Cyprien), *Essai de catalogue descriptif des anciennes tapisseries d'Aubusson et de Felletin* (in B. S. archéol. et hist. du Limousin, 2nd series,

XIX, 1894, X X–1, LI; offprints 1894–1902); *Evrard Jabach, directeur de la manufacture royale d'Aubusson* (†*1695*) (in Réun. Soc. B.-A. des dép., XXIII, 1899, pp. 358–88); — LACROCQ (Louis), *Chroniques des tapisseries anciennes d'Aubusson et de Felletin* (Limoges, 1912 and several other fascicules down to 1934); — MESSELET (J.) and WEIGERT (R.-A.), *Cinq siècles de tapisseries d'Aubusson* (Paris, 1935; catalogue of exhibition at the Musée des Arts décoratifs, November–December 1935); — WEIGERT (R.-A.), *État civil des tapissiers protestants d'Aubusson* (*1674/1685*) *d'après les notes de Louis Lacrocq* (in Bull. Soc. de l'histoire du protestantisme français, 1949, pp. 75–86); — BRAQUEHAYE (Ch.), *La manufacture de Cadillac-sur-Garonne* (in Gaz. des B.-A., 2nd period, XXXVI, 1887, pp. 328–39); — HOUDOY (Jules), *Les tapisseries de haute lice. Histoire de la fabrication lilloise du XIVe au XVIIIe siècle* (Lille, 1871); — MÜNTZ (Eugène), *Les fabriques de tapisseries de Nancy* (in Mém. Soc. archéol. lorraine, 3rd series, XI, 1883); — LOSSKY (Boris), *Les 'Mois de l'année' de la Malgrange au château de Prague*, (in Pays lorrain, 1937, pp. 102–5, fig., pl.); — WEIGERT (R.-A.), *En marge des ateliers de tapisserie lorrains du XVIIIe siècle. Note sur les Bacor* (in Revue historique de la Lorraine, 1950, No. 1, pp. 9–15); — PERNOUD (Régine), *Les tapisseries de Daniel Pepersack et leurs cartons* (in Gaz. des B.-A., 1948, pp. 33–8, fig.); — BOSSEBOEUF (L.), *La manufacture de tapisserie de Tours* (Tours, 1904).

French workshops abroad: — GÖBEL (H.), *op. cit.*, Vol. III; — WEIGERT (R.-A.), *Les 'Grotesques' de Beauvais et les tapisseries de Chevening* (in Bull. Soc. hist. de l'art franç., 1932, pp. 7–21, fig.); — HUTH (Hans), *Zur Geschichte der Berlin Wirkteppiche* (in Jahrbuch der Preussischen Kunstsammlungen, LVI, 1935, pp. 80–91, fig.); — *The Cook after Pieter Aertsen* (in Apollo, XXIX, 1939, p. 266, fig.; woven by E. Serre at St. Petersburg, 1752); — KEIL (Luis), *Algunos dados para a biografia de Pierre-Leonard Mergoux, fundator de fabrica de tapicerias de Tavira* (in B. acad. nac. belas Artes, XIV, 1949, pp. 55–60, fig.).

CHAPTER X

DUMONTHIER (Ernest), *Les tapisseries des Gobelins de l'époque napoléonienne* (in Renaissance de l'art français, May 1923, pp. 234–43, fig.); — JANNEAU (Guillaume), *La renaissance de la tapisserie* (in Tradition française, 1942, pp. 93–102, pl., fig.); *Les manufactures nationales. Nouveaux cartons pour tapisserie* (in Revue des Beaux-Arts de France, October–

Index

Index

Armagnac, Marguerite d', 81
Arming of Pyrrhus, The, 53
Arms of France, 116
arms, coats of, introduced into tapestries, 37, 38, 41, 46, 66, 68, 72, 74, 76, 79–84, 87, 93, 94, 105, 110, 111, 116, 127, 147–9, 158
Arnauld, 128
Arras: abbey of Saint-Waast, 58, 66: Diocesan museum of, 44; captured by Louis XI, 43; thread from, 16, 39, 46; tapestry workshops at, 41, 42, 45, 46, 54–6, 72, 101; technique and style of, 44, 48, 49, 51; and Tournai, 43, 44, 61; tapestries made at or attributed to, 21, 33, 41, 44, 46–50, 52, 54–8, 84, 87; weavers from, 73
Arras, Benoît d', 150
Arras, Jacquart d', 150
Arras, Valentin d', 150
Artemisia, Story of, 102
Arthur, King, 40
Artois, 46
Arts, The, 118
Arts and Sciences, 133
Arzila, Landing under the Walls of, 64
Association des Peintres-Cartonniers de Tapisserie, 160–1
Assumption, 137
Astrée, 132
Astronomy, 67
Aubusson: drawing schools at, 19, 140; Sainte-Croix, 138; tapestry workshops at, 20, 21, 132, 135–42, 149, 158–60; tapestries woven at, 109, 131; weavers from, 127, 134, 150–3, 156
Audenarde, 43, 61, 145, 148
Audran family, 109, 114, 116
Audran, B., 152
Audran, Claude, 114–18, 149, 163
Audran, Gérard, 138
Audran, Jean, 114, 116, 163
Audran, Michel, 114, 120, 163
Augsburg, 151
Aurioli, Bishop Jean d', 85
Austrian State Collections, Vienna, 149
Auxerre, 30, 83
Aveline, 141
Azurara Palace, Lisbon, 70

Babylon, tapestry in, 28
Bacchus, 92
backgrounds, 162
Bacor family, 127, 147, 149, 163
Bacor, F. Josse, 149
Badouyn, Claude, 92, 142

Baert, Jean, 124–5, 145, 148, 163
Bagnolet, château of, 117
Baillet, Bishop Jean, 83
Bailleul, Baudoin de, 44, 57, 61, 164
Bailly, Jacques, 109
Baldishol, Hedmark, 31
Balechon, 141
Banc de France, 127
Banquet, Story of, 69
Baptism, 58
Barbara, St., Martyrdom of, 138
Barberini, Cardinal, 143, 154
Barcelona: museum, 70; weaving at, 150
Bardac, Sigismond, collection, 76
Bargello: *see* Florence
Barraband family, 139, 156, 164
Barraband, Jean I, 151
Barraband, Jean II, 151, 152
Barthélemy, 122
Basle: Segerhof, 142
Bataille, Nicolas, 33–5, 37, 39–41, 46, 164
Bath, The, 78
Bathsheba, Coronation of, 75
Battle of Cassel, 125
Battle of Jarnac, 144
Battle of Landskrona, 127
Battle of Liège, 51
Battle of Lund, 127
Battle of Malmö, 127
Battle of Roncevaux, 62, 64
Battle of Roosebecke, 47, 51
Baubrée, Jean, 44
Baude, Henri, 22
Baudouin: *see* Badouyn
Baumann, 161
Baumetz, Pierre, 40, 164
Bayard, château of, 53
Bayard, Continence of, 122
Bayeux 'tapestry', 13, 31
Bayreuth, Margrave of, 152
Bear-hunt, 50
Beatus, abbot of Liebana, 36
Beaumentiel, Henri de, 58
Beaune, 74, 83, 160
Beauneveu, André, 41
Beautiful Hunts of Guise, 111
Beauvais: cathedral, 21, 57, 74, 88, 126; drawing school at, 19; tapestry weaving at, 15, 19, 20, 119–21, 123–34, 140, 141, 145–8, 158, 159; tapestries from, 80, 115, 116, 142, 152; weavers at, 113, 149
Beckendorf collection, 53
Behagle, Jean, 155, 165
Behagle, Philippe, 124–9, 145, 147, 165
Behagle, Philippe II, 155, 165

Index

Belgium, exhibitions in, 160, 161
Belin: *see* Blain
Bella, Jean, 149
Bellegarde, 136, 140
Beni-Hassan, hypogeum of, 27
Benoist, Barthélemy, 107
Benseman, Jacques, 107
Bérain, Jean I, 115, 126–9, 147, 149, 151–153, 165
Berlin, 127, 150–3
Bernard, St., contemplation of, 74
Bernard, Michel, 47, 165
Berne: Historisches Museum, 52, 63, 154; weavers at, 151, 153–4
Berry, Duc de, 33, 41, 48
Besançon museum, 131
Besnier, Nicolas, 129, 131
Betrayal, The, 50
Bezons, Fair of, 129
Biblia Pauperum, 75, 83, 87
Bièvre river, 101
Bibliothèque Nationale: *see* Paris
Billiet, Nicolas, 145
birds, 32, 110, 125, 126, 129, 137
Björnstorp, castle of, 126
Blain de Fontenoy, J.-B., 114, 117, 128, 131, 152, 165
Blasse, Pierre I, 90, 92, 93, 166
Blasse, Pierre II, 93, 166
Blaye, Jourdain de, Romance of, 48
Blois, 73
Blomaert, Georges, 125, 145, 166
Bloyart, Colart, 69, 166
Blumenthal collection, 78
Boar-hunt, 49
Boccaccio (Staatsbibliothek, Munich), 76
Bohier, Thomas, 78
Boileau, Etienne, *Livre des metiers*, 18, 31
Bondolf, Jean de, 35, 36, 38, 164, 166
Bonnemer, 126
Bonnyn, Jacques, 166
Bordeaux, 65, 121, 160
borders, 21, 69, 87, 89, 93, 94, 103, 104, 109, 110, 112, 115–17, 119, 126, 127, 129, 139, 144, 149
Borgia, Cesare, 136
Bosse, Abraham, 24, 138
Bossy, Albert, gift of, 60
Boston, Museum of Fine Arts, 50, 57, 63, 67, 68, 80, 84, 94
Boucher, François, 114, 117, 120–1, 130–3, 141, 145, 153, 166
Boucherat, Lord Chancellor, 126
Boullongne, Louis de, 112, 115
Bourbon, Duchess of, 59
Bourbon, Cardinal Charles de, 65, 75

Bourbon, Louis de, 90, 135
Bourbon-Vendôme, Cardinal Louis de, 75
Bourdon, Sébastien, 104, 166
Bourges, 41, 73
Boursette, Vincent, 167
Boussac, château of, 79
Bouts, Dirk, 75
Brandenburg, 151
Brauer collection, 94
Brazen Serpent, The, 111
Bredas, Claude, 90
Brenet, 122
Brianchon, Maurice, 161, 167
Briçonnet, Catherine, 78
Britomartis, Drowning of, 94
Brittany, arms of, 38
brocatelle, 24
Bruchsal, Schloss, 127
Bruges, Jean or Hennequin de: *see* Bondolf
Bruges, 59, 60, 68, 80, 103, 106
Brussels: palace of, 57; town hall, 63; Musée de Cinquantenaire, 41, 44, 50, 51, 62, 64, 65, 70; tapestry workshops at, 43, 89–91, 113, 125; tapestry from, 104, 109–11; weavers from, 107, 144, 145, 148
Buckingham Palace, 118
Bullion, M. de, 103
Burbure, 67, 167
Burgundy, house and court of, 43, 53, 57, 60, 64
Burgundy, dukes of, 33, 39, 40, 56, 57, 59, 66, 73, 84: *see also separately under Christian names*
Burning Bush, The, 111
Burning Men, Dance of the, 65–6
Burrell collection, 49, 58, 59
Burtin, Marcel, 161

Cabinet du Roi Louis XIV, 109
Cadillac, 91, 144, 148
Calais, 143
Callot, 122
Caluce, voyage of, 70
Cambrai, 36, 43, 72, 148
Camondo collection, 133
Camousse, 167
Campin, Robert, 44, 58, 61
Campion, 126
Canaye family, 101
Capars, Jean, 167
Capella, Marcianus, *Satyricon*, 30
Capture of Arzila, 64
Capture of Jerusalem, 52

Index

Guérande, Martin, 84
Guéret museum, 138
Guiffrey, J.-J., *Histoires générale des arts appliqués à l'Industrie*, 26, 32, 33, 45, 66, 84, 90, 94
Guignebert, Vincent, 160, 175
guild statutes, 19
Guillard, Charles, 80
Guillaumot, Ch.-A., 114, 175
Guillemart, 161
Guise family, 97
Guise, Beautiful Hunts of, 111
Guise, Charles, Duc de, 51
Guise, François, Duc de, 51
Guise, Duchess of, 90
Guyon, Jacques, 149
Guyot, Laurent, 102, 138, 175

Hainault, Marie de, 135
Halberstadt cathedral, 30
Hallé, Noël, 112, 114
Hanele, Isaac de, 148
Hanstonne, Beuve de: *see* Anton
Hardouin-Mansard, Jules, 113
Hardwick Hall, 49
hatched shading, 145
Hearing, 80
Heart, Offering of the, 48
Hector, Story of, 34, 53, 54
Hector, Pedro Theotonio, 156
Heilbronner, Raoul, sale, 53
Helen, 138
Hellande, Guillaume de, 74
Hellande, Pierre de, Bishop of Beauvais, 57
hemp, 15, 140
Hennequin of Bruges: *see* Bandolf
Henri II, 19, 92–5, 98, 137
Henri III, 97, 136, 144
Henri III, Story of, 144, 148
Henri IV, 19, 96–100, 102, 106, 107, 137, 142, 143
Henri IV, Story of, 122
Henry, Robert, 160
heraldic devices, 32, 38, 80
Héraut, 161
Herbel, Charles, 149
Hercules, Story of, 53, 61, 65, 75, 79
Herkenbald, Trajan and, 52, 62, 63
herms, 109, 149
Heroes, 40–1, 136
Heroines, 41, 79
high-warp tapestry, 13–14, 21, 27, 31–3, 40, 42, 45, 46, 56, 57, 92, 98, 99, 105, 106, 112, 114, 115, 120, 123, 129, 143, 145, 146, 148, 149, 156

Hilaire, Camille, 161
Hinard, Jean-Baptiste, 127, 147, 176
Hinard, Louis, 123, 124, 125, 127, 147, 149, 176
Hippo of Athens, 68
Hirscholm, 156
History of the Great Elector, 151–2
Holophernes, Story of, 148
Holy Sacrament, Story of the, 84
Homberg collection, 67
Hopscotch, 78
Houasse, Michel-Ange, 156
Houasse, René-Antoine, 128, 176
Houel, Nicolas, 102
Hours of the Duc de Berry, 41
Hours of Reims, 87
Huet, Jean-Baptiste, 133, 142, 176
hunting scenes, 137
Hunts, 48–50
Hunts, New, 130
Hunt, Departure for the, 78
Hunt of the Unicorn, 77, 79, 81
Hunts of the Emperor Maximilian, 111
Hunts of Louis XV, 119, 120, 141
Hunts of King Francis, 102
Hunt of the Lion, 70
Huquier, 141

Idoux, 161
Iliad, 28, 118, 132
Illiers, Antoinette d', 136
Illustrations de Gaule et Singularités de Troyes, 88
Indies, Conquest of the, 133
Indies, 111, 112, 155: *see* New Indies
industrial design, school of, 19
Infant gardeners, 109
Ingam, 141
inscriptions, 22, 43, 47, 51–3, 60, 61, 64, 66, 78–84, 87, 94, 109
Inverary Castle, 133
Isle, Garnier d', 114
Issoire, courthouse at, 53
Italian Comedy, 152
Italy, influence of, 23, 83–6, 89, 108

Jabach, Evrard, 140, 176
Jacob and his children, 58
Jacqueline of Bavaria, 52
Jacqueron, Guillaumette, 66
Jacques, Maurice, 114, 117, 121, 176
Jandoygne, Jean de, 176
Janneau, Guillaume, 43, 159
Jans, Jean, 106, 113, 114, 146, 177
Jans, Jean-Jacques, 114, 177

Index

Index